World Christianity

World Christianity

History, Methodologies, Horizons

Edited by

Jehu J. Hanciles

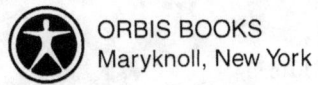
ORBIS BOOKS
Maryknoll, New York

Founded in 1970, Orbis Books endeavors to publish works that enlighten the mind, nourish the spirit, and challenge the conscience. The publishing arm of the Maryknoll Fathers and Brothers, Orbis seeks to explore the global dimensions of the Christian faith and mission, to invite dialogue with diverse cultures and religious traditions, and to serve the cause of reconciliation and peace. The books published reflect the views of their authors and do not represent the official position of the Maryknoll Society. To learn more about Orbis Books, please visit our website at www.orbisbooks.com.

Copyright © 2021 by Jehu J. Hanciles.

Published by Orbis Books, Box 302, Maryknoll, NY 10545-0302.

All rights reserved.

No part of this publication may be reproduced or transmitted in any form or by any means, electronic or mechanical, including photocopying, recording, or any information storage or retrieval system, without prior permission in writing from the publisher.

Queries regarding rights and permissions should be addressed to: Orbis Books, P.O. Box 302, Maryknoll, NY 10545-0302.

Manufactured in the United States of America

Library of Congress Cataloging-in-Publication Data

Names: Hanciles, Jehu, 1964- editor.
Title: World Christianity : history, methodologies, horizons / edited by Jehu J. Hanciles.
Description: Maryknoll, NY : Orbis Books, [2021] | Includes bibliographical references and index. | Summary: "Provides a critical reassessment of the study of world Christianity that connects historical developments to current debates and new trajectories"—Provided by publisher.
Identifiers: LCCN 2021016753 (print) | LCCN 2021016754 (ebook) | ISBN 9781626984486 (print) | ISBN 9781608339112 (ebook)
Subjects: LCSH: Christianity.
Classification: LCC BR121.3 .W669 2021 (print) | LCC BR121.3 (ebook) | DDC 270—dc23
LC record available at https://lccn.loc.gov/2021016753
LC ebook record available at https://lccn.loc.gov/2021016754

Contents

Acknowledgments   vii

Introduction
World Christianity Interrupted: Green Shoots and Growing Pains
Jehu J. Hanciles   ix

Section I: Conception and Institutionalization   1

1. *World Christianity as a Revitalization Movement*
   Dana L. Robert   3

2. *World Christianity: History, Conception, and Interpretation*
   Emma Wild-Wood, Carlos F. Cardoza-Orlandi,
   and Dyron Daughrity   23

3. *World Christianity Curricula: A Perspective from Missiology / Mission Studies*
   Kirsteen Kim   44

Section II: Methodology and Interdisciplinary Approaches   61

4. *Preparing and Equipping Scholars of World Christianity: Deep Understanding, Comparative Imagination, and Theological Awareness*
   Paul Kollman   63

5. *World Christianity and the Challenge of Interdisciplinarity*
   Kwok Pui-lan and Gina A. Zurlo   75

vi   Contents

6. "Worlding" Christianity: Approaches to the Making
   and Breaking of Confessional Boundaries
   Shobana Shankar 97

Section III: Expanding Horizons 117

7. Taking More Seriously the Asian Faces of World Christianity
   Gemma Tulud Cruz 119

8. Granting Full Citizenship to Latin American Christianities
   in World Christianity
   Raimundo C. Barreto 138

9. World Christianity in a Chinese Christian Perspective
   Pan-chiu Lai 158

10. Incorporating Middle Eastern Christianity into World Christianity
    Deanna Ferree Womack 171

11. Generational Transitions and New Conceptions
    Helen Jin Kim 185

Contributors 202

Index 205

Acknowledgments

The process that culminated with the publication of this book dates to a series of very stimulating conversations with a number of colleagues at a world Christianity conference in 2018. The subsequent journey was occasionally challenging but immensely rewarding. Needless to say, a successful outcome required significant contribution from a number of entities. Support for the project within Emory University was considerable and consistent. Dean Jan Love and Associate Dean Jonathan Strom at Candler School of Theology gave full backing to the endeavor, and funding from Emory University's Center for Faculty Development and Excellence made an international consultation in Atlanta possible. As the architect of the project, I was ably served by a core group of Emory faculty who constituted a planning and advisory group: Kwok Pui-lan, Arun Jones, Joy McDougall, Devaka Premawardhana, Deanna F. Womack, and Helen Jin Kim. I am especially grateful to Kwok Pui-lan and Arun Jones, who frequently made themselves available for in-depth consultation.

The contribution and participation of Emory University students (from Candler School of Theology and the Graduate Division of Religion) at the in-person Atlanta consultation was crucial. This select group included Kim Akano, Emmanuel Amponsah, Christy Eubank, Diana Rodriguez-Click, Tala Al-Raheb, Younghwa Kim, Lahronda Little, and Shari Madkins. Above all, I am immensely thankful for the exceptional service provided by Jennifer L. Aycock, who, as the World Christianity program assistant (Candler School of Theology), played a leading role in organizing the international consultation and adeptly coordinated the many complex requirements related to the project.

In addition to the contributors to this volume, an august group of world Christianity scholars (from outside of Emory) participated in the consultation and added considerable value to the undertaking. Klaus

Koschorke, Dale Irvin, and Virginia Garrard provided critical review of consultation papers; while Elias Bongmba, Lalsangkima Pachuau, Joel Cabrita, Afe Adogame, and Daryl Ireland contributed essays that enriched the conversation.

Orbis acquisitions editor Jill Brennan O'Brien handled the publication process with a speed and efficiency that most volume editors would envy. She has my heartfelt gratitude.

The contributors to this volume undertook their tasks with a diligence and determination that defied the grievous constraints of a global pandemic. I, and all those engaged in the study of world Christianity, owe them a debt of gratitude.

Introduction

World Christianity Interrupted: Green Shoots and Growing Pains

Jehu J. Hanciles

In October 2019, an international group of twenty-five scholars (representing a diversity of specialties and institutional affiliations) convened in Atlanta, Georgia, for a two-day consultation to examine core issues and debates central to the relatively new field of world Christianity. The event was preceded by months of preparation and lively scholarly interaction. Like any major international consultation, the planning, preparation, and scheduling complications produced many plot twists. Invitees from different parts of the world, for instance, were forced to pull out very late due to schedule conflicts, and one attendee from Asia was unable to board his flight at the last minute due to new visa regulations. Yet, gloriously, about the time the meeting convened, Gina Zurlo (co-director of the Center for the Study of Global Christianity), one of our participants, made the BBC's list of one hundred inspiring and influential young women from around the world for 2019.[1] With the benefit of hindsight, and a bit of imagination, it is possible to view this constellation of occurrences as evocative of the breakthroughs and breakdowns, the entanglement of promise and predicaments, that constantly attend the growing field of world Christianity.

In Dale Irvin's now familiar and insightful definition, the field of world Christianity "investigates and seeks to understand Christian communities, faith, and practice as they are found on six continents, expressed in diverse ecclesial traditions, and informed by the multitude of historical and cultural experiences in [the] world."[2] Scholars of world Christianity

---

1. "BBC 100 Women 2019: Who Is on the List This Year?", *BBC News* (October 16, 2019), www.bbc.com/news.
2. Dale T. Irvin, "World Christianity: An Introduction," *Journal of World Christianity* 1, no. 1 (2008): 1–26, 1.

vigorously challenge Western-centric approaches and models that still pervade academic discourse. They invariably utilize interdisciplinary methods of inquiry and fresh modes of theoretical analyses to re-envision Christianity as a global religion that from its inception grows and recedes across multiple centers.[3] The study of world Christianity is not always collaborative; but it lends itself, in the words of Emma Wild-Wood, to "a synthetic and collective approach to studying Christian peoples, practices, thought and environment across the globe."[4] A shared commitment to the study of Christianity as a worldwide (polycentric) phenomenon also means that world Christianity scholars are particularly attentive to marginality, show a predilection for a bottom-up analytical framework, and take seriously the dynamic interconnections between seemingly dominant global flows and frequently subversive local forces in the worldwide spread and establishment of the Christian movement.[5]

All this points to the fact that the world Christianity approach is not one thing but a plurality of emphases, models, and interpretative assumptions—all wrapped in a peculiar propensity for boundary-crossing and for exploring intersections in a way that calls master narratives and universalizing constructs into question.[6] Inevitably, however, the field's wide-ranging scope and purview generates its own questions and dilemmas, especially as it becomes more widely accepted.

---

3. On the field's interdisciplinarity and accommodation to plural methods, see Lamin O. Sanneh and Michael J. McClymond, *The Wiley Blackwell Companion to World Christianity* (Malden, MA: John Wiley & Sons, 2016), 6; Irvin, "World Christianity: An Introduction," 2, 11. See also Andrew F. Walls, *The Cross-Cultural Process in Christian History: Studies in the Transmission and Appropriation of Faith* (Maryknoll, NY: Orbis Books, 2002), 30.

4. October 2019 World Christianity Consultation notes; see also Emma Wild-Wood, "What Is the Study of World Christianity?", Center for the Study of World Christianity, October 23, 2019.

5. The critique, in a recent publication, that world Christianity scholarship is preoccupied with "the study of Christianity in very particular territories and locations around the globe, rather than the unitary phenomenon that is usually suggested by the use of the word 'world'"—i.e., that it fails to attend to global connections or ecumenical fellowship—is based on a selective and quite narrow reading of the discourse. It also construes "local appropriation" as an insular process rather than as an integral element in processes of globalization and as indispensable for multidirectional impact. See Joel Cabrita and David Maxwell, "Introduction: Relocating World Christianity," in Joel Cabrita, David Maxwell, and Emma Wild-Wood, eds., *Relocating World Christianity: Interdisciplinary Studies in Universal and Local Expressions of the Christian Faith* (Boston: Brill, 2017), 20.

6. Indeed, Irvin insists that "World Christianity as a field of study is at its best when studying . . . crossings and interstices." Dale T. Irvin, "World Christianity: A Genealogy," *Journal of World Christianity* 9, no. 1 (2019): 18.

Based on the most cursory assessment of the last decade or so, the field of world Christianity is flourishing. World Christianity programs have been established in academic institutions across the United States and Europe; new faculty positions appear to be on the rise; journal articles and book series by major academic publishers devoted to the field of study have increased markedly; academic conferences devoted to the field enjoy robust attendance and attract strong international participation; and the number of graduate students seeking to enroll in world Christianity programs (from diverse entry points) shows no signs of diminishing. These developments, however, have generated significant questions about the nature and scope of the field of study; including whether it is indeed a "field of study," or a "discourse," and how such nomenclature fits into existing guilds or academic training structures.[7] Simply labeling world Christianity a discipline is clearly unsatisfactory; since, as noted above, world Christianity scholarship is not only inherently interdisciplinary (or boundary-crossing), it also accommodates a plurality of methodologies. This all but ensures a proliferation of modes of enquiry and approaches that portend constant flux and potentially trouble a clear identity. Indeed, its far-reaching horizons means that the field's proponents and practitioners often have the sense of building a train that is already moving.

In any event, as the field of study expands and attracts a new generation of scholars from a variety of disciplinary backgrounds, some cogent questions can no longer be ignored: Who are world Christianity scholars? How is either the field or its practitioners different from other specialties in the academy or religion departments? And what constitutes preparation or competence for new graduates interested in teaching world Christianity or advocates keen to incorporate its theoretical models? Even the label "world Christianity" worries some because of semantic issues or the limits of translation into other languages. Meanwhile, others are persuaded that the use of "world Christianities" (plural) is more accurate or compelling,[8] not only because it correctly depicts the great multiplicity of strands, traditions, and expressions that characterize the faith globally but also because it repudiates claims of universality or normativity for Western Christianity.[9] This plural designation appears to be most appealing

---

7. For a recent assessment, see Martha Theodora Frederiks and Dorottya Nagy, eds., *World Christianity: Methodological Considerations* (Boston: Brill, 2021).

8. For a helpful overview of the conceptual issues, see Martha Theodora Frederiks, "World Christianity: Contours of an Approach," in Martha Theodora Frederiks and Dorottya Nagy, eds., *World Christianity: Methodological Considerations* (Boston: Brill, 2021).

9. Proponents include Vietnamese-born Roman Catholic scholar Peter Phan, who argues that the plural designation is particularly important for systematic theol-

in non-Western contexts where the entrenched dominance of the Western Christian tradition foments the need for counternarratives, such as the pointed rebuttal that "[Western Christianity] is only one among other Christianities, no more no less."[10] Chinese scholar Pan-chiu Lai makes a similar point in his chapter in this volume.

Increasingly also, longstanding concerns around the predominantly Protestant orientation of world Christianity scholars (though with notable exceptions) are being overtaken by the thornier issue of whether the study of world Christianity is an insider undertaking shaped by confessional persuasion. How institutional structures (ranging from graduate seminaries to university-based departments) shape world Christianity programs in terms of methodologies, curricula, and academic preparation is another major question—one closely related to the ambiguity surrounding what counts as training in world Christianity or even how competent world Christianity faculty are identified. These questions and more are addressed in this volume.

The wide-ranging impact of institutional structures or settings on the study of world Christianity gets some attention in a few chapters (esp. chapter 3). But this central issue deserves focused treatment for a number of reasons. This volume provides a comprehensive review of the field of study and detailed analysis of a wide range of critical issues, but it also aims to shed some light on pragmatic or strategic elements that have significant bearing on the field of study's development and impact. Moreover, many of the more serious issues considered in the pages that follow are inseparable from the particular institutional environment in which world Christianity programs are designed or developed. In other words, the institutional dimensions of the study of world Christianity are central to any meaningful appraisal of its progress and prospects.

---

ogy. Peter C. Phan, "Doing Theology in World Christianities: Old Tasks, New Ways," in Joel Cabrita et al., eds., *Relocating World Christianity*. Critics point out that the argument overstresses one side of the global-local dialectic and that the Christian movement was marked by great and increasing diversity from the earliest beginnings (in keeping with the faith's universalist vision). Indeed, world Christianity scholars have increasingly rejected the tendency to see the field of study as confined to non-Western realities or a post-Western Christendom era. See Klaus Koschorke, "Transcontinental Links, Enlarged Maps, and Polycentric Structures in the History of World Christianity," *Journal of World Christianity* 6, no. 1 (2016): 29, 32; Dale T. Irvin, "What Is World Christianity," in Jonathan Y. Tan and Anh Q Tran, eds., *World Christianity: Perspectives and Insights* (Maryknoll, NY: Orbis Books, 2016), 12; Sanneh and McClymond, *The Wiley Blackwell Companion to World Christianity*, 3.

10. Phan, "Doing Theology in World Christianities," 121.

The Institutional Question and the Complexities of Incubation[11]

It goes without saying that there is considerable variety in academic institutions that support the study of world Christianity not only in profile, conception, capacity, or setting (e.g., university, seminary, or center) but also from one region to another. The great diversity in institutional contexts, even within the same country, translates into resource inequities (size of faculty and range of expertise, among others) and potential divergence in outcomes (especially in doctoral research and preparation). These and related issues raise questions about what constitutes world Christianity scholarship and how the next generation of scholars is being trained. The point at issue is not that there is need for a central accrediting authority or a homogenization of design and construction material; rather that greater comprehension of the varieties of institutional contexts, designs, and experiences is urgently needed, if only to grasp the fluid contours of academic formation.

Actually, the establishment of world Christianity programs in academic settings is often an indicator of institutional evolution or, as Dana Robert suggests, "a revitalization movement in academic culture" (chapter 1). On occasion successful initiatives are the unanticipated product of new strategic needs, fresh clamor for diversity (in curricula and recruitment), faculty retirements, or even global economic trends. Often, this state of transition and flux is discernible only after the fact. But it means that world Christianity scholars occasionally find themselves in the middle of internal faculty struggles. One consultation participant who had worked in a variety of institutional settings in the United States (including a free-standing seminary, a school of theology, and a religion department in a Christian university) recalls disparate understandings of world Christianity in different institutions, wide variations in openness to new courses (from resistance to active encouragement), a range of attitudes to the intellectual resources of the non-Western world, turf fights over curricula design or course distribution, and contradictory expectations in the wake of a world Christianity appointment.

Transitions and Innovation

The varieties of institutional experiences and challenges received considerable attention at our consultation. By the nature of things, how-

---

11. While I draw mainly on personal experience for the examples and evaluation presented in this section, the overall assessment benefited from the critical insights and views shared by participants at the consultation; in particular, the consultation papers presented by Elias Bongmba, Lalsangkima Pachuau, and Daryl Ireland.

ever, the most concrete examples include private or confidential content and cannot be shared in a publication such as this. However, the issue does deserve attention. The appraisal provided here is more illustrative than exhaustive, in part because it is limited to the U.S. context. It is also framed around my own personal experience, with the subjectivity and limitations that this implies.[12] Of course, concrete examples are snapshots in time; which is to say that the issues or situations have in many cases been resolved or continue to evolve. My ultimate objective, however, is to highlight and analyze the relevance of institutional structures and parameters for the study of world Christianity more broadly, in a way that illuminates the significant bearing of institutional structures on the field of study's progression.

In 2009, while a faculty member in the School of Intercultural Studies (SIS) at Fuller Theological Seminary, I conceived of and spearheaded the founding of the Center for Missiological Research (CMR). By then I had been immersed in the world Christianity discourse and international projects for well over a decade—dating back to my studies under Andrew Walls at the Center for the Study of Christianity in the Non-Western World (now Center for the Study of World Christianity) at the University of Edinburgh. The establishment of the CMR reflected the determination by a handful of faculty, with the full backing of the dean, to create an academic structure based on a vision for doctoral-level missiological study and research that took seriously new global realities (a "post-American" world in which, for instance, American evangelicals had become a minority) as well as the radical shift in foci, topics, and training necessitated by the emergence of Christianity as a non-Western religion. In terms of programs and function, the center was specifically designed to advance the study of world Christianity through PhD studies, public lectures, symposia, postdoctoral fellowships, and partnerships with institutions in Asia and Africa. It also absorbed a preexisting "Global Research Institute" at Fuller that provided postdoctoral writing fellowships for non-Western scholars.

The use of "missiological" in the center's name reflected the institutional environment in which it was conceived and created. A few years earlier, the (then) School of World Mission had changed its name, amidst much debate, to the School of Intercultural Studies. The name change attracted considerable attention and controversy (and probably cost the school some donors). More discerning minds recognized that the old designation was outmoded and emblematic of an American imperial world-

---

12. Since these concrete examples reflect my own personal view and understanding, the names of valuable coworkers (and not a few co-conspirators) are withheld.

view. But the move was ultimately rooted in pragmatism. The "world mission" imprimatur on websites and graduation certificates increasingly jeopardized or constrained employment opportunities for graduates and alumni whose education was specifically designed for service in organizations and ministries throughout the world. (For more on this, see chapter 3.) In naming the new center, however, the key word was "research." Use of "missiological" reflected this concept's embeddedness in the school's DNA, an identification that remained a major source of attraction to prospective graduate students. In essence, "missiological" served the new center's purpose, even though CMR's objectives clearly invested it with a more expansive meaning and application.

The establishment of the Center for Missiological Research exemplifies institutional initiatives that occurred at a time when the transition from mission studies to world Christianity was still underway. This is not to validate the assumption that "world Christianity" is essentially "mission studies" in new clothes. The reality is more complicated than that.[13] But, as Lalsangkima Pachuau noted in a consultation paper, mission or intercultural studies do tend to be important precursors to the study of world Christianity in seminaries. In any case, even though the center's vision adhered to a world Christianity framework, the term "world Christianity" was less in vogue when the CMR was founded than it is today.

Interestingly, the inherent tensions in CMR's "world Christianity" vision were evident from the beginning. They included being Western-based and resourced while promoting an explicit agenda for nurturing scholarship that moved beyond Western perspectives and categories; mining the rich contributions of the discipline of missiology but producing research that is deeply critical of its norms and categories; and the challenge of cultivating a focus on non-Western contexts and experiences (in institutions dominated by Western needs, priorities, models of inquiry, and students) without reinforcing the "us and them" dialectic or feeding an intellectual appetite for the exotic among American students. Navigating these issues required scrupulous programming and policy making. Above all, as is invariably the case for such initiatives, the fact that it took place in an auspicious and enabling environment made a ton of difference. But even that goes only so far.

---

13. There is some truth in this, but it is also simplistic. I agree with Dale Irwin that world Christianity has multiple roots, of which missiology may be one of the most significant; Dale T. Irvin, "World Christianity, a Genealogy," *Journal of World Christianity* 9, no. 1 (2019). See also, James Strasburg, "Creating, Practicing, and Researching a Global Faith: Conceptualizations of World Christianity in the American Protestant Pastor and Seminary Classroom," *Journal of World Christianity* 6, no. 2 (2016).

The fact that Fuller Theological Seminary is nondenominational mattered (in the U.S. context), since this eliminated preoccupation with a narrow constituency or the training needs of a particular polity.[14] Fuller boasted a large and diverse student population (with a sizeable Korean program) and was also invested or embedded in global partnerships and networks that represented a wide array of ideological commitments. Academic programs were wide-ranging, and the existence of a School of Psychology (among other factors) ensured robust connections to the world outside the church or institutional Christianity. Incidentally, the global financial crisis (ca. 2007–2008) fostered even greater receptiveness to new academic initiatives that emphasized the needs of the global church and called for recruitment strategies with a wider lens. But Fuller's prominence within the evangelical academic constellation, combined with the School of Intercultural Studies' international reputation, all but ensured widespread interest and enrollment.

Yet, for a new center with an innovative academic vision, there were impediments aplenty. Limited financial resources for scholarships and increasingly inhospitable (post-9/11) American immigration policies translated into low international enrollment from countries or regions in the non-Western world[15]—despite strong partnerships with institutions in Asia and Africa. All too often, non-Western applicants who had sponsorship lacked the academic requirements; and, in a time of purse tightening, many American donors (organizations and individuals) were even more skittish than usual about funding non-Western students who in many instances failed to return to their home countries after costly education in the United States. Moreover, opportunities for graduate/postgraduate theological education were growing rapidly in parts of Asia and Africa, where prospective students could study for a tiny fraction of the cost of an American education and avoid the severe disruptions and dilemmas of relocation to the West. (The study of world Christianity in the United States and Europe continues to face significant challenges in these areas.)

Furthermore, even in a favorable environment, organizational structures and ingrained academic traditions troubled the CMR game plan. Fuller comprised three schools (Theology, Psychology, and Intercultural Studies) with distinctive academic profiles. The tensions and discon-

---

14. Though it maintained strong commitment to an evangelical ethos, an evangelical identity was not a prerequisite for student enrollment.

15. In the 2003–2004 academic year, the number of foreign students in the United States declined for the first time in thirty years, with a corresponding decline in foreign applications to American graduate schools; see "A Survey of Higher Education: Wandering Scholars," *The Economist*, September 10, 2005.

nection between the schools of theology and intercultural studies were longstanding. This state of affairs meant that, though widely celebrated, the CMR initiative (and, by extension, the study of world Christianity it promoted) was perceived as a special project associated with the unique interests of an individual school. A mere handful of faculty members in the School of Theology were associated with world Christianity scholarship. Quite simply, intra-institutional silos and programmatic "lanes" (fortified by decades of mutual resistance and misunderstandings) rendered the wider interdisciplinary collaboration and cross-fertilization envisaged by the CMR initiative largely aspirational—at least in the short term. Change came over time, facilitated by farsighted leadership, new interpersonal alliances, and (to be honest) a few faculty retirements!

However, as many know all too well, such positive change in institutional dynamics is not a foregone conclusion. In many institutional settings in the United States and elsewhere, the interdisciplinary or multimethod approach that the study of world Christianity calls for are constrained or impeded by traditional academic divisions or entrenched curricular demarcations.

Modules and Nomenclature

If missiology or intercultural studies provide a natural transition point in many seminaries and university-based schools of theology/divinity, the study of religion frequently serves the same purpose in secular or "nonsectarian" university settings. Elias Bongmba, who led the effort to create a graduate track in "Global Christianity" at Rice University (a private liberal arts research institution in Houston, Texas), reports in his consultation paper that the new track was rooted in the historical study of religion and heavily linked to historical studies. Since the history of religions approach is somewhat modular, in the sense that it treats Christianity as one of the religions of the world, faculty collaboration is essential. As such, in departments of religion with strong capacity and diversity, the study of world Christianity readily draws on faculty with expertise in a wide range of related disciplines, perspectives, and regional contexts (see also chapter 3). It is easy to imagine that the establishment of world Christianity programs in different institutions around the world draws on available resources in similar fashion, allowing world Christianity practitioners and close allies to craft courses and concentrations with new interdisciplinary approaches or methods in innovative ways.

The recently established Global Christianity program at Emory University is distinctive in at least one respect: it is based on cooperation between the Candler School of Theology (which has a separate world

Christianity program at the master's level) and Emory's Department of Religion in the College of Arts.[16] This setup reflects the fact that all PhD studies in religion at the university are housed within the Graduate Division of Religion (GDR), which is comprised of faculty from both the School of Theology and the College of Arts and Sciences. With some fifty faculty and close to twice as many students, the GDR constitutes one of the largest PhD programs in religion and theology in the United States, with great resources for studying religious cultures around the world and a strong interdisciplinary academic culture. Emory's Global Christianity program is accessed in one of two ways: as "a field of emphasis" within the Historical Studies in Theology and Religion course of study (one of nine[17]), or as a "GDR concentration." The latter allows PhD students in units across the GDR to incorporate world Christianity approaches and theoretical models in developing their research projects and to work closely with world Christianity faculty. This multi-unit architecture and multimodular approach maximizes use of resources but also adds layers of complexity that are unlikely to be present where the faculty and students of the program are all located in one center or department.

The descriptors "world" and "global" are used interchangeably by world Christianity scholars and are treated as synonymous in the relevant literature.[18] In some university settings (in the United States), however,

---

16. This is noteworthy only because strong or systematic collaboration between schools of theology and departments of religion within the same university is rare in the U.S. context. At Boston University, to cite one example, the study of Christianity was removed from the Graduate Program of Religion and confined to the School of Theology.

17. Changes to the structure of these nine courses of study are imminent. At the time of this writing, they are American Religious Cultures; Ethics and Society; Hebrew Bible; Historical Studies in Theology and Religion; Jewish Religious Cultures; New Testament; Person, Community, and Religious Life; Theological Studies; and West and South Asian Religions.

18. A major exception was eminent world Christianity scholar Lamin Sanneh, who viewed "global Christianity" as synonymous with Western imperial expansion, and interchangeable with "Christendom"; in sharp contrast with "world Christianity," which he associated with "the spontaneous coming into being of Christian communities" and "the variety of indigenous responses" among populations that had not been Christian. See Lamin O. Sanneh, *Whose Religion Is Christianity?: The Gospel Beyond the West* (Grand Rapids, MI: Eerdmans, 2003), 22 (see also pp. 75, 78, 92). This conceptualization has several weaknesses: the failure to recognize that Western Christianity is itself rooted in indigenous responses; the unhelpful notion that "world Christianity" is a post-Christendom phenomenon (which Sanneh himself refutes elsewhere); and the once common, but now widely challenged, understanding of globalization as a one-directional, Western-controlled process. As noted below, others are equally convinced that "world" (not "global") is laden with imperialistic or hegemonic intent!

the establishment of world Christianity programs inadvertently activates contentious claims that one term or the other is symbolic of Western hegemony. This appears to have fostered a divergence in institutional usage. In seminaries and divinity schools (in the United States), both labels are used; whereas in university (religious) departments, the "global" nomenclature is widely favored.[19] The predilection for "global" in university religion departments is possibly rooted in deep aversion to phrases like "world religions" or "world mission," an aversion that is generally absent or muted in divinity schools or schools of theology, even within the same institutional setting.[20] At Boston University, renowned world Christianity scholar Dana Robert chose to use "global" when she founded the Center for Global Christianity and Mission in order "to fit in better with university nomenclature."[21] This, interestingly, made her the Truman Collins Professor of *World Christianity* and History of Mission, and Director of the Center for *Global Christianity* and Mission, at the same institution (italics added)!

The "world" versus "global" argument perhaps exemplifies the many parochialisms of Western academia. In reality, either term can be used with hegemonic connotations. What matters, as Dana Robert notes, "is *how* they're being used, rather than *which* is being used."[22] But even if such debates act as a lightning rod for latent misperceptions, they do alert world Christianity scholars to the heavy ideological baggage that the field of study carries, at least in the eyes of outsiders (or even sympathetic colleagues). They also showcase the kinds of institutional concessions and trade-offs that world Christianity programs must still make in some institutional settings in order to be taken seriously or even to get out of the starting gate.

---

19. Examples include Boston University, Duke University, Emory University, Rice University, and the University of Washington. Whether the same is true of the European context, where world Christianity programs or units are relatively fewer but linguistic differences are a factor, is difficult to say. It is, however, interesting to note a similar contrast between the Center for the Study of World Christianity (linked to Edinburgh University's Divinity School) and the Global Christianity and Interreligious Relations program in the Centre for Theology and Religious Studies (at Lund University).

20. Thus, while "world Christianity" is the nomenclature of choice within Emory's Candler School of Theology (used for a named academic chair and the relevant program), "global Christianity" is strongly favored within the department of religion.

21. Dana L. Robert and Aaron Hollander, "Beyond Unity and Diversity: A Conversation with Dana Robert on Mission, Ecumenism, and Global Christianities," *Ecumenical Trends* (June 2019): 3.

22. Ibid., 3.

Some Answers, More Questions

It bears reiterating that the institutional realities that shape the study of world Christianity (in the United States and elsewhere) vary greatly. Many more factors are undoubtedly at play in institutional settings outside the North Atlantic world. From a certain perspective, the diversity of institutional arrangements conceivably adds to the strength of the field. At the same time, the differences often translate into disparities and inequities that increase as the field of study spreads globally. But should it? Do genuine efforts to promote world Christianity, as an academic field or scholarly discourse, outside the North Atlantic world in which it originated, raise ethical questions related to acute disparity of resources and the risk of captivity to Western academic models and structures? Questions of this nature are coming more fully into view as the field of study grows in appeal and acceptance (see chapter 2).

"World" as construct and concrete reality has been integral to world Christianity discourse from its inception. But the prominence of Africanist scholars in the development of the field of study means that the African context can feature prominently in its formation. For this reason, few areas of development promise to be more fertile or fascinating than the increasing contribution by scholars located in, or immersed in the study of, other regions of the world. Still, on a larger canvas, scholarly involvement and contribution from the non-Western world (or Global South) remains relatively limited. The study of world Christianity, at least in terms of academic profile and programmatic initiatives, is largely confined to (and dominated by) Western-based institutions or entities. In fact, as things stand, there is increasing likelihood that the field will become wholly captive to North Atlantic (Anglophone) academic structures and intellectual categories. This raises the undesirable possibility that a field of study attentive to marginality and "committed to engage with Christians worldwide" might end up as an embodiment of the inequities it seeks to confront: a fixation with Western academic priorities, or a propensity to settle for extraction of research data and knowledge from non-Western contexts in place of meaningful collaboration and exchange with non-Western voices. Whether or not this is realized, the mere prospect is worrisome.

All of this is not to suggest that the field of world Christianity is in a state of crisis or, for that matter, at an inflection point. As noted above, it is flourishing in the North Atlantic world. As such, the pressing issues mentioned above can be perceived in one of two ways: as either the fruits of prosperity or as representing growing pains (or both?). What matters is that they cannot be dismissed as inconsequential. Most indicate areas of persistent confusion or potential disruption. Disruption is not necessarily a bad thing in academic discourse. World Christianity scholarship is itself disruptive of Western paradigms and disciplinary boundaries that insulate intellectual production. But disruption is not a goal or grand design. The field of study must tend to shared commitments and core frameworks or risk loss of (intramural) congruency. An ingrained penchant for boundary-crossing makes for provocative analyses and exciting findings; but without conceptual parameters of its own, however flexible, hermeneutical coherence is likely to erode over time. In any case, these issues require serious attention and debate. For this reason alone, an appraisal of this rapidly shifting terrain promises to be a vital resource for both experienced and emerging scholars.

Overview of the Book

The chapters in this volume (divided into three sections) provide a critical reassessment of the field of world Christianity in a way that connects historical developments to emergent dilemmas (or incipient debates) and promising trajectories. The contributors, who comprise an international and diverse group of world Christianity scholars, explore topics that range from basic questions of conception and North Atlantic lineage to more complex issues pertaining to institutional life, intersection with an expanding array of established academic fields and specialties, and the critical issues raised by fresh intellectual engagement and exchange with different regions of the world. The treatment aims not to resolve all questions but to deeply scrutinize their significance, elucidate what is at stake (pitfalls and possibilities), and appraise the issues in a way that moves the conversation forward.

The three chapters in section one cover issues of conceptualization and institutionalization. In chapter 1, **Dana Robert** draws on her extensive experience in the world Christianity field of study to provide a front-row view of its evolution since the early 1990s. This intriguing review includes useful accounts of critical milestones and major debates. The rich details are enlivened by a personal narrative that often gives a "behind the scenes" vibe that many readers will relish.

In the first of two collaborative chapters (chapter 2), **Emma Wild-Wood, Carlos Cardoza-Orlandi**, and **Dyron Daughrity** reappraise the complex strands that shaped the rise of the study of world Christianity in the Global North, primarily as a "corrective to an understanding of Christianity as a Western phenomenon." The authors describe and evaluate major aspects of the field of study's origins and ongoing development. Among other things, they outline recent critique (of early concepts, emphases, and glaring limitations), examine new challenges that lie ahead as world Christianity becomes more established within Western institutions and spreads globally, and make a case for an approach that is expansive, inclusive, and relational.

In chapter 3, **Kirsteen Kim** probes the key issues of how the interdisciplinary nature of the study of world Christianity might impact student preparation and employment prospects. This detailed assessment draws on her considerable international experience and intimate familiarity with institutional structures. Taking a different approach to the genealogical question, she identifies six major disciplines that are foundational to the rise of the field of world Christianity. She evaluates the approach that each provides to the study of world Christianity and briefly reviews implications for program design and curricular development.

The second section of the volume focuses on methodology and interdisciplinary approaches. Which core elements constitute training and preparation in world Christianity scholarship is an increasingly urgent question, especially given the field of study's growing scope. This query forms the centerpiece of **Paul Kollman**'s contribution (chapter 4), in which he scrutinizes the value of world Christianity as a theoretical framework and proposes certain "scholarly dispositions" that he considers vital for world Christianity scholarship. The strong interdisciplinary (or integrative) character of the study of world Christianity is greatly valued but seldom evaluated. In chapter 5, **Kwok Pui-lan** and **Gina Zurlo**, two scholars from different disciplinary backgrounds, diagnose the benefits and challenges of using multiple methods and theories (beyond history and theology). Drawing on sociology of religion, gender studies, and migration studies, they examine the complications and contributions produced by the intersection of world Christianity scholarship with a growing number of disciplines, and call for more South-to-South engagement.

In a manner that incorporates elements of both methodology and conception, **Shobana Shankar** interrogates the two concepts that comprise "world Christianity" in chapter 6. She makes the case that the use of "world" as a verb—hence, *"worlding"*—is more capacious (as method) because it conveys the boundary-defying nature of lived religion; and this, in turn, exposes tensions with "Christianity," which is associated with confessional particularity and bounded existence. This tension, Shankar argues, inhibits world Christianity scholarship in terms of its ability to address religious phenomena that occur in "in-between" spaces, where Christian and non-Christian intersect for instance. Using historical examples from Northern Nigeria, she explains how a *"worlding"* approach can reshape understanding of world Christianity and its capacity to contribute to studies of religion and globalization more broadly.

The volume's final section is devoted to the study of fields or regions that have not typically received strong attention in the study of Christianity and exemplify the rich fruits that await fuller engagement or interaction. While many acknowledge that failure to fully incorporate the perspectives, histories, and debates of the diverse regions of the Global South impoverishes the study of world Christianity, few make the case as forcefully or insightfully as **Gemma Tulud Cruz** does in chapter 7. Her assessment focuses on Asia, a region where Western Christian influences remain dominant (despite the region's status as the birthplace of the Christian movement). She calls for comprehensive and creative (re)engagement with Asian experiences (encompassing the massive Asian diaspora) within world Christianity scholarship, but also cautions that this requires confronting many challenges, such as the politics of scholarship, imbalances in academic publishing, and the marginalization of non-Western contexts and epistemologies.

Despite growing interest in Latin America among world Christianity scholars, writes **Raimundo Barreto** in chapter 8, the field of study has had minimal engagement with Latin American scholarship or its academic world. Reasons for this include the predominantly Anglophone and Protestant character of world Christianity scholarship and the focus on Africa that marked its early development. In forthright terms and compelling analysis, Barreto explains why full interaction with Latin America's history, religious world, and intellectual traditions is urgently needed in the study of world Christianity. Despite the language barriers, he notes, vital areas of intellectual convergence between the two and recent developments in Latin America's academic realm portend copious rewards for mutual engagement.

In chapter 9, the focus turns to China. **Pan-chiu Lai**, a Chinese Christian theologian and world Christianity scholar based in Hong Kong, has long promoted the world Christianity approach and methodologies in his teaching and writings. Here, he examines crucial ways in which the world Christianity discourse can equip Chinese Christian scholars not only to address the misleading but entrenched conception of Christianity as a "Western" religion in Chinese academia, but also to make distinctive contributions to the study of Christianity "as a cross-cultural and multilingual movement." Central to his analysis is a theoretical model that makes full use of the Chinese cultural, philosophical, and religious heritage to enrich theological discourse and the study of religion.

Inadequate attention to the Christian traditions of the Middle East in historical studies of Christianity, as **Deanna Ferree Womack** notes (chapter 10), is commonplace; and this marginalization is evident, though perhaps to a lesser degree, in the study of world Christianity. In this fascinating overview, Womack analyzes the reasons behind the neglect of Middle Eastern Christianity (past and present) in the relevant literature and offers explanations for the dearth of scholars of Middle Eastern Christianity who identify with the world Christianity field of study. She advances persuasive arguments for world Christianity scholarship to give substantial attention to Middle Eastern Christianity and engage its scholars more fully.

Depending on one's perspective, the study of world Christianity is now attracting a third generation of scholars, who bring their own unique and pressing issues or questions to the field of study. In some respects, the process will be disruptive; especially because, as **Helen Jin Kim** observes (chapter 11), new scholars engage the field from a greater multiplicity of academic disciplines, regional focus, and methodologies. In this final essay (one that fittingly connects past, present, and future), Kim reviews the field of study's progression and emphasizes the rich and enduring intellectual legacy of its pioneers. She demonstrates how critical insights advanced by early Africanists (with regard to empire and mission, for instance) furnish important analytical tools for a transnational approach to the study of multidisciplinary field of transpacific Korean Christianity.

Only two of the chapters in this volume are multi-authored. But the volume as a whole showcases the collaborative approach of world Christianity scholarship insofar as most of the chapters benefited from wider conversations and reveal the considerable gains of an in-person consultation.[23] In the final analysis, the volume explores important and pressing issues with a depth of coverage and multiplicity of perspectives that a single-authored monograph is unlikely to achieve. By combining the input and insights of both seasoned and rising scholars it also presents an intergenerational dialectic that is often absent in such treatments. The deeply pragmatic nature of some of the issues under consideration also encouraged a framework that combined scholarly appraisal and pragmatic evaluation. The result is a rich and instructive trove of material that will be a valuable resource and reference for both experienced scholars and entrants, as well as the growing cadre of interested inquirers eager to find out more about this growing and exciting field.

---

23. In addition to the authors of the chapters in this volume, the list of consultation participants include (in alphabetized order): Afe Adogame, Elias Bongmba, Joel Cabrita, Virginia (Ginny) Garrard, Daryl Ireland, Dale Irvin, Arun Jones, Klaus Koschorke, Joy McDougall, and Devaka Premawardhana. (Dana Robert is the only contributor to this volume who was not present at the consultation itself.)

Section I

Conception and Institutionalization

1

World Christianity as a Revitalization Movement

Dana L. Robert

Since its conceptualization by anthropologist Anthony F. C. Wallace in 1956, the "revitalization movement" has become one of the best-known descriptors of how cultural innovation takes place. Wallace began by studying a Seneca prophet, Handsome Lake, who pioneered a new religion.[1] As he began comparing similar prophetic figures, Wallace speculated that in "thousands" of examples, communal religio-cultural change proceeded along recognized pathways. The revitalization movement is "a deliberate, organized, conscious effort by members of a society to construct a more satisfying culture."[2] The society or "social organism" proceeds along a "mazeway," a self-understanding that provides meaning for the collective and integrates its varied parts. "Stress" occurs when the mazeway no longer aligns with "reality." Intersection with foreign elements, new contexts, and new needs all challenge the existing mazeway. Society must either tolerate the stress or construct a new mazeway that makes sense of its new realities. Some also try to force realities to match the existing mazeway. Wallace writes, "The effort to work a change in mazeway and 'real' system together so as to permit more effective stress reduction is the effort at revitalization; and the collaboration of a number of persons in such an effort is called a revitalization movement."[3] Once the new mazeway aligns with the perceived reality of the social organism, social stress is reduced and a new religio-cultural movement is born.

---

1. Anthony F. C. Wallace, "Revitalization Movements," *American Anthropologist* 58, no. 2 (1956): 264–81. Many thanks for helpful feedback on this article from Gerald Anderson, David Hollinger, and Robert Hefner.
2. Ibid., 265.
3. Ibid., 267.

After multiple actors use "communication, organization, adaptation, cultural transformation, and routinization" to reformulate the mazeway, a new "steady state" results, and revitalization has occurred.[4]

At the risk of trivializing Wallace's important model, I suggest that "world Christianity" represents a revitalization movement in academic culture. As one of the early adopters of the new "mazeway," I shall explore how the old mazeway no longer made sense to a subset of academics—those interested in the growth of Christianity in Africa, Asia, and Latin America after the mid-twentieth century. A host of collaborators from mission studies, religious studies, history, and the social sciences collectively constructed a new mazeway through "communication, organization, adaptation, cultural transformation, and routinization." By 1992, the shorthand "world Christianity" was affixed to the new discourse. By the turn of the century, increasing numbers of stakeholders from diverse fields began adopting it. As we enter arguably the third generation of world Christianity scholars, projects like this book represent its routinization and achievement of "steady state." Of course, the exciting reality about academic discourses is that there is no such thing as a permanent equilibrium—the very process of routinization gives birth to new cultural innovations, such that one generation's discovery is the next generation's obsolete mazeway. But as Wallace observed, the old myths, insights, dreams, and accretions persist and inform the future, and even become the source of new revitalization.

As I reflect on the construction of world Christianity as an academic discourse, I am struck by how much its emergence felt like religious conversion. One of its chief instigators, Andrew Walls, recalled as much: when teaching about second-century Christianity in West Africa in the early 1960s, he realized that his students were dealing with the same issues in their churches. They knew more about spiritual controversies, healing and exorcism, and church planting than he did. After he returned to Scotland, he made it his mission to bring knowledge of vibrant African Christianity to the Western academy. During the 1980s, initial groups of scholars gathered at Walls's Centre for the Study of Christianity in the Non-Western World in Aberdeen and then Edinburgh; at the Overseas Ministries Study Center (OMSC) in New Haven, Connecticut; and at consultations in Boston and other locations, and light bulbs started going off.

Collaborative conversation among scholars and practitioners, many with firsthand experience in the global South, showed that the depressing tropes of inevitable secularization and Western denominational malaise were not the center of the story. Western colonialist oppression, while

---

4. Ibid., 268.

important to face and to reject, was not what defined Christian identity worldwide. Rather than mission history being a tale of expanding empire with outposts run by colonial-era missionaries, it became clear that the margins and the center were always shifting. The local and the global constantly intersected. The seemingly powerless used their faith to create new identities. The founding of indigenous churches, the spread of liberation theologies, the global flow of Pentecostal worship—all these were signs of vitality, not a death spiral of the Christian faith. World Christianity was not the story of Western denominations and institutions bound by rigid doctrine generated by powerful gatekeepers. Rather, as "social organism," it included women and children who worshiped under trees in Africa, migrant preachers who traversed urban spaces across the Americas, Catholic sisters who led base Christian communities, Asian religious minorities who pushed for social change, eastern Europeans who brought down the Iron Curtain, and globe-trotting pilgrims from everywhere to everywhere.

From Baton Rouge to Boston: An Intellectual Journey

The voyage of discovery to "world Christianity" began with multiple individuals and small nodes of exploration that eventually coalesced. When I began my doctoral work in religious studies at Yale in 1978, there was no such academic field as world Christianity. I called my own evolving mental map "comparative Christianity," once I realized that Christianity did not look the same from one culture to the next. As a history major in the mid-1970s at Louisiana State University, I had found myself writing papers on religious history in every course I took, whether it was studying Huguenots in "Western civilization," the imperial religion in the Roman Republic, Orthodoxy in Russian history, or the Catholic Left in U.S. history. With a visiting Belgian missionary from Zaire named Fr. Jaak Senyaeve,[5] I studied African independent churches and African Catholicism.

As soon as I entered Yale University's Religious Studies Department, I signed up for comparative doctrine with theologian George Lindbeck and the "expansion of Christianity" under the successor of Kenneth Scott Latourette, mission professor Charles Forman. Both Lindbeck and Forman were the children of missionaries. Having grown up in Asia, they

---

5. Father Jaak was a White Father who spent sixty-seven years as a missionary. He taught for one semester at LSU around 1976. He was at one point vice president of the Catholic University in Kinshasa. He later returned to LSU for a few years in the 1990s. http://thepelicans.org.uk/obituaries/obits17.htm#seynaeve.

pushed beyond Western academic formulations and the categories of the nation-state. Both men remained connected to Christianity in other parts of the world. As official Lutheran observer at the Second Vatican Council, and a son and brother of missionaries, Lindbeck speculated that *Gesundschrumpfen*, downsizing for the state of health, was not the only possible path forward for Christianity in the world. For my term paper on the Catholic charismatic movement in the fall of 1978, I was able to read every book on pentecostalism in the Yale Divinity School library—something that would be impossible today because of the huge amount of research on the subject since then.[6]

My advisor, Sydney Ahlstrom, whose magnificent *Religious History of the American People* had come out just a few years before, had officially declared that the Puritan tradition in American religion collapsed in the 1960s.[7] He told me that the study of evangelicalism was boring, as it contained no new ideas. Rather, the "secular city" and religious pluralism were now the dominant paradigms in American religion. My graduate school cohorts had long discussions about breaking free from Ahlstrom's intellectual approach, but also building upon his interest in diversity by studying Christianity as a religion of the people, of women and immigrants, and the poor.[8] To do this, we needed different tools than the "high" sources that intellectual historians like Ahlstrom favored. To pursue my personal interest in "comparative Christianity," I took directed studies in missiology with Charles Forman,[9] studied on my own for an extra doctoral examination in African Christianity, and wrote my dissertation on

---

6. I remember one conversation in his office in which Lindbeck and I agreed that the most satisfying church service was a Roman Catholic charismatic mass. Lindbeck was formulating his "post-liberal" linguistic theory, and we students read the photocopied proofs before it came out. George A. Lindbeck, *The Nature of Doctrine: Religion and Theology in a Postliberal Age* (Philadelphia: Westminster Press, 1984).

7. Sydney E. Ahlstrom, *A Religious History of the American People* (New Haven: Yale University Press, 1972). I went to Yale to study with Prof. Ahlstrom. Sadly, he died of amyotrophic lateral sclerosis in 1984. Four of us doctoral students were the pallbearers at the funeral.

8. Some of their revised dissertations became important books: Robert A. Orsi, *The Madonna of 115th Street: Faith and Community in Italian Harlem, 1881–1950* (New Haven: Yale University Press, 1985); Robert Bruce Mullin, *Episcopal Vision/American Reality: High Church Social Thought in Evangelical America* (New Haven: Yale University Press, 1986); Ann D. Braude, *Radical Spirits: Spiritualism and Women's Rights in Nineteenth-Century America* (Boston: Beacon Press, 1989).

9. Forman was an expert on Christianity in Oceania. See Charles W. Forman, *The Island Churches of the South Pacific: Emergence in the Twentieth Century* (Maryknoll, NY: Orbis Books, 1982).

what was then the virtually unexplored subject of late-nineteenth-century American evangelical mission history.[10]

The point of this personal narrative is not to claim some kind of unique insight but to illustrate how discontent with the reigning narrative of Western institutional church history was bubbling up in the mid- to late 1970s. Whether it was the push toward social history, popular Catholicism, women's studies, Pentecostalism, or evangelical missions, younger scholars were no longer content to be limited by the theologies of mainline Protestantism, with its guilt complexes and inevitable decline. Interest in popular religion was reinforced by larger social trends: with Jimmy Carter becoming the Democratic nominee for the U.S. presidency, *Newsweek* magazine declared 1976 the "year of the evangelical." Similarly problematic was the idea of secularization as a totalizing global narrative. If the theories of sociologists were correct, and religion would die as education and modernization spread,[11] then why study it at all? Surely the history of Christianity had more to offer than the patriarchal narrative of Western kings and popes.

In 1984, I landed a term appointment to teach mission studies at the Boston University School of Theology. Like other old mainline institutions, the school of Norman Vincent Peale, Georgia Harkness, Martin Luther King Jr., and other notables had seen its department of mission and ecumenism collapse during the Vietnam War–era general reaction against colonialism. From within the post-Christian context of secularizing New England, it was willing to try something new on a minimal

---

10. Ahlstrom's decline meant that Forman and Lindbeck became my dissertation readers. To replace Ahlstrom's area of expertise, William R. Hutchison of Harvard graciously agreed to become my second reader. He was writing his book on American mission theory, and so we had interesting discussions. See William R. Hutchison, *Errand to the World: American Protestant Thought and Foreign Missions* (Chicago: University of Chicago Press, 1987). My dissertation was published in Korean, but its revision some years later resulted in Dana L. Robert, *"Occupy Until I Come": A. T. Pierson and the Evangelization of the World* (Grand Rapids, MI: Eerdmans, 2003).

11. José Casanova writes movingly of the dominance of "grand theory" secularization in his own sociological training and how it took him twenty-five years to "unlearn" it and theorize the existence of "multiple modernities," not all of which are secularizing. "Fifty years ago, as I was finishing my studies in theology at the University of Innsbruck, Austria, and starting my graduate studies in sociology at the New School for Social Research in New York, the theory of secularization was the dominant paradigm through which the social sciences and much of Christian theology were looking at religion in the modern world. In a sense, in the last twenty-five years I had to unlearn or at least rethink much of what I had learned as a sociologist of religion in the previous twenty-five years." José Casanova, "Global Religious and Secular Dynamics: The Modern System of Classification," *Brill Research Perspectives in Religion and Politics* 1, no. 1 (2019): 2.

budget. An inexperienced twenty-seven-year-old was all they could afford to hire to "revive" the grand ecumenical tradition. The first course I taught was "The Emergence of the Church in the Third World"—a survey of selected themes in Asia, Africa, and Latin America—my dream come true of "comparative Christianity." There were no textbooks, professional journals, or academic associations interested in this topic except for the old missionaries who attended the American Society of Missiology.

But I found dialogue partners in Boston. In the Boston Theological Institute (BTI), a consortium of nine seminaries, I joined the faculty committee on "international mission." We met monthly to compare ideas, plan an annual ecumenical conference on Christianity beyond Western borders, provide support for international students, and similar activities.[12] Our faculty committee on mission studies included legendary Afghanistan missionary J. Christy Wilson of Gordon-Conwell Theological Seminary; Lamin Sanneh of Harvard Divinity School; Indologist Frank Clooney SJ, of Boston College; former Episcopal missionary Ivan Kaufman of Episcopal Divinity School; and Peter Schineller SJ, future provincial in Nigeria and a Weston School of Theology Jesuit. The new dean at Andover-Newton Seminary, Orlando Costas, had also arrived in Boston in 1984, and he soon became a close colleague through our monthly meetings. Costas was the first Latinx dean of a U.S. seminary, and he saw himself as a bridge figure between Latin American and North American Christianity.[13] Through the BTI faculty mission committee, Boston became one of the nodes committed to collaborative exploration of Christianity in Asia, Africa, and Latin America.

My dialogue partners from within Boston University were social scientists connected with the Institute for the Study of Economic Culture, founded in 1985 by sociologist Peter Berger.[14] Although he was a

---

12. Over the years, the faculty composition of the committee changed according to the interests of the BTI schools. Other notable members of the committee since I joined in 1984 have included Ian Douglas, Ray Helmick, Daniel Jeyaraj, Rodney Petersen, Margaret Guider, Todd Johnson, and Luke Veronis. In addition to the annual Orlando E. Costas Consultations on Mission and Ecumenism, our committee sponsored one of the Edinburgh 2010 conferences. Proceedings were published as Todd M. Johnson, Rodney L. Petersen, Gina A. Bellofatto, and Travis L. Myers, eds., *2010 Boston: The Changing Contours of World Mission and Christianity* (Eugene, OR: Pickwick Publications, 2012).

13. Orlando E. Costas was one of the most important missiologists of the late-twentieth century. I sent students to him for work in mission theology, and he sent them to me for work in mission history. Sadly, Costas died prematurely at age forty-five, in 1987. See Orlando E. Costas, *Christ Outside the Gate: Mission Beyond Christendom* (Maryknoll, NY: Orbis Books, 1982).

14. In the late 1980s, Berger's institute changed its name to the Institute on Culture, Religion, and World Affairs (CURA). https://www.bu.edu/cura/. Some of Berger's

prophet of secularization, Berger was also a self-professed conservative Lutheran with a well-deserved reputation for creative brilliance. Among liberal academics, he was seen as a maverick because of his interest in comparative capitalism. With powerful supporters in the grant-making world, Berger began sponsoring research into the surprising growth of Christianity, starting in 1986 with funding sociologists David and Bernice Martin's groundbreaking research on pentecostalism in Central America. David Martin had already rejected the secularization "grand narrative," and the publication of his research on Pentecostalism in 1989 further contradicted it.[15]

In April of 1988, Berger's associate director, Islam scholar Robert Hefner, held a small working conference on conversion to world religions as part of his interest in the "world building" function of religious systems. With the dawning recognition that Christian conversion represented fascinating case studies of local societies changing in dialogue with global religions, for the published volume Hefner pulled together comparative studies of Christian conversion.[16] The conference drew together such notables as Jean Comaroff, then writing what would become *Of Revelation and Revolution* (1991); John Barker, scholar of Christianity in Oceania; and Terence Ranger, expert on Zimbabwean Christianity. At the conference, my role as mission historian was to press the anthropologists to take seriously the self-referenced religiosity of the people they were studying, and not to bury their testimonies in theories that disregarded their agency.

Thus by the late 1980s, scholars in Boston were feeling the stress upon the old, inadequate mazeways. Although the mission professors and the social scientists were not in formal dialogue with each other, the global flow and public impact of world religions—especially Christianity and Islam—

---

best known books include Peter L. Berger and Thomas Luckmann, *The Social Construction of Reality: A Treatise in the Sociology of Knowledge* (Garden City, NY: Anchor Books, 1966); Peter L. Berger, *The Sacred Canopy: Elements of a Sociological Theory of Religion* (Garden City, NY: Doubleday, 1967); Peter L. Berger, *A Rumor of Angels: Modern Society and the Rediscovery of the Supernatural* (Garden City, NY: Doubleday, 1969); and Peter L. Berger, *The Heretical Imperative: Contemporary Possibilities of Religious Affirmation* (New York: Anchor Press, 1980).

15. David Martin, *Tongues of Fire: The Explosion of Protestantism in Latin America* (Oxford: Blackwell, 1989). Robert Hefner indicates that as a historical sociologist, David Martin in his 1960s publications resisted grand theories and rather postulated multiple secularizations. See Robert Hefner, "Religion as Raft in a Stormy Sea: David Martin and the Study of Global Pentecostalism," *Nations and Nationalism* (forthcoming). Hefner notes that Martin's view of secularization was contingent on local circumstances, and thus he was sensitive to the growth of evangelicalism and pentecostalism. Email to author, August 3, 2020.

16. Robert W. Hefner, ed., *Conversion to Christianity: Historical and Anthropological Perspectives on a Great Transformation* (Berkeley: University of California Press, 1993).

were on everyone's mind.[17] Clearly Christianity was growing around the world, not disappearing. Despite privatization of religious belief, it was paradoxically, through globalization, a world-building system.[18] Christianity should be studied as a world religion rather than merely a Western export.[19] Amidst our discontent with the academic status quos of Western church history, the secularization theory of sociologists, and the neglect of Christianity by anthropologists, we saw something new.

Peter Berger allowed me to admit doctoral students into his "major" of religion and culture, in order to study a combination of mission theology, history of Christianity in the non-Western world, and social sciences. When my colleague in early Christianity, Howard Clark Kee, decided to write a book on the social history of Christianity as replacement for the outdated classic overview textbook by Williston Walker, I wrote a section on the emerging Christianity of Asia, Africa, and Latin America. Although my "epilogue" was inadequate and limited, its publication in 1991 declared that the mainstream history of Christianity needed to incorporate the growing churches beyond Europe and North America.[20]

1989: Revitalization Begins

Even as we in Boston and groups of scholars in the United Kingdom and other locations collectively groped toward something now named "world

---

17. The dialogue among mission studies, Christianity in the global South, and anthropology and sociology took place indirectly through joint participation in CURA seminars and with graduate students at Boston University, who studied missiology and world Christianity in the theology school, and anthropology and sociology in the graduate school. A brilliant scholar of Islam, Hefner also directed CURA projects on pentecostalism and is one of the few scholars to compare popular Islam with pentecostalism. See especially Robert W. Hefner, ed., *Global Pentecostalism in the 21st Century* (Bloomington: Indiana University, 2013); *The New Cambridge History of Islam*, vol. 6. *Muslims and Modernity: Culture and Society since 1800* (Cambridge: Cambridge University Press, 2010).

18. Roman Catholic sociologist José Casanova made this point in *Public Religions in the Modern World* (Chicago: University of Chicago Press, 1994).

19. Hefner pressed this issue in *Conversion to Christianity*. I used his definition of conversion in my book *Christian Mission: How Christianity Became a World Religion* (Chichester: Wiley-Blackwell, 2009), 152.

20. Howard Clark Kee et al., *Christianity: A Social and Cultural History* (New York: Macmillan, 1991). Howard Kee also attended Hefner's conference on conversion to world religions and contributed a paper to Hefner's volume on *Conversion to Christianity*. It is important to mention that the world history and global history movements also emerged in the 1980s. Although religion was not a chief focus of groups like the World History Association (founded in 1982), the importance of transnationalism, globalization, and cultural encounters beyond Europe was influencing both secular and religious historians by the 1980s.

Christianity," there was not yet a coherent field or discourse. The tipping point came in 1989. Changing contexts and grant funding made possible a series of networked conversations that led to the shaping of world Christianity as a field of study. First, of course, was the growing recognition that secularization was not a universal pattern. In 1989 the Berlin Wall fell and the Iron Curtain began collapsing—chiseled away by hymn-singing German youth, the Roman Catholic-inspired Polish Solidarity movement, and others. As Soviet communist empire failed, nationalism and religious belief revived. No longer could religio-ethnic identities be discarded on the trash heap of history.

A second development in 1989 was the holding of international meetings by both the ecumenical and evangelical clusters of mission leaders and the linkage of church growth and social justice as templates for both groups. "The papal encyclical *Redemptoris missio*, released the following year (1990), meant that the major branches of Christianity—Roman Catholicism, Ecumenical Protestantism, Orthodoxy, and Evangelicalism—were moving forward in tandem toward mission renewal and appreciation for growing ecclesial diversity."[21]

Another important development in 1989 was the publication of Lamin Sanneh's *Translating the Message*.[22] Published in the American Society of Missiology series, this work popularized the "translatability" theory developed by Sanneh and Walls. This concept emphasized indigenous control of the Christianization process. Despite colonial imposition, Sanneh argued, peoples everywhere brought their own meanings, including concepts of God, into their understanding of the faith. Furthermore, since the Bible was not written in a cosmic sacred language, it could be translated into any language and carry with it people's cultures. As put forth by Sanneh, the concept of translatability allowed scholars and practitioners to move beyond the pit of despair in which Christianity was the religion of European imperialists, and was rather potentially a source of liberation—a metaphor for Christianity as incarnational faith.

On top of the political and theoretical developments of 1989, funding from the Pew Charitable Trusts brought into dialogue several clusters of scholars eager to launch a new paradigm. The core group were those with the most at stake—mission scholars and historians. Mission studies was considered a "churchy" intellectual backwater that needed to engage

---

21. Part of this section is quoted from Dana L. Robert, "Naming 'World Christianity': Historical and Personal Perspectives on the Yale-Edinburgh Conference in World Christianity and Mission History," *International Bulletin of Mission Research* 44, no. 2 (2020): 111–28, here 119.

22. Lamin O. Sanneh, *Translating the Message: The Missionary Impact on Culture* (Maryknoll, NY: Orbis Books, 1989).

broader academic currents, and historians were the faculty responsible for identity formation, for "telling the story," especially in theological schools. Mission scholars, most with considerable experience in Africa, Asia, and Latin America, had front-row seats on the changes in the world Christian population, and they felt the urgency of moving beyond Western paradigms of Christian history.

The men behind the scenes, launching the new movement, were Joel Carpenter and Gerald Anderson. Carpenter had moved from his position as head of the Institute for the Study of American Evangelicals (ISAE), founded 1982 at Wheaton College, to the program office at the Pew Charitable Trusts. Given that ISAE had sponsored the first-ever conference on evangelical mission history in 1986, Carpenter knew the time was right to push for the globalization of conversations to revision mission history.[23] But he needed a partner grounded in the global church. He found that in Gerald Anderson, historian, missiologist, and former missionary in the Philippines, now head of the Overseas Ministries Study Center, and editor of the largest circulation journal in mission studies, the *IBMR (International Bulletin of Mission Research)*. The OMSC had moved to New Haven in 1987 to gain access to the Day Missions Library at Yale Divinity School.[24] Anderson identified the important stakeholders for a pilot project called SISMIC, the Scholars Initiative for Studies in Mission and International Christianity. Fortuitously, Lamin Sanneh had just joined Yale Divinity School in the chair previously held by Forman, and before that, Latourette. Andrew Walls was already a frequent visitor to New Haven, as he did research in the Day Missions Library. In addition to the notables, Anderson gathered "a team of eighteen scholars to advise Pew for what became a multimillion-dollar infusion of research funds for the study of mission history and Christianity worldwide."[25] Andrew Walls, with his rich experience both teaching in Africa and founding a religious studies department in the United Kingdom, "gave a keynote address to SISMIC that laid out the needed agenda for next steps: documentation and preservation of sources, collaborative research projects, and the de-Westernization of curricula in church history were all necessary goals. To move mission studies out of its academic isolation, Walls

---

23. Joel Carpenter also played a key role in the Pew funding for CURA at Boston University. Pew was attempting to fund "centers of excellence" into research on religion and public affairs, and in that context supported Peter Berger's institute.

24. In 2020, the OMSC moved to Princeton Theological Seminary in New Jersey.

25. Robert, "Naming 'World Christianity,'" 119. I was the youngest of the eighteen scholars who gathered to advise SISMIC.

strongly advocated for investment in research that would integrate it with other academic disciplines."[26]

With the report from SISMIC in hand, in 1992 the Pew Trusts started awarding major research advancement grants to scholars for large collaborative projects in non-Western Christianity. Carpenter recalls that "'from 1990 through 1995, Pew's religion program made grants totaling over $13 million in this field,' about $1 million 'in programs and projects at the Edinburgh Centre.'"[27] From 1992 to 1999, the Research Enablement Program (REP) channeled Pew funds into 110 individual scholarly projects on all aspects of world Christianity. The REP promoted interdisciplinary scholarship by supporting projects in history, anthropology, political science, intercultural studies, religious studies, and missiology. It also funded scholarly consultations, translations, and planning grants.[28] Scholars who received REP grants and attended seminars in Nashville, led by the REP committee, realized that not only was the study of Christianity larger and more interesting than had been supposed, but that interdisciplinarity and intersections between global flows and local contexts were central to its study.

As a member both of SISMIC and then of the REP selection committee throughout the existence of the project, I had a birds-eye view of the revitalization of the academic study of Christianity. Under the leadership of Gerald Anderson, the REP committee read all the applications from both beginning and established scholars, participated in the annual seminars, and saw firsthand how scholars in multiple disciplines began integrating their particular projects into a larger intellectual framework. The REP committee was itself interdisciplinary, though composed of scholars willing to be identified with Christianity as a growing reality—not a very large group in the early 1990s. Historians included Robert Frykenberg (India) and Dan Bays (China). Global theologians included John Pobee (Ghana), José Míguez-Bonino (Argentina), David Kerr (Islam), and Mary Motte (Catholicism). Paul Hiebert covered anthropology. On the REP committee, I was a full generation younger than the committee elders.[29] As a university-based scholar of mission history, I especially appreciated how our annual

---

26. Ibid. See Andrew F. Walls, "Structural Problems in Mission Studies," *International Bulletin of Mission Research* 15, no. 4 (1991): 146–55.

27. Robert, "Naming 'World Christianity,'" 120. E-mail from Joel Carpenter to Dana Robert, February 28, 2019.

28. Gerald H. Anderson and Geoffrey A. Little, *Research Enablement Program Assessment, 1992–1999* (New Haven: OMSC, 1999), 2.

29. Dana L. Robert, "Locating *Relocating World Christianity: Interdisciplinary Studies in Universal and Local Expressions of the Christian Faith*," *International Bulletin of Mission Research* 43, no. 2 (April 2019): 131.

seminars brought theologians and social scientists together, and lowered the barriers between ostensibly "Christian" and "secular" scholarship.

The REP program essentially gave permission to scholars to think about their local and individual research projects through a larger lens of global and local intersections, within the context of Christianity as a world religion. As scholars returned to their home institutions, they took with them a sense of collaborative energy. This, in essence, was the revitalization movement. Although the intellectual agendas now encapsulated by the term "world Christianity" had been launched, the term itself did not appear in the titles of any of the individual REP projects, although the term "world church" was used in one.

World Christianity Rises

The Pew-funded projects of the 1990s succeeded in bringing together multiple nodes of research into networked, mutual conversation. Among them, in 1992 occurred "the first major instance of use of the term 'World Christianity' in the conference 'From Christendom to World Christianity.'"[30] Co-sponsored by the OMSC at Yale Divinity School and the Centre for the Study of Christianity in the Non-Western World at Edinburgh University, the Yale-Edinburgh Conference:

> underscored the commonalities and intersections among what were usually told as separate mission histories. Held in the 500th anniversary year of Columbus's so-called discovery of America, the term "World Christianity" signified a postcolonial stance of moving beyond the European Christendom model of the old Latourette model of mission history, to that of indigenous initiative and Christianity as a multicultural religion not tied to one hemisphere.[31]

A listserv staffed by Martha Smalley of the Day Missions Library at Yale Divinity School maintained the collaborative conversation, and the

---

30. Robert, "Naming 'World Christianity,'" 121. Yale-Edinburgh Group on World Christianity and the History of Mission, Yale University, http://divinity-adhoc.library.yale.edu/Yale-Edinburgh. Two conferences were held the first year. The term "world Christianity" had come into use among ecumenical Protestants in the 1940s, but its usage collapsed during the turbulent 1960s. On the earlier use of the term "world Christianity," see Dana L. Robert, "The Giants of 'World Christianity': Historiographic Foundations from Latourette and Van Dusen to Andrew Walls," in William Burrows, Mark Gornik, and Janice McLean, eds., *Understanding World Christianity: The Vision and Work of Andrew F. Walls* (Maryknoll, NY: Orbis Books, 2011), 141–54.

31. Robert, "Naming 'World Christianity,'" 121.

Yale-Edinburgh Conference extended from one year to the next, alternating between Yale/OMSC and Edinburgh. In 1996, Pew Trusts funding underwrote the ambitious Currents in World Christianity Project (CWC), a multiyear initiative involving interested scholars from around the world. Directed by historian Brian Stanley at Cambridge University, CWC represented the merger and expansion of two projects: the North Atlantic Missiology Project and a global evangelicalism project directed by Australian Mark Hutchinson. Its series of international conferences resulted in over thirty volumes published by Eerdmans/Curzon presses.[32]

By the late 1990s, the idea of studying Christianity as a world religion had expanded beyond the practical and historical concerns that launched it. A growing cadre of doctoral students in Edinburgh, Boston, Princeton Seminary, Fuller School of Intercultural Studies, and other locations began producing exciting research. Different academic guilds began paying attention. Given the predominance of Christian historians who shaped the first phase, it is not surprising that the American Society of Church History became the first guild to hold a session on "world Christianity": in 1999, Lamin Sanneh and I gave invited plenary addresses on the new approach.[33] Meanwhile,

> in Munich in 1997, church historian Klaus Koschorke launched a conference series on "non-Western" Christianity that eventually shifted its focus to the "polycentric" nature of worldwide Christianity.[34] Historians began publishing revisionist textbooks that focused on the worldwide nature of the history of Christianity.[35]

---

32. The resulting series, edited by Brian Stanley and Robert Frykenberg, was titled "Studies in the History of Christian Missions." For a list of publications, see the Eerdmans website, https://www.eerdmans.com. Stanley became head of the Edinburgh center in 2009.

33. Dana L. Robert, "Shifting Southward: Global Christianity since 1945," *International Bulletin of Missionary Research* 24, no. 2 (April 2000): 50–58. As far as I know, Lamin Sanneh did not publish his speech.

34. The volume of the third conference first used the term "world Christianity." See Klaus Koschorke, ed., *African Identities and World Christianity in the Twentieth Century: Proceedings of the Third International Munich-Freising Conference on the History of Christianity in the Non-Western World* (September 15–17, 2004) (Wiesbaden: Harrassowitz, 2005).

35. Groundbreaking works included Howard Clark Kee, ed., *Christianity: A Social and Cultural History* (New York: Macmillan, 1991). In the second edition of Kee's volume, published in 1998 by Prentice-Hall, Dana Robert expanded her epilogue, "Christianity in Asia, Africa, and Latin America," into a section entitled "Christianity in the Wider World," including a chapter entitled "World Christianity"; Adrian Hastings, ed., *A World History of Christianity* (Grand Rapids, MI: Eerdmans, 1999); Wilbert Shenk, ed., *Enlarging the Story: Perspectives on Writing World Christian History* (Maryknoll, NY:

... By the early twenty-first century, the terms "World Christianity" and "Global Christianity" were proliferating as shorthand for an interdisciplinary focus on Christianity in Asia, Africa, and Latin America, and on Christianity as transnational networking. Documentation and research centers began appearing, looking to the model founded by Andrew Walls in Aberdeen.[36]

Regional documentation centers were founded, such as Michael Poon's Centre for the Study of Christianity in Asia at Trinity Theological College (Singapore). And as I noted in the *IBMR*,

In 2001 Boston University chartered the Center for Global Christianity and Mission, located in the School of Theology. In 2003 the demography project of David Barrett and Todd Johnson moved to Gordon-Conwell Seminary under the name Center for the Study of Global Christianity. After the publication in 2002 of Philip Jenkins's blockbuster *The Next Christendom*, the discourse of World Christianity rapidly accelerated.[37]

In 2005, Peter Phan and Dale Irvin organized a world Christianity group within the American Academy of Religion (AAR).[38]

The new discourse of world Christianity was not universally welcomed, even though the launching of the idea was useful in justifying certain kinds of research into local/global intersections. The traditional focus of many anthropologists on locality resisted the kind of globalism inherent in the concept. Nevertheless, rising water lifts all boats, and the matrix of world Christianity informed the launching of the anthropology of Christianity as a scholarly emphasis.[39] Similarly, historical research

---

Orbis Books, 2002); Dale T. Irvin and Scott W. Sunquist, *History of the World Christian Movement*, 2 vols. (Maryknoll, NY: Orbis Books, 2001, 2012).

36. Robert, "Naming 'World Christianity,'" 121.

37. Philip Jenkins, *The Next Christendom: The Coming of Global Christianity* (Oxford: Oxford University Press, 2002).

38. Robert, "Naming 'World Christianity,'" 121–22. Peter Phan had received an REP grant during the mid-1990s for his work on Alexander de Rhodes. The president of the American Academy of Religion asked Phan to organize a group on the theme "Christianity as a World Religion." During the November 2005 organizational meeting, Peter Phan and Dale Irvin switched the name to the "World Christianity" group; e-mail correspondence with Dale Irvin and Peter Phan, August 1, 2017. Dale Irvin, in particular, has played a key role in mainstreaming world Christianity into the AAR.

39. Joel Robbins points to Jenkins's volume as a motivating force behind the anthropology of Christianity. Joel Robbins, "Anthropological Perspectives on World Christianity," in Joel Cabrita, David Maxwell, and Emma Wild-Wood, eds., *Relocating World Christianity: Interdisciplinary Studies in Universal and Local Expressions of*

was traditionally tied closely to particular contexts and chronologies. Just as not all historians embraced the world history movement, also expanding at that time, not all historians embraced world Christianity. To the extent that world Christianity implied a theological universalism, critics accused it of inheriting hegemonic tendencies from the old colonial mission history framework that gave it birth. That most of its founders were themselves Christian scholars, many of whom had been missionaries or studied evangelicalism, raised suspicion about its motives among some scholars in religious studies.

Creative Tensions within World Christianity Discourse

From within the early conversations of those who basically welcomed the idea, differences of opinion naturally emerged over time. As with any revitalization movement, multiple streams and new contexts brought different emphases into the common discussion. First, the creative tension between locality and globality produced a range of opinions regarding which comes first, the chicken or the egg? And which is more important—the local context or the global flows? While everyone agreed that local impacted global and that global impacted local, the proportionate weight of each was not clear. Initially, the celebration of local contexts—of indigenous agency, new churches, and the like—seemed to take priority. This focus was important as a corrective to the dominant Western narrative. The language of "world" was seen to express the primacy of locality. To Andrew Walls and Lamin Sanneh, two of the framers of the early discourse, the concept of "world" in "world Christianity" implied the prioritization of local studies and indigenous initiatives. So, for example, they rejected the use of "global Christianity," seeing it as buying into the older hegemonic assumptions of mission-generated Christian expansionism.[40]

Christianity (Leiden: Brill, 2017), 241–42. Already in the 1990s, many recipients of REP grants were anthropologists who shaped the field, including John Barker, Brian Howell, J. D. Y. Peel, Charles Farhadian, and Erica Bornstein. An influential early text of importance both to world Christianity and to the launching of the anthropology of Christianity was Elizabeth E. Brusco, *The Reformation of Machismo: Evangelical Conversion and Gender in Colombia* (Austin: University of Texas Press, 1995).

40. On the definition of these terms, see Dana Robert and Aaron Hollander, "Beyond Unity and Diversity: A Conversation with Dana Robert on Mission, Ecumenism, and Global Christianities," *Ecumenical Trends* 48, no. 6 (June 2019): 2–9, 15. See also the discussion of nomenclature in Lamin Sanneh and Michael J. McClymond, "Introduction," in Lamin Sanneh and Michael McClymond, eds., *The Wiley Blackwell Companion to World Christianity* (Malden, MA: Wiley-Blackwell, 2016), 4–6; Todd M. Johnson and Sandra S. Kim, "Describing the Worldwide Christian Phenomenon," *International Bulletin of Missionary Research* 29, no. 2 (April 2005): 80–84.

With my husband, M. L. Daneel, who is an expert on Shona religions, I did field research in Zimbabwe and edited a multivolume project on "African Initiatives in Christian Mission."[41] I also participated in the Institute on Culture, Religion, and World Affairs (CURA) at Boston University, through which Peter Berger, Robert Hefner, and David Martin were researching globalization and the public role of religion, comparative pentecostalism and its economic impact, and related topics. In 2001 I named our new center the Center for Global Christianity and Mission. The deliberate use of the term "global" signaled the interdisciplinary scholarly concern for the public role of religion, as consistent with our university-based research priorities. The "mission" part of the title was meant to signal that Christian practices were not foreign to the scholarly task. Around the same time, the Center for the Study of Global Christianity—founded as the demography project of David Barrett, editor of the first edition of the *World Christianity Encyclopedia*—moved to neighboring seminary Gordon-Conwell Theological School. One example of the Boston continuum of discussion along the "global religion" axis is that Todd Johnson, head of the Christian demography center at Gordon-Conwell, was able to link with Peter Berger at CURA. And so it resulted that the World Religion Database, also run by Johnson and his associates, was launched at Boston University.[42]

In addition to the creative tension between locality and globality, including its expression in the terms "world" versus "global," a second issue that emerged after the turn of the century was whether to enforce the language of pluralization within the notion of Christianity itself. Since world Christianity operated in the tension between a universal tradition and local manifestations of it, should the new mazeway be called "world Christianities"? A leading proponent of the plural form was Peter Phan, one of the leaders of the discourse as it entered the American Academy of Religion. As a Roman Catholic theologian, not coincidentally investigated by doctrinal watchdogs for his support of an interreligious Christianity, Phan wanted to support the multiculturalism of the faith by use of the plural. Though

---

41. From 1995 to 2011, M. L. Daneel and I edited a thirteen-volume series on African Initiatives in Christian Mission. Twelve volumes were published by the University of South Africa Press, and one by Africa World Press.

42. Peter Berger was initially skeptical of the project, located at Gordon-Conwell. I helped convince him to accept it as part of CURA. For the World Religion Database, see https://worldreligiondatabase.org/. In 2008, Peter Berger and I wrote a large (unsuccessful) grant proposal for a three-year project on "world Christianity and international affairs." The project would have launched a formal collaboration between CURA and the CGCM, with the goal of researching world Christianity and transnationalism, world Christianity and ethnicity and identity, and world Christianity and humanitarian relief and development.

animated by different motives, his position aligned with new trends among some religious studies scholars. Walls and Sanneh preferred the singular, as a visible resistance to the idea that some forms of Christianity might not be as truly Christian as others. In other words, "new" Christianity was just as much fully authentic Christianity as old forms of the faith. From my social location within a university-based seminary, I also prefer the singular, because I have heard religious studies scholars argue that there is no such thing as the religion "Christianity," since it is so diverse. In other words, attention to diversity has been turned on its head as a basis from which to argue against the idea of Christianity as a world religion. Both as a Protestant and as a university-based historian, in which division and particularity are the default, I prefer to retain the idea that Christianity is a world religion, with diverse manifestations, rather than potentially multiple religions that lack historical continuity. As my colleague Robert Hefner notes by comparison, the idea of plural Islams proved to be repugnant to Muslim scholars, regardless of the ethnic diversity within the faith. In my opinion, alignment of emic and etic perspectives is better served by normally referring to Christianity (singular) rather than Christianities (plural).

A third issue that emerged in the new discourse was the extent to which studying world Christianity was itself an indication of belief in certain kinds of Christian vitality. Can true believers teach world Christianity, or must they first be put through the ringer of secular religious studies theory? Conversely, can non-Christians research and write about world Christianity? I would say "yes" to both propositions. As a revitalization movement, the existence of the academic discourse of world Christianity has unleashed huge creativity for scholarship among African, Asian, and Latin American scholars. It has also generated major research in secular history departments and area studies programs. In practice, however, there are biases against both. I have seen departments unable or unwilling to hire scholars, many of color, who are "too Christian" in how they approach the subject matter. Conversely, I have seen groups of world Christianity aficionados not wish to admit that secular scholars can generate exceptional research from outside a Christian framework. In my opinion, the beauty of thinking about world Christianity as a scholarly revitalization movement is that diversity of approach and a continuum of faith perspectives are integral parts of that movement. While it is a fact that Christian scholars had strong reason to adopt the new mazeway, its routinization means that Christian belief is not assumed. At the same time, the study of world Christianity has provided a door into academia for studies of healing, spiritual practices, conversion, and beliefs in supernaturalism, especially in a global context where pentecostalism has become a huge force.

A fourth and final tension that emerged within world Christianity discourse is the question of whether it is a lens through which to analyze a range of questions applied to any time or place, or if it is a field of study. The origins of the nomenclature leaned toward a field or subject of study, viz., Christianity in Africa, Asia, and Latin America. The idea of the "Third World," "Two-Thirds World," or "global South" reflects the origins of the discourse as a corrective to the traditional overfocus on European and North American Christianity. To consider world Christianity a field also opened the door to hiring people into an academic specialization. Especially in history departments that hire people into periods or major themes, the addition of world Christianity language allowed the designation of someone with specialization in modern Africa, Asia, or Latin America. Another advantage of thinking of world Christianity as a field is that it often opened hiring to much-needed persons of color, unlike fields such as medieval church history or modern European history. The acceptance of world Christianity as a field resulted in a plethora of job postings in North American institutions.

But as the corrective nature of the field description became less necessary and the utility of the transnational or global/local lens became attractive to scholars in all historical periods and in all regions of the world, some scholars pushed back against the idea that world Christianity is primarily a field of study limited to Africa, Asia, and Latin America. The attraction of the field ironically made European Christianity the outlier, the poster child of decline and collapse against which non-Western vitality could be triumphantly compared. But if world Christianity was actually a lens through which to research local/global encounters, and they impacted each other, then the study of European Christianity or Christianity in past eras could also be considered legitimate topics within the framework. The explosion of studies on Orthodoxy is a case in point. Another example from sixteenth-century studies, the traditional split between Protestant Reformation versus Catholic conquest models, is less meaningful when world Christianity is used as a lens of analysis. Similarly, studies of the Black Atlantic are marvelous examples of how world Christianity is a helpful framework, both from the perspective of world Christianity as a field and as a lens. As a lens of vision, all periods of history can find world Christianity nomenclature to be generative.

In 2013, the Center for Global Christianity and Mission at Boston University and the Center for the Study of Global Christianity at Gordon-Conwell co-sponsored a forum for the heads of world Christianity centers. Given the proliferation of research centers, it seemed important to gather the American and British stakeholders to compare information about funding, priorities, and the relationship between research and teaching. Over thirty scholars attended from world Christianity centers, including several scholars from continental Europe and additional graduate students.[43] One of the most interesting parts of the conference was a vigorous discussion as to whether world Christianity was a perspective or a field. Most participants saw the utility of both approaches, depending upon the scholarly context. In some institutions, Christianity was an opening wedge for studies of the non-Western world and for hiring diverse kinds of scholars. In other institutions, using world Christianity as a lens of vision allowed more traditional fields to connect with current relevant topics such as globalization, religion and migration, diasporic movements, cultural hybridity, and the relationship between Christianity and politics. Revitalization, in short, looks different depending upon the context.

The Messy Mazeway

As I reflect on over forty years of interest in what I used to call "comparative Christianity," I see the faces of dialogue partners along the way; and I recognize that while we have each walked our own paths, we have also walked together. Among these dialogue partners are those who don't even realize they have been part of a scholarly conversation. Two vignettes will illustrate this, both from the late 1980s. One day around 1986, I went home to my Boston apartment from a day of teaching about missions and colonialism. I was a bit depressed and wondering why I was spending my time teaching seminarians about Christian mission, when its footprint included oppression and violence. As I went into my little kitchen to get some water, I could hear the voices of workers drifting down the air shaft. Their accents sounded like they were from somewhere in south Asia, and they chatted as they worked in an apartment above me. Then they began singing a familiar evangelical hymn in their own language. Here were migrants, far from home, affirming their identities through singing a hymn that had crossed the ocean and back again, com-

---

43. Although graduate students took notes on the conference discussions, the primary purpose of the World Christianity Forum was to assist the heads of the centers. Proceedings were not published. Eleven world Christianity centers were represented, as well as key interlocutors. Participants included Joel Carpenter, Elias Dantas, Martha Frederiks, Bryan Froehle, Jehu Hanciles, Dale Irvin, Douglas Jacobsen, Elizabeth Koepping, Xi Lian, Christine Lienemann-Perrin, Michael McClymond, Jim Miller, Sung-Deuk Oak, and Emma Wild-Wood. Sociologist Nancy T. Ammerman gave the keynote address. "World Christianity Forum Program Booklet," October 17–19, 2013, Boston University School of Theology.

forting both them and me with the familiar tune. I felt revived. Despite it all, Christian history was not only about racism and colonialism, but also about self-selected identities and multicultural community.

A few years later, I was teaching a seminar in the Boston University School of Theology on the fourth floor. Again the topic was Christianity, imperialism, and colonialism. The noise from the street grew so loud that I stopped and went over to the window. There in front of the building was a van (labeled the "Mishnah mobile") that was blaring music, while young Orthodox Jewish men with beards, sidelocks, and black hats handed out pamphlets. Next to them were robed Hare Krishnas with shaved heads, beating drums and inviting students to free vegetarian dinners. While adherents of two other religions were evangelizing on the streets of Boston, the Christians were up in the ivory tower dissecting the history of Christian evangelization. The street noise reminded the class that putting Western Christians into the center of the picture is not an accurate portrayal of the world today. Christianity was not the only evangelistic game in town, and the United States had become a nation of coexisting but competing religions—and of no religion at all.

These two stories remind me that the study of world Christianity is messy—and it should be. It cannot be boxed and domesticated. The model of the revitalization movement is multilayered, widespread, and not controlled by the prophets who launched it. Like the academic discourse itself, the issues it raises are morphing, ongoing, and proceeding down multiple paths, depending on their context. New questions emerge in dialogue with the issues of the day. In an age of collapsing academic infrastructures and structural inequality, how do we support collaborative multilingual and multicultural projects that explore the meaning of Christianity as world religion? How do we anchor research centers and other nodes of generative creativity when we lack funding and resources? Does our research address unequal power, racism, and gender-based violence in the context of Christian community life worldwide, while also appreciating the variety of local/global intersections that make the faith possible? How do we put sociological theories of "multiple modernities" and "lived religion" into conversation with emic notions of pentecostal and evangelical vitality? How do boundary-crossing relationships create ecumenical Christian community, even amid political divisions, pandemics, and climate change? How do stories of local transformation impact global flows? All these questions, and more, reside in the mazeway called world Christianity.

2

World Christianity: History, Conception, and Interpretation

EMMA WILD-WOOD,
CARLOS F. CARDOZA-ORLANDI,
AND DYRON DAUGHRITY[*]

The rapid expansion of Christianity across the globe, particularly during the twentieth century, has been studied and mapped by a variety of scholars in the humanities and social sciences since the 1980s. Christianity as a vehicle for social, cultural, and political change throughout the world is gaining interest among anthropologists, sociologists, historians, theologians, and political scientists. Some of these scholars formed networks to develop this study. In the last ten years, a large number of textbooks that introduce "world Christianity" have been published—an indication of its arrival as a study area. More recently, scholars have turned to discussing the methods and approaches by which world Christianity should be studied as a distinct academic endeavor.[1] This chapter examines the historical development of this interdisciplinary study area and shows how it has been conceived and interpreted over the last forty years. Scholars have grappled with its place in the academy in the Western world and across the globe. They have discussed its composite disciplines and considered whether it is best understood as a contribution to

---

[*]With thanks to all the delegates of the October 2019 conference on world Christianity at the Candler School of Theology at Emory University, and particularly Joel Cabrita, whose paper was particularly helpful in the writing of this chapter.

1. See, for example, Joel Cabrita, David Maxwell, and Emma Wild-Wood, eds., *Relocating World Christianity: Interdisciplinary Studies in Local and Universal Expressions of the Christian Faith* (Leiden: Brill, 2017); Martha Fredricks and Dorottya Nagy, eds., *The Study of World Christianity: Approaches, Methods, Case-Studies* (Leiden: Brill, 2020).

constructive theological endeavor or to current or historical analysis of lived religious realities.

A survey of the history of the study of "world Christianity" provides some brief reflections on the terms of reference and the institutions that encouraged its study in Northern Hemisphere academic-confessional circles as well as outlining the complex factors that have, over time, shaped what is now a lively new study area.[2] By understanding the evolution of this area, we gain a deeper, more nuanced understanding of the current scholarly state of play and are able to reflect on how we may wish to maintain or change the status quo. We turn first to the institutions and networks that supported its advance. Then we will explore the research agenda that drove the development of world Christianity as its own discipline.

Institutions, Networks, and Projects

The genealogy of world Christianity is complex. The origins of the term can be found within ecumenical circles of the interwar and postwar period where it was used to reflect an idealistic hope for a worldwide Christian fraternity detached from the horrors of war.[3] However, the current use of the term developed as a postcolonial corrective to the modern missionary and ecumenical movements in an attempt to learn from mistakes undermining effective church partnerships in the late twentieth century. Its study arose within familiar academic structures in order to challenge existing norms. It emerged in the 1970s and 1980s to critique some Western assumptions about Christianity, not least those found in traditional faculties of theology.

A pioneering example of the promotion of this approach was the Centre for the Study of Christianity in the Non-Western World (CSCNWW), established by Andrew Walls in 1983 at the University of Aberdeen (it moved to the University of Edinburgh in 1987).[4] The title of the center is instructive. The term "non-Western" was deployed to challenge the nor-

---

2. For a discussion of the earlier history of the term, see Joel Cabrita and David Maxwell, "Introduction," in Cabrita et al., *Relocating World Christianity*, 1–44; Dana L. Robert, "Naming 'World Christianity': Historical and Personal Perspectives on the Yale-Edinburgh Conference in World Christianity and Mission History," *International Bulletin of Mission Research* 44, no. 2 (2020): 112–16.

3. For example, see Francis John McConnell, *Human Needs and World Christianity* (New York: Friendship Press, 1929), and Henry P. Van Dusen, *World Christianity: Yesterday, Today and Tomorrow* (Nashville, TN: Abingdon-Cokesbury Press, 1947).

4. For more information, see Brian Stanley, "Founding the Centre for the Study of Christianity in the Non-Western World," in William R. Burrows, Mark R. Gornik, and Janice A. McLean, eds., *Understanding World Christianity: The Vision and Work of Andrew F. Walls* (Maryknoll, NY: Orbis Books, 2011), 51–59.

mativity of Eurocentric subjects, categories, and objectives. The center was intended to educate the Western academy about the vibrant and growing Christian movements outside the West, which were developing theologies and spiritualities in response to different cultural and religious contexts. A number of scholars connected with the center came from the global South, including Kwame Bediako, founder of the Akrofi-Christaller Institute of Theology, Mission, and Culture, Ghana, and Marcella Althaus-Reid, a feminist liberation theologian from Argentina. It also welcomed international students—particularly those from the global South—who wanted to study their own Christian traditions. The term "non-Western" in the center's title has been justifiably criticized for the negative, "defining against" phrasing that serves to reinforce Eurocentrism. The change of title to the Centre for the Study of World Christianity (CSWC) in 2009, under the directorship of Brian Stanley, a historian of the global modern missionary movement, was a recognition that the "West" can no longer examine the "rest" and call it the "the world" as if it stood outside it. It was also an acknowledgment of the importance of the study of global connections and comparisons. The close friendship between Walls and Lamin Sanneh, who moved from Aberdeen to Yale University, prompted the first Yale-Edinburgh conference on the history of Christian mission and world Christianity in 1992. The title of that conference, "From Christendom to World Christianity," is perhaps the first reference to the term world Christianity as it is currently used. Sanneh's presence at Yale Divinity School revived study in the history of missions previously researched by Kenneth Scott Latourette, as well as interest in the Day Missions Library as a repository of information about the global spread of Christianity in the modern era.

Another significant center for the study of world Christianity in the United Kingdom was the federation of mission and education colleges at Selly Oak, Birmingham, ca. 1920–2005.[5] The main purpose of Selly Oak Colleges was to train European missionaries for mission, largely outside Europe. Students from partner churches also contributed to the life and worship of the colleges.[6] As a federation, the colleges were ecumenical, evangelical, and missional, and provided cultural training in the appreciation of context and Christianity. In the tradition of practical ecumenism of the modern missionary movement, Selly Oak taught theology

---

5. The colleges included the Harold Turner collection of documents on New Religious Movements, including African initiated and pentecostal churches, which is now part of the University of Birmingham, www./birmingham.ac.uk/schools/ptr/dept.

6. Daniel O'Connor, "All Change at Selly Oak," *Church Times*, November 2, 2006. Selly Oak Colleges was merged into The Queen's Foundation and the University of Birmingham.

and hermeneutics from around the globe, the history of mission and the worldwide church, and the art of cross-cultural communication. These subjects were taught as "mission studies." One of the most prominent faculty members was R. S. Sugirtharajah, who edited the seminal *Voices from the Margins: Interpreting the Bible in the Third World* (1991). The reduction and restructuring of missionary training led to the demise of the federation and the diminution of practical mission studies with a global focus in the United Kingdom, at the same time that world Christianity was becoming more prominent as an area of study.[7] However, there was overlap in content, approach, and personnel among emerging networks of world Christianity.

By the 1990s, the study of world Christianity had begun to develop a distinct sense of itself, through its development of formal research connections across the Atlantic. Pew Charitable Trusts supported the historical North Atlantic Missionary Project and the contemporary Currents in World Christianity initiative (starting in 1999). The Pew Research Enablement Program (led by Joel Carpenter in the 1990s) supported the projects of scholars from a range of disciplines. In Munich, beginning in 1997, Klaus Koschorke spearheaded conferences that developed a concern for the "polycentric" nature of Christianity across the globe. More academic posts and centers were established. In 1999 the American Society of Church History invited Dana Robert and Lamin Sanneh to present papers on the "new" worldwide approach to Christian history.[8] The publication of Philip Jenkins's pivotal book *The Next Christendom* in 2002 brought the scholarship produced in these initiatives to wider attention and encouraged a turn to Christianity in some areas of anthropology and sociology. By the dawn of the twenty-first century, the North Atlantic academy was beginning to recognize the importance of studying the variety and diversity of Christianity worldwide using interdisciplinary methods.

The study of Christianity as a world religion arose, in the first instance, from a peculiarly Western need usually within departments of theology and religious studies, even as students from Africa, Latin America, and Asia also wished to study their own traditions within a (Western) university setting. James Strasburg's historical trajectory of the study area shows that early positions in world Christianity usually followed faculty lines in mission studies that had developed since 1910 in

---

7. Colleges like Redcliffe and All Nations still remain, and ministerial training has developed a missiological component.

8. See Dana L. Robert, "Locating *Relocating World Christianity*: Interdisciplinary Studies in Universal and Local Expressions of the Christian Faith," *International Bulletin of Mission Research*, 43, no. 2 (2019).

the United States.⁹ Strasburg identifies four reasons for the title change from "mission studies" to "world Christianity": (1) as a strategy to avoid the colonial legacy of European and U.S. Christian missionary endeavors while upholding Christian mission as one of the marks of the church; (2) a "balancing act" between the growing crisis in the ecumenical movement, the inertia of the missional impact of the Lausanne Movement, and the growth of pentecostalism; (3) the increasing awareness of the decline of Christianity in Europe and the United States and the vitality of Christianity in the global South; and (4) the growing number of global South scholars in European and U.S. theological and religious academic institutions.

The development of the study of world Christianity as a corrective to Western discourses on religion has always been a collaborative endeavor with scholars from the global South. Institutional change, however, has been slow and uncomfortable. Carlos Cardoza-Orlandi taught world Christianity in three different institutions in the United States from 1994 and is aware that the particular approach of world Christianity is also bound up with the kind of institutions that have begun to make space for world Christianity and the disciplines or departments in which it is placed. The term prompts strong postmodern and postcolonial assumptions that potentially set boundaries in the imaginations of students and faculty.¹⁰ It triggers ideological affiliations within faculty circles, exacerbating tensions and turf fights in curricula design, course distribution, and department association. Scholars from the global South teaching in the North are often expected to be experts on their own region. Cardoza-Orlandi is originally from Puerto Rico and has frequently been expected to lead immersion courses on Latin America and the Caribbean and to teach courses on Latin American liberation theology, thereby joining the ranks of liberationists in the faculty. In short, he was expected to be the voice for his region of origin as it was understood by the institutions for whom he worked. During his career he has navigated the changing tides of institutional assumptions, disciplines' ambiguity, and deep assumptions about "younger churches" and the marginality of world Christianity. Where once there would have been little reference to Latin America,

---

9. James Strasburg, "Creating, Practicing, and Researching a Global Faith: Conceptualizations of World Christianity in the American Protestant Pastorate and Seminary Classroom, 1893 to the Present," *Journal of World Christianity* 6, no. 2 (2016): 223–31.

10. For discussion of the difference between diversity and pluralism in the West and in African theological studies, see Kwame Bediako, "Whose Religion Is Christianity? Reflections on Opportunities and Challenges in Christian Theological Scholarship: The African Dimension," in Andrew Walls and Cathy Ross, eds., *Mission in the Twenty-first Century* (Maryknoll, NY: Orbis Books, 2008), 109–10.

now it is safely compartmentalized and unable to intrude on the core focus of the faculty.

Conceptualization of Research Agendas

The development of the institutions, networks, and projects above has been identified with a necessary corrective to an understanding of Christianity as a Western phenomenon and connected with the disciplines of history and theology. The emerging field of world Christianity was interdisciplinary at a time when interdisciplinarity was still novel and when religious studies and theology were claiming distinct disciplinary paths.[11] It was also influenced by ecumenical and missiological thought. An examination of the research agendas emerging from world Christianity during its development provides a perspective of its historical evolution that allows for freedom in advocating for new directions to be followed in future world Christianity studies. In other words, a historical understanding of the term yields an appreciation of the noninevitability of the current scholarly priorities of the field. What has constituted world Christianity has changed over time—rather than always occupying the same static territory—so it is yet capable of further change and redefinition.

The pioneers of world Christianity were concerned that unified, global expressions of Christianity did not sufficiently recognize the range and variety of Christian movements around the world. They critiqued the globalism of an earlier generation of mission scholars who understood contextual expressions of Christianity as deviations from a norm.[12] Rather, scholars of world Christianity contended that these Christian movements demanded attention and reflection because they offered a corrective to the secularization theories prevalent in much of religious studies. For example, non-Western manifestations of Christian faith held theological insights for declining European churches and showed that Christianity had already been encountering other faith traditions in religiously plural settings when that still seemed rather novel in the global North.

Mainly Protestant, male missiologist-academics became—in the context of decolonization and independence of the 1960s and 1970s—increasingly disillusioned with missionary enterprise as traditionally understood and turned to what they regarded as a more politically progressive notion of world Christianity. The corrective work of pioneers gave attention to

---

11. For a restatement of this position, see D. Weibe, "Religious Studies," in J. R. Hinnells, ed., *The Routledge Companion to the Study of Religion* (London: Routledge, 2005).

12. Robert, "Naming 'World Christianity,'" 8.

the local and distinct expressions of Christianity around the globe. It is this interest that defined the first decades of the study of world Christianity. It became shaped by a focus on the "local" authenticity of Christianity as it had taken root in different regions across the world, in pluriform manner, largely or entirely independent of European or North American cultural and religious influence. This focus can be called the "indigeneity" approach.[13] Demonstrating that Christianity did not need to be a foreign European import was significant for the pioneering contributors to the new field of world Christianity. World Christianity scholarship was, with some exceptions, characterized by a commitment to fine-grained regional studies of Christianity, focusing on how local factors had shaped appropriations of the faith. This was particularly true for the study of Christianity in Africa, where the pioneering studies of the 1960s had focused on the culturally "authentic" independent churches while scholars' later interest in missionary churches had similarly emphasized the manner in which Africans appropriated and made their own a Northern-Hemisphere religious tradition.

The African continent and an Africanist scholarly agenda have been significant in shaping the world Christianity field as a whole. This was both in terms of the scholars who had historically dominated the field (Sanneh, Walls, Adrian Hastings, Kwame Bediako, and others) and in terms of the ongoing and continuing importance of African research agendas in shaping the field of world Christianity, for example, in the ubiquity of the influential notion of "translatability" and local agency (itself pioneered within an African context by Sanneh and Walls).[14] The Afro-optimism that had swept the continent in this period significantly shaped scholarly research agendas, resulting in the emergence of new departments of history devoted to examining African rather than European perspectives on the continent's history, and the founding of new journals such as the *Journal of African History* (1960) and the *Journal of Religion in Africa* (1967).[15] When European colonialism ended with the independence of African nations, many thought that Christianity would wither with the departure of colonial administrators and missionaries. On the contrary, the com-

---

13. Paul Kollman, "Classifying African Christianities: Past Present and Future," *Journal of Religion in Africa*, 40 (2010): 3–32.

14. For a retrospective of Sanneh's work, see J. Kwabena Asamoah-Gyadu, "Reform, Renewal and Revival: Lamin O. Sanneh and the Place of Africa in World Christianity," *Exchange* 49, no. 1 (2020): 53–77, and David Tonghou Ngong, "Domination and Resistance: Lamin Sanneh, Eboussi Boulaga, and the Reinterpretation of Christianity in Africa," *Exchange* 49, no. 2 (2020): 93–109.

15. The founding editor of the *Journal of Religion in Africa* was Andrew Walls. Adrian Hastings was his successor.

mitment of Africans to Christianity grew significantly from the 1960s. In largely implicit ways, factors particular to the continent imprinted a legacy on the development of world Christianity that shapes how it operates in the present day.

World Christianity was interdisciplinary from the start. It aimed to bring together historians, anthropologists, and theologians—among others—from an early date.[16] Nevertheless, a particular focus on the collection and analysis of archival sources gave modern historians prominence in world Christianity. Martha Smalley of the Day Missions Library, Terry Barringer at the Royal Commonwealth collection in Cambridge, and Rosemary Seton, the archivist at the School of Oriental and African Studies in London supported a number of database projects.[17] This engagement with the identification and cataloguing of historical sources was also taken up with enthusiasm by Michael Poon at the Centre for the Study of Christianity in Asia, Trinity Theological College, Singapore.

The pioneers of world Christianity were also ecumenists and engaged in interfaith relations, as Dale Irvin has pointed out.[18] The inter- and postwar ecumenical thinking called for institutional unity to solidify international fellowships and respond to the crises of war.[19] The merger of the International Missionary Council with the World Council of Churches (WCC) in 1961 widened the fissure between conservative evangelical missiologists and the ecumenical movement.[20] However, many mission scholars and theologians, some of whom worked in the WCC, contributed greatly to early discussions on world Christianity. They include Catherine Bliss, John Mbiti, Stephen Neill, Lesslie Newbigin, John Pobee, and Ruth Rouse.[21] They were also part of a movement to replace the integrative theology of ecumenical unity with contextual theologies that celebrated

---

16. Robert, "Locating *Relocating World Christianity*," 126–33.

17. Missionary Periodicals Database, Mundus, Gateway to Missionary Collections in the UK, 1999–2002, https://www.soas.ac.uk/library/archives/links/missionary; and projects to catalogue and copy church archives worldwide, supported by the Latourette fund.

18. Dale Irvin's "World Christianity, A Genealogy," *Journal of World Christianity* 9, no. 1 (2019): 5–18, further grounds his thesis, perhaps first proposed in his essay "World Christianity: An Introduction," *Journal of World Christianity* 1, no. 1 (2008): 1–26.

19. See T. Johnson and S. Kim, "Describing the Worldwide Christian Phenomenon," *International Bulletin of Missionary Research* 29, no. 2 (2000): 80–84.

20. Kirsteen Kim, "Mission: Integrated or Autonomous? Implications for the Study of World Christianity," 62–80, and Emma Wild-Wood, "Introduction: Ecumenism and Independency in World Christianity," 1–19, both in Alexander Chow and Emma Wild-Wood, eds., *Ecumenism and Independency in World Christianity: Historical Studies in Honour of Brian Stanley* (Leiden: Brill, 2020).

21. Aruna Gnanadason, "Women in the Ecumenical Movement," in *International Review of Mission* 81, no. 322 (April 1992): 237–46.

the diversity of Christianity.[22] The WCC supported networks of scholars like the Ecumenical Association of Third World Theologians (est. 1972) and the Circle of Concerned African Women Theologians (est. 1989) in their search for fresh theological responses that addressed regional concerns. In a move that mirrored and informed the development of world Christianity, diversity, indigeneity, and authenticity influenced the theological endeavor. Indian theologians like M. M. Thomas and Stanley Samartha developed an intellectual engagement with other religious traditions of India. From the late 1960s, Latin American liberation theologies contributed to an awareness, in both Catholic and Protestant circles, of the need for a contextualized Christian experience and agenda—one with a focus on social and political justice that included a critique of the structures of the church. One of the critical ecumenical publications that illustrates this awareness was *Iglesia y Sociedad* (ISAL, 1964).[23] The Caribbean Council of Churches (CCC) created the ecclesial and theological conditions that drove the emergence of theologies of emancipation, interreligious dialogue, and geopolitical collaboration. The CCC became a link between the African Council of Churches and the Latin American Council of Churches in developing theologies addressing race, ethnicity, and gender issues.[24] From the 1970s, theologians based in the West who were convinced by the insights emerging from across the globe developed an "intercultural" and often "interreligious" theology.[25] James Mackie, for example, the founding editor of the pioneering journal in the field, *Studies in World Christianity* (SWC), was a Catholic theologian with deep ecumenical sympathies who, influenced by Vatican II, critiqued the familiar Christian explanations of the relationship between religions and culture. Mackie argued that questions of Christian morality should be placed "in the context of cultures developing and declining, interacting and excluding" rather than in "more abstract and theoretical forms."[26] This was part

---

22. Robert, "Naming 'World Christianity,'" 116.

23. For more information on Protestant history in English, see the following: Orlando Costas, *Christ outside the Gate: Mission beyond Christendom* (Maryknoll, NY: Orbis Books, 1982); Carlos F. Cardoza-Orlandi, *From Christian Continent to Mission Field: The Missional Discourse of the Committee on Cooperation in Latin America and Protestants Latin Americans, (1910–1938)* (Ann Arbor, MI: ProQuest Dissertation Publishing, 1999). A more recent publication that captures *las voces más evangélicas* is David C. Kirkpatrick's *A Gospel for the Poor: Global Social Christianity and the Latin American Evangelical Left* (Philadelphia: University of Pennsylvania Press, 2019).

24. For more information, see Carlos F. Cardoza-Orlandi, "Caribbean, 1960–1998," in *A History of the Ecumenical Movement, Volume III* (Geneva: WCC, 2004), 523–32.

25. Emma Wild-Wood, "Afterword: Relocating Unity and Theology," in Cabrita et al., *Relocating World Christianity*, 327, 332–33.

26. James Mackie, "Editorial," *Studies in World Christianity* 3, no. 1 (1997): 1.

of his vision, "to promote theology/science of religion by providing a truly international forum in which a true 'dialogue of equals' can take place."[27] World Christianity, as it developed as a field of research, was influenced by developments in missiology and ecumenical and interreligious theology that critiqued concepts of mission and unity of the postwar years and focused on indigeneity and context. World Christianity also drew from history, the social sciences, and area studies, particularly African studies. It paid keen attention to sources. By the beginning of the twenty-first century, it was distinct from the areas of study that had formed it and was increasingly focused on analyzing the many cultural manifestations of Christianity worldwide, rather than focusing on constructive theology or missiology.

New Interpretations of World Christianity

The historical perspective on the study of world Christianity has prepared the ground for explaining some of the new directions the field has taken recently. The localized agenda has come under scrutiny in the last few years, and there is a turn to examining the field's connections across the globe. Interconnectedness, hybridity, and transcultural concerns in the study of Christianity are emerging as fresh foci for inquiry. Brian Stanley's *Christianity in the Twentieth Century* (2018) approaches this vast topic by employing a comparative model to study the way in which Christians in different parts of the world respond to similar issues. The edited volume *Relocating World Christianity: Interdisciplinary Studies in Local and Universal Expressions of the Christian Faith* (2017) encouraged a comparative, transnational perspective on the study of world Christianity. Rather than an exclusive focus on regional microhistories, it was interested in the complex interplay between local and transnational factors in the history of Christianity worldwide. It was written to stimulate a different kind of research agenda; it enquired into how local Christians imagined themselves as part of a worldwide church, and it asked about the importance of regional and international networks, connections, and movements in the history of Christianity. *Relocating World Christianity* featured essays by historians, anthropologists, theologians, and religious studies scholars that demonstrated this connected, comparative method. Themes were examined such as migration and diaspora, the role of new media in forming transnational religious communities, the importance of print networks, and the way in which debates about theology occurred through the platform of international conferences and widely read transnational

---

27. James Mackie, "Editorial," *Studies in World Christianity* 1, no. 1 (1995): 2.

journals and magazines. Throughout, the goal was to infuse "world" with a sense of connection: How have Christians forged their distinctive religious and cultural identities through imagining themselves to stand in some form of relation (not necessarily a harmonious one) with believers in other parts of the world? How can world Christianity define itself as a profoundly relational field, one devoted to the study of connective comparisons?

Historian of India Chandra Mallampalli has probed the concept of "translatability" (employed by both Walls and Sanneh and commonly used within world Christianity discourse) to signify the positive possibilities whereby indigenous cultures can find new meaning within Christianity, and vice versa. Mallampalli takes this discussion from its Africanist milieu and asks what conversion might mean within an Indian milieu. In India, Christian conversion is best explained in terms of loss and disruption due to the very small (2.3 percent) Christian minority in India, compared to a large majority of Hindus (80 percent) and a significant minority of Muslims (14 percent). When Indians become Christians, they join a small minority, often disconnected from their own communities. Some reify traditions they have inherited from Western forms of Christianity, like the use of the King James Version of the Bible.[28] They readily associate with Christian movements across the globe. At the same time, the *Ghar Wapsi* (Home Coming) reconversion movements back to Hinduism have impacted Christians disproportionately, compared to Muslims. In a Hindu-Sanskritic context, Mallampalli says, conversion is not a positive "translation" of culture within a new Christian form. Conversion instead implies loss or desertion of Indian linguistic-religious identity. Bearing Mallampalli's model in mind might help scholars of world Christianity to invest more heavily in idioms of breakage and rupture—rather than complementarity and continuity as is implied in the translatability model—in analyzing the impact of the faith on regional contexts.

Christian conversion and culture may not always exist in a harmonious relationship, a point the anthropologist of Christianity Joel Robbins has also made.[29] Observations from India by Dyron Daughrity also

---

28. Dyron Daughrity, "The King's English in a Tamil Tongue: Missions, Paternalism, and Hybridity in South India," *Missio Dei* 4, no. 1 (February 2013), http://missiodeijournal.com.

29. Chandra Mallampalli, "The Orientalist Framework of Christian Conversion in India: Three Venues of 'Inducement' from Colonial Times to Present," in Cabrita et al., *Relocating World Christianity*, 162–88; Joel Robbins, *Becoming Sinners: Christianity and Moral Torment in a Papua New Guinea Society* (Berkeley: University of California Press, 2004). See also Eliza F. Kent, "Secret Christians of Sivakasi: Gender, Syncretism, and Crypto-Religion in Early Twentieth-Century South India," *Journal of the Academy*

push continuity questions toward issues of hybridity, multiple belonging, and new blended religious traditions. Many Indians incorporate Christ into their Hindu practice. The Khrist Bhakta Movement is one of many movements in India that exists so interstitially between Christianity and Hinduism that it is difficult to ascertain which religious tradition is more prevalent.[30] In a hostile context there are few reasons to explicitly identify as Christian when simply returning, at least nominally, to Hinduism could make life much easier. A cross-cultural, interreligious bricolage is prevalent, even common, in many expressions of Christianity worldwide. Indian studies have begun to influence the world Christianity discourse, and we may expect the rise in studies on China over the last ten years to contribute increasingly to the theoretical discussions within world Christianity.[31]

The work of Klaus Koschorke and his associates has also shifted away from the indigeneity/localization model and embraced a more connected, comparative approach. Koschorke argues that the church has always had multiple centers of influence and gravity. He says that instead of reconstructing more local histories of Christianity (what Koschorke calls the "add-and-stir" model of world Christianity[32]), the field should explore the multidirectional transcontinental links between these multiple sites of Christendom. Rather than "world" merely denoting an aggregate of regional Christian "area studies" (in the style of many similar world Christianity volumes), or simply a nod to Western Christian agencies with international reach (in the style of older, early-twentieth-century studies of supposedly "world" Christianity), Christianity is being studied as a global phenomenon, composed of multiple lateral South–South, as well as North–South, linkages, networks, and connections.

This turn to the transnational is distinct from a naïve return to the interwar rhetoric of an unproblematic, international Christian ecumene.

---

of Religion 79, no. 3 (September 2011): 676–701. For an example of how such a discussion is illustrated in a majority Christian context, see Carlos F. Cardoza-Orlandi, "What Is Jesus Doing among the Spirits? Questions from a Mission Studies Scholar to Grass-roots Caribbean Charismatic *Evangélicos*," in David H. Jensen, ed., *Always Being Reformed: Challenges and Prospects for the Future of Reformed Theology* (Eugene, OR: Wipf & Stock, 2016).

30. See Jerome Sylvester, *Khristbhakta Movement: Hermeneutics of a Religio-Cultural Phenomenon* (Delhi: ISPCK, 2013).

31. See, for example, Chan Kei Thong, *Faith of Our Fathers: God in Ancient China* (Shanghai: China Publishing Group, 2006); and Kim-kwong Chan's *Understanding World Christianity: China* (Minneapolis: Fortress Press, 2019). Earlier scholars of Christian mission in China include Jessie Lutz and Gary Tiedemann.

32. Cited in Cabrita and Maxwell, "Introduction: Relocating World Christianity," in Cabrita et al., *Relocating World Christianity*, 24.

Connection and lateral networks do not imply the absence of hierarchies and structures of power—financial, political, and otherwise. Indeed, one of the drawbacks of much globalization rhetoric (one of the main ways social-scientific scholars currently conceive of interconnectedness between different parts of the world) is that it ignores the extent to which such networks are rarely constituted "evenly." To paraphrase historian Frederick Cooper: The world is filled with lumps; that is, places where power coalesces surrounded by those where it does not, places where social relations become dense amidst others that are diffuse. Structures and networks penetrate certain places and do certain things with great intensity, but their effects tail off elsewhere.[33] Identifying the "lumpiness" of international networks is an excellent methodological starting point for contemporary scholars of world Christianity.

For example, anthropologist Naures Atto has written about Middle Eastern Christians who debate the pros and cons of leaving their "homeland" for Western countries when confronted with extreme hardship. Some Christians choose to stay in their homeland despite the dangers (often citing their ancestral rights to the territory), but the financially disadvantaged who lack fortuitous transnational connections are forced to stay.[34] This echoes a broader argument made by many scholars of migration, which is that certain social categories of refugees are more likely than others to get "stuck" in situations of conflict and danger. Diaspora studies of the kaleidoscopic forms of Christianity that exist today in the large cities in the West indicate the opportunities and pitfalls of global markets and travel that raise questions of interdependency and injustice. A stark reminder of the lumpiness of power is presented regularly in news commentaries on the rise of nativist-popularist governments across the globe and, most powerfully, in the reported societal effects of the Covid-19 pandemic. Rather than being seduced by the myth of unlimited mobility, ease of movement, and access to social goods, scholars need to recognize the severe constraints experienced by those Christians who seek to exercise their right to belong to a worldwide ecumene.

In recent years the historic and geographic scope of world Christianity has been challenged. Dyron Daughrity has highlighted the risk of ignoring Eastern forms of the faith.[35] While Orthodoxy is relatively small

---

33. Frederick Cooper, "What Is the Concept of Globalization Good for? An African Historian's Perspective," *African Affairs*, 100, no. 399 (2001): 190.

34. Naures Atto, "The Death Throes of Indigenous Christians in the Middle East: Assyrians Living under the Islamic State," in Cabrita et al., *Relocating World Christianity*, 281–301.

35. Dyron Daughrity, "Christianity Is Moving from North to South—So What About the East?" *International Bulletin of Missionary Research* 35, no. 1 (January 2011):

on a global scale, in Eastern Europe it is the most common form of Christianity. In the Middle East, nearly one in three Christians is a member of an Orthodox church.[36] In light of the global political significance of these contexts, world Christianity should provide a better understanding of these ancient forms of Christian faith. Ignoring the East perpetuates a Western bias against Orthodoxy and impoverishes Western Christians, many of whom are unable properly to understand Orthodox history and theology. It also means the historical frame of world Christianity begins at the very earliest in the sixteenth century. Irvin and Sunquist's multivolume *History of the World Christian Movement*[37] helps break historical silos and challenge the "Western" worldview of Christianity's movement and vitality. Walls and Bediako are unusual in their comparative study of Christian origins and the early church in order to understand the rapid growth of Christianity in Africa.[38] The conceptualization of world Christianity as a transnational, transtemporal phenomenon may encourage such developments.

Another significant shift that requires mention is the turn toward ethnography. While the methods and findings of social science have played a role in world Christianity since the 1980s through the field of religious studies, there is a fresh appreciation of ethnographic fieldwork that is most evident in the world Christianity conference that has been held annually at Princeton Theological Seminary since 2018, convened by Afe Adogame, Raimundo Barreto, and Richard Fox Young. A greater attention to the best methods of data collection and a concern about the overreliance on the archives of Western mission organizations as sources for Christianity worldwide is a welcome addition to the internal critique of the field.

World Christianity across the Globe

This chapter has described the study of world Christianity as a product of Western institutions attempting to correct previous assumptions and

---

18–22. See also Dorottya Nagy on concepts of Eastern Europe in "World Christianity as a Theological Approach: A Reflection on Central and Eastern Europe,' in Cabrita et al., *Relocating World Christianity*, 143–61.

36. See Dyron Daughrity, *The Changing World of Christianity: The Global History of a Borderless Religion* (New York: Peter Lang, 2010), 23.

37. Dale T. Irvin and Scott W. Sunquist, *History of the World Christian Movement*, 2 vols. (Maryknoll, NY: Orbis Books, 2001, 2012).

38. Andrew Walls, "Eusebius Tries Again: Reconceiving the Study of Christian History," in *International Bulletin of Missionary Research* 24, no. 3 (July 2000): 105–11; Kwame Bediako, *Theology and Identity: The Impact of Culture upon Christian Thought in the Second Century and in Modern Africa* (Oxford: Regnum, 1992).

methods of Western scholarship and of Christian unity. The field has also developed a wide network of scholars around the globe who associate with world-Christianity approaches and contribute to the production of knowledge of Christianity in Africa or theologies of Asia and the like.[39] Two significant questions arise for the study of world Christianity today. First, is it of use to the academy outside the Western world, or does it so derive its rationale from North Atlantic academic structures or norms that it has little purchase beyond them? And second, does it perpetuate dominant—and dominating—models of enquiry that are extractive or excluding?

The network of institutions in the global South whose scholars draw on world-Christianity approaches have emphasized diversity in teaching and research in order to (1) eradicate curricular expectations of the colonial era; (2) acknowledge their own history, culture, and intellectual engagement; and (3) respond to national or regional academic expectations. Institutional change taking place in Africa, Asia, and Latin America has been accompanied by curriculum reform. In Africa, seminaries have developed into privately chartered universities as a result of neoliberal policy changes.[40] As limited resources came under increased pressure, there was a greater need for lay training of Christians in all occupations, which prompted a greater incentive for integration into teaching of contemporary issues (gender, HIV and AIDS, human rights, disability, conflict resolution, interfaith, environment, etc.) and church-state relations and politics. In broad terms, some of these issues are similar to the concerns of all universities to give students of humanities and social sciences the knowledge and "transferable skills" they will need to take up professional roles in society. However, the specific concerns may be distinct, and the language and the values may be different. Curriculum reform often focuses on national interests, but is also concerned about the international connections of universities.[41] Institutions in Africa, Asia, and Latin Amer-

---

39. A partial list of Andrew Walls's PhD students, for example, illustrates the influence of his approach in institutions across the globe.

40. One recorded reflection comes from St. Paul's University Limuru, Kenya: Esther Mombo and C. B. Peter. "Leadership and Theological Education," in Titre Ande, ed., *A Guide to Leadership* (London: SPCK, 2010). For a wider discussion on theological education in Africa, see Isabel Apawo Phiri and Dietrich Werner, eds., *Handbook of Theological Education in Africa* (Oxford, OR: Wipf & Stock, 2015).

41. There is also an increasing concern that, having mounted a challenge to Western theologies and Western curricula, African universities now face the challenge of commodification. See Nontando M. Adebe, "Commodification, Decolonisation and Theological Education in Africa: Renewed Challenges for African theologians," *HTS Teologiese studies/Theological studies* 73, no. 3 (2017): 1–10.

ica may or may not use the discourse of "world Christianity," but they will certainly adapt its approaches to their own circumstances.

The study of world Christianity is unfamiliar in many institutions in Latin America and the Caribbean, and particularly among *evangélicos* and *pentecostales*.[42] Only among elite theologians with global connections will the term *cristianismo mundial* have some meaning. A particular direction was set in Cuba in the early 1990s, when sociologists addressed a group of theologians from the Seminario Evangélico de Matanzas and the Academia de la Religión. They discussed the growth of religious expressions and Christianity's vitality in the region. Yet the most prevalent thread of academic reflection from that early interaction remains the conspiracy theory of the imperial and colonizing agenda of the United States or Europe in Latin America and the Caribbean. Moreover, while many social scientists emphasize the relationship between Christianity's growth and its connection to the market economy (i.e., religion as a commodity), there appears to be little academic concern for the religious and theological dimensions of Christianity's lived experience. There also appears to be little interest in the lived experience of religious people on the continent. Meanwhile, some of the ecumenical and missional organizations in Latin America and the Caribbean are either in crisis or their emphasis is on practical mission work, including South-to-South work. Most of the theologies and practices of *pentecostales*, *evangélicos*, and non-denominational *evangélicos* have an evangelistic drive with the expectation of church growth. Cardoza-Orlandi views this range of theologies and practices as providing a laboratory to explore polycentric structures, the spectrum of competition to collaboration among Christian communities, and international partnerships of different missional inclinations. In Asia, the influence of the study of world Christianity is variable. Pan-chiu Lai, writing from Hong Kong, finds that the discourse of world Christianity offers a challenge to the assumption in East Asia that Christianity is a Western religion and provides an explanation for the compatibility of Christianity with Chinese identity and thus is useful in a Chinese religious studies setting.[43]

If a world Christianity approach has enabled academic institutions in Africa, Latin America, and Asia to examine their own local and indig-

---

42. Recently, the Seminario Evangélico de Matanzas, with the collaboration of the University of La Habana, created ISECRE, Instituto Superior Ecuménico de Ciencias de las Religiones, Teologías y Religiones Caribeñas. Further collaboration with faculty from the University of Puerto Rico and the Seminario Evangélico de Puerto Rico is currently underway.

43. Untitled working paper presented to Emory colloquium ("World Christianity: Issues, Questions, Debates") in 2019.

enous forms of Christianity without comparing them with other parts of the globe, how might the shift to a transnational and connective approach to the study of world Christianity be useful in the global South? This question cannot be fully answered here. However, it does suggest that there is some reflective work to be done on the importance of attention and collaboration by North American and European institutions where world Christianity is prominent. It is important to ask whether studies of world Christianity are extractive. That is, do they use material generated in one part of the globe, or among one group of people, for aims that serve the purposes of the North Atlantic academy and *not* the people among whom the research has been carried out?

The recent return to public consciousness of issues of racial and cultural difference, in the face of growing nativist populism on both sides of the Atlantic, has generated renewed attention in certain academic subjects to the necessity of "decolonizing the curriculum." Again, the debate has returned to how the Western academy can improve itself by deliberately listening to voices that have often been ignored and unheard because they do not seem to fit the agenda, or because their books are not published with a well-known Western publisher. Many of the concerns raised in "decolonizing the curriculum" discussions have already been incorporated into the way in which world Christianity has been done. This is not a moment of self-congratulation—the cultural lens most often used to frame world Christianity studies can relativize race and poverty and locate it at a safe distance from the academy. It does not always articulate fully the injustices around race and poverty.

It is difficult to overturn cultural biases that have existed in cultural and political consciousness for generations. World Christianity scholars are among the best positioned to address these prejudicial lines of thinking. How might this take place in the academy itself? Cardoza-Orlandi was welcomed as a "missionized" instructor teaching Christian mission in a context of church decline. However, students and staff did not expect him to challenge assumptions about course content. They were unprepared to accept in theological and ministerial curricula concepts such as "the feminization of evangelization," "the polycentricity of the Christian religion," and "the Trinity as a divine *mestizaje*." Nevertheless, he discovered that being located in Christian mission provided fragile, but legitimate, opportunities to integrate Christian mission (including ecumenics, cross-cultural mission, and interfaith studies) with an interdisciplinary world-Christianity approach. It allowed space to illustrate the agency of the global South Christian community, particularly poor women of color, in living out their faith and the living faith and challenges of those communities faithfully giving Christian witness in contexts rich in religious, linguistic, and cultural diversity, and overwhelmed by environmental deterioration, war conditions, and extreme poverty.

Studies in world Christianity have created a bridge between constructive theological studies and the largely secular academy. Depending on the institution, the field may operate with more or less secular assumptions built into its approach. However, secularity is not necessarily a normative position in institutions elsewhere in the globe that recognize the public role of religion, whether they are secular, state institutions, or in the burgeoning sector of faith-based tertiary education providers. Scholars in the field of world Christianity come from a variety of faith commitments and in some cases even a context of no faith. The question of secularity or faith as a norm in academic inquiry is likely to remain an important topic in the field.

Scholars of world Christianity across the globe need one another if our work is not to be naïve, or extractive, or overly insistent on a normative confessional or secular position. The corrective project that Walls and others began[44] is not over—the North Atlantic academy still requires its norms, structures, and content to be challenged. A "sustained and thoughtful interaction between academics across different geographical regions" is required in order to "modify the objectification and suppositions of alterity that can still insert themselves into academic work."[45] Global networks of scholars studying aspects of Christianity is valuable. The North Atlantic academy, in particular, should avoid extraction or exoticization by attending to how and with whom it carries out research. The final part of this section examines how scholars might collaborate with one another, as we might use different methods and hold different assumptions about scholarship or curriculum content to achieve an expansive, inclusive, and relational approach to the worldwide study of world Christianity.

An expansive approach includes developing the potential for theological material and method to enrich historical and social scientific approaches and vice versa. The academic community is far from united in its pursuit of knowledge and understanding. In particular, significant fractures exist within the ranks of those who study religion. There has been, for example, a long-standing debate about the nature and objectives of religious studies and its relationship to theology, which has largely

---

44. Andrew Walls refers to this in his recent article, "Overseas Ministries and the Subversion of Theological Education," *International Bulletin of Mission Research* 45, no. 1 (2021): 7–14.

45. "Afterword: Relocating Unity and Theology," in Cabrita et al., *Relocating World Christianity*, 338–40, quoted and referenced at some length here.

been formed by the Western academy. Some scholars still adhere to a clear distinction between studying *about* and being educated *in* a religious tradition. They express concern about the intrusion of theology into their fields: for them, it confuses the subject of study with the method of study and addresses the metaphysical, moral, and existential in a manner that is unconventional in post-Enlightenment disciplines long assumed to be secular and expunged of doctrinal influence.[46] However, there is a growing recognition that social scientific claims are no more unmotivated than any other, and that social scientific categories have marginalized Christian categories while being a product of them. This acknowledgment has provoked a call to adopt something from the people under study, describe the people under study in their own terms, and be willing to recover certain indigenous categories (theological or otherwise) and to identify their beneficial ways of being.

An inclusive approach is one in which scholars study "with" and "in" world Christianity, learning from those who are shaping their disciplines in ways different from those that exist in the Western academy. Some scholars are part of the communities they study and contribute to studies in world Christianity as a form of scholarship that is emotionally engaged. The Western academy has traditionally expected a critical distance. Those of us who have been academically trained to maintain that distance need to attend to scholars who are activist in intent, often programmatic, and committed to the outcomes they elucidate in their writing, for example, in response to immediate problems facing their own churches and societies. Activist scholars are critical of forms of thought that they consider to be insufficiently relevant to society. Their ideas challenge the distinction between private and public expression.

One way in which Cardoza-Orlandi's research is expansive and inclusive is through *testimonio*, which he understands as a sub-category of Peter Phan's similar *participatory* method.[47] Testimony is the embodiment of the complex movement and flow of religious identity for both an individual and community. Researchers ask, What are the testimonies of a community in its context—for example, in its relation to people of other faiths, to the experience of war, to environmental change, or to unexpected events? They inquire as to whose testimonies are embodied (women?

---

46. Daniel Weibe, "Religious Studies," in J. R. Hinnells, ed., *The Routledge Companion to the Study of Religion* (London: Routledge, 2005).

47. Peter Phan, "Doing Theology in World Christianity," *Journal of World Christianity* 1, no. 1 (2008): 27–41. Phan uses the term "myth" to describe the agency of common people. By using the term, he leaves open the source of the myth—it comes from all religions and cosmologies. Cardoza-Orlandi prefers to use "testimony" since it is closer to his own charismatic *evangélico* tradition.

children? slaves? missionaries? pastors and/or priests? disabled people? immigrants? refugees? theologians? creation?). How do these testimonies intersect and interact with each other? In this approach, the agency of embodiment and the forces that shape the embodiment are explored. Are these *testimonios* coherent or in continuity with other *testimonios* in the same context, in other regions and in other historical periods? If not, what explains the discontinuities or incoherencies? This interdisciplinary endeavor builds a theoretical and theological framework to grapple with questions of identity/hybridity, theology, power, and communication. For this expansive and inclusive approach to be successful it requires a relational component.

Relational reflexivity seeks to comprehend the other on their own terms, through a process of personal and disciplinary reflexivity; it also engages in dialogue and exchange of assumptions and belief together. It is particularly important where there are significant doubts about the premises and rationale of the other. This relational reflexivity is focused not on the other but on the encounter between two or more parties.[48] It includes a dialogue about the attitudes, values, and assumptions of scholars involved with research as a corporate exercise and integrated into the research. It is a sharing of a self-examination process, in order to recognize the subjectivities of those involved in their different contexts and agendas.

In the field of pedagogy, bell hooks's reflections on theory and practice are insightful. In her book *Teaching to Transgress: Education as the Practice of Freedom*, she states, "When our lived experience of theorizing is fundamentally linked to processes of self-discovery, of collective liberation, no gap exists between theory and practice. Indeed, what such experiences makes more evident is the bond between the two—that ultimately reciprocal process wherein one enables the other."[49]

Engaging in self- or collective discovery and freedom by using the category of testimony presents world Christianity scholars with a vocational identity embedded in an approach to research.

Conclusion

Over time, the study of world Christianity has become a synthetic and collective approach to peoples, practices, thought, and environment across

---

48. For more discussion on this, see O. Lievik, "Interreligious Studies: A Relational Approach to the Study of Religion," *Journal of Interreligious Studies* 13 (2014): 15–19; V. Kuster, "From Contextualization to Glocalization: Intercultural Theology and Postcolonial Critique," *Exchange* 45, no. 3 (2016): 203–6.

49. bell hooks, *Teaching to Transgress: Education as the Practice of Freedom* (New York: Routledge, 1994), 61.

the globe. It attends to diversity and interconnectedness. It often prioritizes marginality (in its various forms) and deploys the lens of culture as a frame of study. It uses a variety of methods and works across disciplines (drawing particularly, but not exclusively, upon history, theology, and ethnography). It is committed to engage with Christians worldwide. It is informed by scholarship in other parts of the globe and is based primarily in the North Atlantic as a corrective to Western-centric scholarship.

This chapter has examined how "world Christianity" became shorthand for the study of Christianity in very particular territories and locations around the globe, rather than the more unitary phenomenon usually suggested by the use of the word "world," and indeed by older invocations of world Christianity in the interwar period as an ecumenical international fellowship. Scholarship became largely invested in studying how Christians imprint local concerns upon a universal faith rather than how a universal faith provides a basis for imagined and actual solidarities between highly divergent believers across the world.[50] The chapter has shown two ways in which the emergence of the field of world Christianity developed as a corrective to the content and approach of theology and religious studies and mission training in British institutions. These changes included the recognition of the importance of partnerships in the world church as well as the enrichment of scholarship in the West by exchange and by providing doctoral education for church leaders from the global South.

If the study of world Christianity is to continue to offer a critique of norms and structures (which all academic subjects should be prepared to do), then it would do well to engage with the changes taking place in other disciplines but also to continue engaging with scholars across the globe. It should also retain a certain fluidity. Fixing or highly differentiating the field may minimize some of its most critical strengths, its intra- and interdisciplinarities, which provide opportunities to "place us in opposition to any system of education or culture that would have us be passive recipients of knowledge."[51] Ultimately, a fluid identity helps to contribute perspectives and knowledge that enrich the theological and religious formation of students and institutions.

---

50. Joel Cabrita and David Maxwell, "Introduction: Relocating World Christianity," in Cabrita et al., *Relocating World Christianity*, 20.

51. bell hooks, *Teaching Critical Thinking: Practical Wisdom* (New York: Routledge, 2010), 185.

3

World Christianity Curricula: A Perspective from Missiology/ Mission Studies

KIRSTEEN KIM

Students and Employment

From where I sit as associate dean of a missiological research center (at Fuller Seminary's School of Intercultural Studies), "world Christianity" is an alternative name for missiology or mission studies in North America that, like intercultural studies, avoids problems having to do with the term "mission." These problems are (a) the colonial legacy and the intentional connotations of "mission," both of which are questioned in the Western academy; and (b) the inadvisability of having "mission" on the CVs of those who intend to work in contexts inhospitable to Christianity or religion in general. The inhospitable context may be in places where a non-Christian faith is defended or where the ideology is strongly secular (including in parts of Europe).[1] If indeed "world Christianity" is seen as a more acceptable alternative, then many of the potential students of world Christianity come from the same pool as those who apply for missiology or intercultural studies at the masters' degree level. These mainly aim to work in churches, Christian nonprofits, or FBOs (faith-based organizations), or to teach in seminaries or universities. Although the

---

1. Fuller Theological Seminary might have chosen "world Christianity" or, more likely, "global Christianity" as a new name for the school, but its motivation was more toward the latter problem. See Elizabeth "Betsy" Glanville, "Name Change at Fuller's School of World Mission to School of Intercultural Studies," in Robert A. Danielson and Larry W. Caldwell, eds., *What's in a Name? Assessing Mission Studies Program Titles: The 2015 Proceedings of the Association of Professors of Missions* (Wilmore, KY: First Fruits Press, 2015), 11–23, https://place.asburyseminary.edu/academicbooks/12/.

label "intercultural studies" may create a deception that it is not explicitly religious, "world Christianity" does not have an advantage with respect to problem "b." However, because it avoids problem "a," it may attract more students of theology (especially church history), cultural studies, and religious studies who are planning to begin an academic career. In addition, compared to "missiology," "world Christianity" would disadvantage graduates less for posts in development studies, which distances itself from explicitly religious agendas. Both world Christianity and intercultural studies have an advantage over missiology in attracting students put off by missiology, or even theology, because of its colonial heritage, orientation to the West, and association with white supremacy.

Regarding prospects for employment, opportunities in churches, Christian nonprofits or FBOs, or seminaries and universities after studying "world Christianity" are depressed at present due to (a) the weakness of churches that have historically valued higher education and their seminaries; (b) the withdrawal of the United States from international engagement under President Donald Trump and the current disruption to international travel (due to the COVID-19 pandemic) that is causing mission and development agencies to reconsider their work abroad; (c) the tenuous position of theology and religious studies in universities and academia in the West; and (d) the undermining of the humanities by the promotion of the sciences, which are thought to contribute more to the global economy and to the students' own earning potential. However, for the reasons above, general employment prospects may be stronger than in the closely related field of missiology.

The extent to which "world Christianity" prepares students for employment in churches, agencies, and academic institutions depends on *what* is taught in the curriculum, and *how* it is taught. In the next section, I will review and assess different ways in which "world Christianity" is understood and presented.

The Nature of World Christianity

As Dale Irvin has shown, the field of world Christianity has multiple origins and represents a confluence of interests. Irvin argues that its origins lie in the ecumenical movement and, more specifically, "the search for unity, mission, and interreligious dialogue."[2] I largely agree with this analysis, but I would like to enlarge the picture still further from my perspective to describe contemporary world Christianity as the confluence

---

2. Dale T. Irvin, "World Christianity: A Genealogy," *Journal of World Christianity* 9, no. 1 (2019): 5.

of six fields of study: mission history; cultural anthropology and area studies; ecumenism and intercultural theology; studies of globalization and development; religious studies; and post- or de-colonial studies that aim to decenter the West in theology. The content, method, and outcomes of a program in world Christianity will vary according to which of these is in view.

World Christianity as Mission History

In her address to the 2019 meeting of the Yale-Edinburgh Group on World Christianity and the History of Christian Mission, Dana Robert traced the rapid emergence of the discipline of world Christianity in the last thirty years and especially its links to mission history.[3] According to Robert, the first occasion in which the term "world Christianity" was used for a research project was when the North Atlantic Missiology Project, funded by Pew Charitable Trust at the University of Cambridge, was succeeded by the project Currents in World Christianity—both projects being directed by Brian Stanley. While it was led by Stanley and Lamin Sanneh, the Yale-Edinburgh Group itself interpreted world Christianity as a historical discipline, but Robert pointed out that the recent passing of Sanneh and the retirement of Stanley would now signal a new phase in its existence.

Teaching world Christianity as history is a strength in that there is a common disciplinary approach. This method has yielded much fruit that has been disseminated at the highest academic levels. In this way, mission and intercultural issues are penetrating university departments of history as well as religious studies. Sometimes, in the West, world Christianity as history continues the privileging of the history of European or white mission enterprises, whose primary sources are easiest to access, and therefore suggests that world Christianity is the product of Western colonialism and hegemony.[4] Nevertheless, there are significant efforts to rewrite church history in light of the ancient polycentric nature of the

---

3. Dana Robert's lecture, entitled "Naming 'World Christianity': The Yale-Edinburgh Conference in Historical Perspective," can be viewed at https://www.youtube.com.

4. A further project proposed at Cambridge in the early twenty-first century—Christianity in the First Millennium, which might have corrected this misconception—did not get funding. However, another project, covering two millennia and led by Dr. Sara Parvis at the University of Edinburgh (2006–2009), produced "interactive mapping for teaching world Christianity." See https://www.ed.ac.uk/divinity/research/resources/animated-maps.

Christian movement.[5] Furthermore, even when using mostly sources generated by Western missions, it is nevertheless possible to discern and recognize the initiatives of local people.[6]

World Christianity as Cultural Anthropology and Area Studies

Another way of studying world Christianity is through cultural studies and area studies. The origins of this approach lie in the strong interest in contextualization and inculturation in missiology and in the emergence of new forms of Christianity and new forms of theological expression[7] arising in different non-Western regions. Area studies with an interest in culture represents the approach of Andrew Walls's Center for the Study of Christianity in the Non-Western World, which documented the growth of Christianity in Africa and Asia especially.[8] It is continued by the *Studies in World Christianity* journal and by some of Walls's students.[9] In the United States, anthropology has arguably been a more dominant mode of inquiry for missiology than history in both Protestant and Catholic schools. Postwar missiology in particular was oriented to support a growing movement of world evangelization and therefore emphasized its practical nature and utilized the social sciences, especially the growing fields of cross-cultural communication and cultural anthropology. Evidence for this is that the journal of the American Society for Missiology, now *Missiology*, was originally entitled *Practical Anthropology*.[10] This may partly explain the ease with which intercultural studies was adopted as a synonym for missiology in member schools of the Association of Theological Schools, instead of world Christianity.

The strength of a cultural and regional approach is its validation of, and attention to, the particular and diverse expressions of Christian faith that make up world Christianity. Fuller Theological Seminary School of

---

5. See, for example, Dale T. Irvin and Scott W. Sunquist, *History of the World Christian Movement*, 2 vols. (Maryknoll, NY: Orbis Books, 2001, 2012).

6. Klaus Koschorke, ed., *Polycentric Structures of World Christianity* (Studies in the History of Christianity in Asia, Africa, Latin America 20; Wiesbaden: Harrassowitz, 2014).

7. Such as liberation theology, Indian Christian theology, and Minjung theology.

8. Founded in Aberdeen in 1982, the Centre moved to Edinburgh in 1987, where it is now the Centre for the Study of World Christianity.

9. As seen in the 2nd International Interdisciplinary Conference on World Christianity at Princeton Seminary in 2019, which was entitled "Currents, Perspectives and Ethnographic Methodologies."

10. See Wilbert R. Shenk, *History of the American Society of Missiology, 1973–2013* (Elkhart, IN: Institute of Mennonite Studies, 2014), 24–25.

World Mission,[11] which was dominated at the time by cultural anthropologists, pioneered the adoption by evangelicals of methods of contextualization that raised interest in local expressions of faith.[12] In addition, it may (but does not necessarily) give voice to church leaders and theologians outside Western academies who may address different issues from a different starting point.[13]

However, there are several weaknesses with the cultural approach. First, fragmenting world Christianity into regions neglects what is arguably the field's greatest strength: its ability to identify the connections between regions and peoples.[14] Second, there is a danger that Christianity in a particular region or among a particular people encourages essentialist, and even racist, caricatures.[15] Related to this is a simplifying approach that neglects minority voices in any particular region, such as African Americans in the United States, Dalits in India, or Palestinian Christians in Israel. World Christianity, as with missiology, may rely on older theories of culture, whereas, especially because of attention to migration and societal plurality, the meaning of culture and context has more recently become de-territorialized, hyperdifferentiated, and more clearly hybridized,[16] and culture has become a question of identity rather than society.[17]

---

11. What is now the School of Intercultural Studies went by this name from its founding in 1965 until 2003.

12. Lausanne Committee for World Evangelization, *The Willowbank Report: Consultation on Gospel and Culture* (Lausanne Occasional Paper 2; Lausanne Committee for World Evangelization, 1978). See https://www.lausanne.org/content/lop/lop-2.

13. Its attention to contextualization may explain why Fuller's School of World Mission also led the way in rethinking church history as "multipolar, global Christian story and not as just a Western story." James Strasburg, "Creating, Practicing, and Researching a Global Faith: Conceptualizations of World Christianity in the American Protestant Pastorate and Seminary Classroom, 1893 to the Present," *Journal of World Christianity* 6, no. 2 (2016): 217–36, at 231.

14. Joel Cabrita, David Maxwell, and Emma Wild-Wood, eds., *Relocating World Christianity: Interdisciplinary Studies in Universal and Local Expressions of the Christian Faith* (Theology and Mission in World Christianity; Leiden: Brill, 2017).

15. Martha Frederiks and Dorottya Nagy, eds., *Religion, Migration and Identity: Methodological Explorations* (Theology and Mission in World Christianity; Leiden: Brill, 2016).

16. Robert Schreiter, *The New Catholicity: Theology between the Global and the Local* (Maryknoll, NY: Orbis Books, 1997), 26–27.

17. Peter C. Phan, "The Experience of Migration as a Source of Intercultural Theology," in Elaine Padilla and Peter Phan, eds., *Contemporary Issues of Migration and Theology* (New York: Palgrave Macmillan, 2013), 185–98. See also Kirsteen Kim, "Doing Theology for the Church's Mission: The Appropriation of Culture," in Jason Sexton and Paul Weston, eds., *The End of Theology: Shaping Theology for the Sake of Mission* (Minneapolis, MN: Fortress Press, 2016), 73–99.

World Christianity as Ecumenism and Intercultural Theology

The ecumenical movement grew out of, and in close relation to, the missionary movement. Ecumenism was defined by the World Council of Churches in 1951 as applying to "everything that relates to the whole task of the whole church to bring the Gospel to the whole world." It was therefore said to cover both the missionary movement and the movement for unity.[18] Not only theologically but also practically, twentieth-century missiology in the historic Protestant churches was closely linked with ecumenics.[19] The background in ecumenical studies is significant for world Christianity insofar as its ethos is toward inclusion and comprehensive coverage of all manifestations of Christian faith across and within all regions.

It was in the context of departments of mission and ecumenics that the term "intercultural theology" was coined by Walter Hollenweger, Hans Margull, and Richard Friedli in the 1970s as they reflected on contemporary Christian diversity.[20] From the mission perspective, Hollenweger and his colleagues were convinced that the non-Western forms of Christianity that they were documenting were discontinuous with European theology due to the social, political, cultural, and religious diversity of their contexts.[21] From an ecumenical perspective, the catholicity or universality of Christianity was seen to admit, and even demand, an "exchange of theologies" that would challenge churches, including in the West, which became too local or provincialized.[22] At this stage, intercultural theology was an intra-Christian enterprise,[23] an exercise in "theological giving and receiving that characterises the history of Christianity in its post-colonial and polycentric period."[24] It recognized the stress on "partnership in mission" of the International Missionary Council in the context of the independence of former mission churches.[25] Led by German institutions,

---

18. Central Committee of the World Council of Churches, "The Calling of the Church to Mission and to Unity," *Ecumenical Review* 4, no. 1 (October 1951): 66–71, at 68.

19. As documented by Irvin in the case of the United States; Dale T. Irvin, "World Christianity, A Genealogy," *Journal of World Christianity* 9, no. 1 (2019).

20. Walter Hollenweger, "Intercultural Theology: Some Remarks on the Term," in Martha Frederiks, Meindert Dijkstra, and Anton Houtepen, eds., *Towards an Intercultural Theology* (Zoetermeer: Meinema, 2003), 89–95.

21. Werner Ustorf, "The Cultural Origins of 'Intercultural' Theology," in Mark J. Cartledge and David Cheetham, eds., *Intercultural Theology: Approaches and Themes* (London: SCM, 2011), 17.

22. Ibid., 14.

23. Hollenweger, "Intercultural Theology," 91.

24. Ustorf, "The Cultural Origins of 'Intercultural' Theology," 14.

25. Graham Kings, director of the Henry Martyn Centre in the Cambridge Theological Foundation (now the Cambridge Centre for Christianity Worldwide), was

intercultural theology has more recently been adopted in Europe as the preferred alternative to the colonial term "mission studies."[26] In 2008 the Academic Association for Theology and the German Association for Mission Studies (DGMW) proposed "intercultural theology" because it recognized the importance of crossing cultural and religious boundaries in the twenty-first century and the historical partnership of missiology with cultural studies.[27]

World Christianity as intercultural theology sets the discipline clearly within the domain of theological studies rather than history or anthropology. If this is the context, then it has many strengths in internationalizing theology (see below). However, depending on how theology is understood, this context could be a limitation for its interdisciplinarity, especially when it comes to the social sciences. More specific objections are that, rather than helping to overcome Eurocentrism in missiology, the new name redefined it within the very European categories of culture and religion.[28] A critic from Africa regarded it as a retrograde step toward parochial and ethnic theology,[29] and another from Asia found it neglectful of the social and political questions.[30]

Another contentious aspect of the development of intercultural theology in Europe has to do with the enlargement of ecumenical openness to include other faiths. This is demonstrated by the establishment of the scholarly guild as The European Society for Intercultural Theology *and Interreligious Studies* (ESITIS; italics added).[31] David Cheetham, one of the leaders of ESITIS, argues that the combination is justified because, at the

---

instrumental in the shift at Cambridge away from the history of missions and toward world Christianity. An Anglican clergyman who had served with the Church Mission Society in Kenya and formed strong relations with African scholars, Kings took partnership in mission very seriously and wished to move beyond the study of colonial missions (which is very easy to do in the British context because the archives are there) to raise the profile of mission initiatives in and from other continents. One of the board members of the HMC was Louise Pirouet, author of one of the first studies of African missionaries: *Black Evangelists: The Spread of Christianity in Uganda, 1891–1914* (London: Collings, 1978).

26. Ustorf, "The Cultural Origins of 'Intercultural' Theology."
27. The Religious Studies and Mission Studies section of the Academic Association for Theology (WGTh) and the Administrative Board of the German Association for Mission Studies (DGMW), "Mission Studies as Intercultural Theology and Its Relationship to Religious Studies," *Mission Studies* 25 (2008): 103–8.
28. Ustorf, "The Cultural Origins of 'Intercultural' Theology," 25.
29. Francis Anekwe Oborji, "Missiology in Its Relation to Intercultural Theology and Religious Studies," *Mission Studies* 25 (2008): 113–14.
30. Ken Christoph Miyamoto, "A Response to 'Mission Studies as Intercultural Studies and Its Relationship to Religious Studies,'" *Mission Studies* 25 (2008): 109–10.
31. Margull and Friedli were keen for intercultural theology to open up to "interreligious theology" in order for Christianity to realize its vulnerability as one

very least, a "thick description" of different cultural expressions of Christianity must always take into account the religious and philosophical influences on the culture and also that Christian theology can be considered part of a wider discipline of religious studies.[32] He further notes that intercultural theology "is a *methodological* rather than an ideological commitment" (italics original). That is, it is not aimed at challenging doctrine and it does not necessarily imply religious pluralism, although some may wish to construct "global theologies in the context of interreligious dialogue."[33] Clearly world Christianity is committed to an intra-Christian focus, but it does have an important relationship to religious studies that will be considered below.

World Christianity as Globalization and Development

World Christianity can be studied as an example of globalization or as a movement of economic and social development. In global history, there are few movements as global and diverse as Christianity, or global institutions that have shown the same level of expansion and sociopolitical influence as the Roman Catholic Church. Christian churches, and their alliances, have long been of interest geopolitically. What is more, since Max Weber, attention has been drawn to the possible economic effects of particular forms of faith,[34] and criticism of the purported ecological effects of Christianity lie in the origins of ecology.[35]

Examples of forms of Christianity that have been of interest to scholars of globalization and development include missionary movements that allied with colonial governments to reshape societies through language, work, health care, education, and technological innovation, and also Christianity as an independence movement (for example, the Ethiopian churches in southern Africa), a form of nationalism (for example, in Korea), and an influence in nation building (such as in India).[36] Global

---

religion among many, unlike Hollenweger, who saw intercultural theology as an intra-Christian endeavor. Ustorf, "The Cultural Origins of 'Intercultural' Theology," 19.

32. David Cheetham, "Intercultural Theology and Interreligious Studies," in Mark J. Cartledge and David Cheetham, eds., *Intercultural Theology: Approaches and Themes* (London: SCM, 2011), 51, 59–60.

33. "Introduction," in Mark J. Cartledge and David Cheetham, eds., *Intercultural Theology: Approaches and Themes* (London: SCM, 2011), 1–3.

34. Max Weber, *The Protestant Ethic and the Spirit of Capitalism*, trans. Talcott Parsons (London: Allen & Unwin, 1930).

35. Namely, the influential article by Lynn White Jr., "The Historical Roots of Our Ecologic Crisis," *Science* 155, no. 3767 (1967): 1203–7.

36. For these examples, see Sebastian Kim and Kirsteen Kim, *Christianity as a World Religion*, 2nd edn. (London: Bloomsbury, 2016).

pentecostalism has recently been subjected to scrutiny by scholars of globalization and development for its (positive or negative) effects on poverty and its possible community empowerment. Despite the secularist nature of development discourse since the 1960s, in this millennium, scholars of development and some governmental development agencies have identified church networks as channels of development. Some have gone further to recognize the contribution of faith-based organizations (FBOs) and even to see churches as development organizations for their own communities.[37]

In this respect, the study of world Christianity connects with the origins of Protestant missiology in the late-nineteenth-century project of world evangelization, discussed at the World Missionary Conference at Edinburgh in 1910, which saw a Christian world as its goal.[38] For U.S. Americans, that goal may have been primarily religious; for Europeans in the context of empire, it was also developmental, as shown by European criticism of U.S. activism.[39] The social Christianity of approximately 1880 to 1940, along with the rise of socialism, influenced the missionary movement to understand evangelization more in social and moral terms.[40] The considerable social involvement of Christian missions laid the ground for the collaboration of European Christians with the post–Second World War agenda of development.[41]

Its significant social and political dimensions are often missing from programs that have their origins in mission studies or missiology,[42] but the study of world Christianity could legitimately emphasize these,

---

37. See Emma Tomalin, ed., *The Routledge Handbook of Religions and Global Development* (London: Routledge, 2015).

38. Brian Stanley, *The World Missionary Conference, Edinburgh 1910* (Studies in the History of Christian Missions; Grand Rapids, MI: Eerdmans, 2009), 13–16.

39. As documented in James Strasburg, "Creating, Practicing, and Researching a Global Faith: Conceptualizations of World Christianity in the American Protestant Pastorate and Seminary Classroom, 1893 to the Present," *Journal of World Christianity* 6, no. 2 (2016): 217–36 at 219–23. For background, see Henning Wrogemann, *Intercultural Theology*, vol. 2. *Theology of Mission*, trans. Karl E. Böhmer (Downers Grove, IL: IVP, 2018), 33–58.

40. For an overview of the movement, see Paul T. Phillips, *A Kingdom on Earth* (University Park, PA: Pennsylvania State University, 1996).

41. Philip Fountain, "Proselytizing Development," in Tomalin, *The Routledge Handbook of Religions and Global Development*, 80–97.

42. As a practically oriented topic, missiology has often neglected self-reflection on the social and political situation of the missionary or of the church or mission organization, which has contributed to the ease with which missions (and FBOs) have been co-opted by governments.

although this approach can also be covered under the heading of public theology (where that is treated globally).[43]

World Christianity as Religious Studies

In the UK context at least, since the 1980s, departments of theology in secular universities have become departments of theology and religion, religious studies and theology, or similar, and increasingly are now just departments of religion or religious studies. Religious studies has its origins in the fields of comparative religion and history of religion of the late nineteenth century. European empires tended to associate particular faiths with particular groups of people. So religious studies also owes much of its current growth to agendas of interreligious peacemaking in the context of the growth in Western societies of religious plurality and the desire for religious harmony globally, which can be shown to be in continuity with the ecumenical movement.[44] Postwar theoretical influences include the work of Wilfred Cantwell Smith in the comparative history of religion, from which he proposed "world theology";[45] the development of theologies of religious pluralism, most notably by John Hick;[46] and the recent development of comparative theology on the one hand[47] and the characterization of religions as incommensurable worldviews on the other.[48]

Religion is a contested category. Academic religious studies has mostly adopted the world religions paradigm, the origins of which lie in Western classification of "the rest."[49] The world religions paradigm uses a methodology of religious relativism that aims to treat religions on their own terms. However, Christianity has until recently been represented as the religion of the West, without acknowledging its ancient Asian and Afri-

---

43. As, for example, in the Global Network for Public Theology and in the *International Journal of Public Theology*.

44. Kirsteen Kim, "Peace and Migrations: From Ecumenical Dialogue to Interreligious Interpretation," in Luca Ferracci and Alberto Melloni, eds., *A History of the Desire for Christian Unity*, vol. 7 (John XXIII Foundation; Leiden: Brill; Rome: Il Mulino, forthcoming).

45. Wilfred Cantwell Smith, *Towards a World Theology: Faith and the Comparative History of Religion* (Philadelphia: Westminster, 1981).

46. John Hick, *God and the Universe of Faiths* (London: Macmillan, 1973).

47. Francis X. Clooney, *Comparative Theology: Deep Learning across Religious Borders* (Chichester, UK: Wiley-Blackwell, 2010).

48. Perry Schmidt-Leukel, *Religious Pluralism and Interreligious Theology* (Maryknoll, NY: Orbis Books, 2017).

49. Tomoko Masuzawa, *The Invention of World Religions, Or, How European Universalism Was Preserved in the Language of Pluralism* (Chicago: University of Chicago Press, 2005).

can origins and manifestations or the contemporary worldwide nature of Christianity today.[50] However, the use of sociology of religion within religious studies has made it possible to consider Christianity under the heading of world religions rather than separating it off as a separate category. Social studies of religious communities, their practices, and their influence on wider society have helped break through the politically motivated constructs of religion. Contemporary worldwide pentecostalism especially has been studied in this way by sociologists as a new religious movement.[51] World Christianity has become a means of recasting Christianity as globally widespread, locally rooted, and interconnected for religious studies scholars.[52]

One of the weaknesses of sociological studies is that theology is not often included in the methods of analysis, and therefore the significance of the self-understanding of Christianity—and other religions—is not appreciated. The reasons for their growth, decline, or impact are instead attributed entirely to social, economic, or political factors. The growing field of anthropology of Christianity goes some way toward addressing this problem and could be included in the study of world Christianity.[53]

World Christianity as Decentering Europe in Theology

If world Christianity is taught in the context of theology, then it will promote an intra-Christian approach that at the very least takes seriously "the methodological implications for undertaking theology in light of a sheer expansion of data brought about by globalisation, inculturation and non-Western theologies."[54] It will encourage a kind of theology that recognizes that many Christian churches are only tenuously connected with the historic traditions developed in Europe—and that some are more of a reaction to them—and it will take seriously the cultural, religious, and political realities from which different Christian communities arise.[55] In

---

50. This is one of the reasons for the recent plethora of texts on Christianity that attend to its global nature. For a recent example, see Vince Bantu, *A Multitude of Peoples: Engaging Ancient Christianity's Global Identity* (Missiological Engagements Series; Downers Grove, IL: IVP Academic, 2020).

51. For example, David Martin, *Pentecostalism: The World Their Parish* (Oxford: Blackwell, 2002).

52. Our own attempt to address this problem for religious studies students and teachers is Sebastian Kim and Kirsteen Kim, *Christianity as a World Religion*, 2nd edn. (London: Bloomsbury, 2016).

53. See, for example, the book series edited by Joel Robbins, *The Anthropology of Christianity* (University of California Press).

54. "Introduction," in Cartledge and Cheetham, *Intercultural Theology*, 1.

55. Henning Wrogemann, *Intercultural Theology*, vol. 1. *Intercultural Hermeneu-*

doing so it will contribute to the postcolonial agenda to decenter Europe and to challenge white privilege, and even supremacy, in academic and church theology.[56]

The reality of world Christianity demands new approaches in all the traditional theological disciplines. So far scholars of world Christianity have directed their contribution to questions of church and Christian history, with considerable success (see above). However, the significance of this history and of contemporary world Christianity has been given less attention in biblical studies, practical theology, or doctrine and systematics. World Christianity challenges biblical studies to recognize the contradiction that the Bible's origins are not European and yet methods of interpretation are dominated by European perspectives.[57] Differences in biblical hermeneutics are a major source of tension between Christians in the global North and South especially,[58] and so it is important that greater attention is given to how decisions are made about what is the correct interpretation.[59] The study of practical theology is readily shaped to local contexts, but rarely in the West does it take world Christianity into account. If it did, it would diversify its sources to consider methods and examples from outside the West. Furthermore, by focusing on local contexts, wherever they are in the world, practical theologians may fail to understand the significance of globalization as sets of processes that increasingly penetrate all localities and link all regions together through recognized and unrecognized systems.[60]

Bringing a world Christianity perspective to Christian doctrine and systematic theology is the most challenging task, given the strength of

---

tics, trans. Karl E. Böhmer (Downers Grove: IVP, 2012), 20. Cf. Kirsteen Kim, "Gender Issues in Intercultural Perspective," in Cartledge and Cheetham, *Intercultural Theology*, 91–92.

56. For example, Willie James Jennings, *After Whiteness: An Education in Belonging* (Theological Education between the Times; Grand Rapids, MI: Eerdmans, 2020). As Dana Robert points out, all disciplines benefit from being approached from a global perspective. Dana Robert and Aaron Hollander, "Beyond Unity and Diversity: A Conversation with Dana Robert on Mission, Ecumenism, and Global Christianities," *Ecumenical Trends* (June 2019): 2–15, at 6.

57. For examples from elsewhere, see Mercy Amba Oduyoye and Hendrik M. Vroom, eds., *One Gospel—Many Cultures* (Amsterdam: Rodopi, 2003); R. S. Sugirtharajah, ed., *Voices from the Margin*, 20th anniversary (Maryknoll, NY: Orbis Books, 2016).

58. See, for example, Philip Jenkins, *The New Faces of Christianity: Believing the Bible in the Global South* (Oxford: Oxford University Press, 2006).

59. For example, Joshua D. Broggi, *Diversity in the Structure of Christian Reasoning* (Leiden: Brill, 2015).

60. Kirsteen Kim, *Joining in with the Spirit Connecting World Church and Local Mission* (London: SCM Press, 2012).

European traditions and the widespread tendency to regard some form of Western theology as normative. There has certainly been impact from other regions on Western theology. In fact, three of the most influential theological developments of the late twentieth century—liberation theology, theology of inculturation, and theology of dialogue—were all stimulated by issues that particularly concerned the churches of, and were articulated by theologians from, the majority world.[61] By the end of the twentieth century, theologies from Africa, Asia, and Latin America were included in standard Protestant theological textbooks in English, but they were not integral to them.[62] Moreover, the influence of the theologians of the majority world was not often acknowledged in the text or footnotes of the work of the leading Western theologians.[63] Making theology a truly global conversation should be an aim of world Christianity in a seminary setting.[64]

There are conscious attempts in Western theology to address these issues, which include the global theology of Veli-Matti Kärkkäinen,[65] the attention to the theological implications of migration by Peter Phan and Elaine Padilla,[66] and the Theology and Mission in World Christianity series.[67] However, two aspects of Western theological method present particular difficulties for taking account of world Christianity and decentering Europe in theology. The first is that the predominant historical-theological approach stimulated by *ressourcement* theology, although it recognizes the significance of context, takes a chronological line from the Bible and the church fathers to Europe and the West. The second is that Western philosophical hermeneutics, as appropriated by European theology, continues to rely on a Gadamerian approach that assumes a shared history of interpretation—a tradition, or culture, which is "uniform, self-

---

61. Ibid.

62. See, for example, David Ford, *The Modern Theologians*, 2nd ed. (Oxford: Wiley-Blackwell, 1997); Alister McGrath, *Christian Theology*, 3rd ed. (Oxford: Wiley-Blackwell, 2001).

63. For the case of Jürgen Moltmann, see Susanne Hennecke, "Related by Freedom: The Impact of Third-world Theologians on the Thinking of Jürgen Moltmann," *Exchange* 32, no. 4 (2003): 292–309.

64. For global conversation, see Kirsteen Kim, *The Holy Spirit in the World: A Global Conversation* (Maryknoll, NY: Orbis Books, 2007).

65. Kärkkäinen has published a series of "global introductions" to a number of doctrinal issues with Baker Academic: *Pneumatology* (2002); *Christology* (2003); and *The Doctrine of God* (2004).

66. Peter C. Phan and Elaine Padilla, eds., *Contemporary Issues of Migration and Theology* (New York: Palgrave Macmillan, 2013). See also Peter Phan's book series, Theology in Global Perspective (Orbis Books).

67. Theology and Mission in World Christianity series (Brill), edited by Kirsteen Kim, Stephen B. Bevans, and Miikka Ruokanen.

contained or inescapable."⁶⁸ Hence, Gadamer is limited when it comes to Europeans interpreting texts that come from an external historical context (even though, of course, the Bible and the ancient creeds fall into that category). Nor does Gadamerian hermeneutics allow for what happens when a Christian text is read by someone, whether Christian or not, from a non-European tradition of interpretation.⁶⁹ From this perspective, the postliberal theology of the late twentieth century exacerbated the problem and encouraged theological separatism, even European exceptionalism.⁷⁰ Further attention to theological method and hermeneutics is necessary before world Christianity can decenter Europe in theology.

Learning Outcomes, Structures, and Faculty

Based on the analysis above, world Christianity is an interdisciplinary field of study. However, factors such as disciplinary boundaries, funding specifications for projects, or curricular limitations may limit its scope. Consequently, the learning outcomes for a program on world Christianity will look significantly different according to the way in which the title is understood.

Potential learning outcomes that correspond to the categories above include:

- (History) Write a critical history of a particular Christian movement from Africa, Asia, Latin America, the Caribbean, or Oceania.
- (Anthropology) Produce a thick description of a particular contemporary Christian community in context.
- (Ecumenism) Read intertextually two expressions of Christian theology from differing cultural settings.
- (Globalization) Assess the extent to which a particular form of Christianity is empowering the community economically.
- (Religious Studies) Compare a Christian movement with another movement from a different religious tradition.

---

68. Joshua D. Broggi, *Diversity in the Structure of Christian Reasoning* (Leiden: Brill, 2015), 88–143; Wrogemann, *Intercultural Theology*, vol. 1. *Intercultural Hermeneutics*, 59.

69. Broggi, *Diversity in the Structure of Christian Reasoning*, 127–29. See also David W. Congdon, "Emancipatory Intercultural Hermeneutics: Interpreting Theo Sundermeier's Differenzhermeneutik," *Mission Studies* 33 (2016): 127–46.

70. Kirsteen Kim, "Globalisation after Empires: World Christianity and the Theological De-centring of Europe," in Philip Ziegler, ed., *Edinburgh Critical History of Christian Theology*, vol. 6. *Twentieth Century* (Edinburgh: Edinburgh University Press, forthcoming).

- (Theology) Analyze a theological work from a postcolonial or race perspective.

However, these are so wide-ranging and demand such a breadth of expertise that they are likely unachievable in any single course. So, it is wise to limit a particular program to a selection of the six categories according to the strength of the disciplinary context (history, anthropology, ecumenics, globalization, religious studies, or theology). Faculty expertise will also significantly affect the program in any particular institution, and not only for reasons of methodology; an exceptionally large faculty would be needed to cover every region and community. The temptation is often to exclude the West from the study of world Christianity.[71] However, to do this will distort the discipline for two main reasons. First, Christianity in the contemporary West is integral to world Christianity as a global movement, which is interconnected by global flows that cannot be properly understood without it. Second, studying European and Western Christianities among the others puts them in world perspective and decenters them.

Structurally, there are several important program considerations. First, because world Christianity is potentially such a wide subject, it is important that at least one course required early in the program is about world Christianity as a discipline. This should be designed to help students navigate the field and make other course selections. Second, if a thesis or dissertation is involved, the ethos of world Christianity is such that it is desirable that students should study a context other than their own. It is sometimes assumed that students from overseas will focus their research on their own context; but if Western students can research any global context, then students from other continents should be encouraged to do the same. Third, if the student body is diverse, then this strength should be utilized in the classroom. Courses should be structured in such a way that the students themselves, and their interaction, facilitate learning. Fourth, since Christianity is a globalized movement, online resources can be used to provide visual and audio introductions to different regions and churches (without re-enforcing stereotypes, with awareness that not all communities have an online presence, and understanding that the algorithms of search engines limit what is found). Fifth, a course in world Christianity will be enhanced by linking up with faculty, and even class-

---

71. Cf. Dana Robert and Aaron Hollander, "Beyond Unity and Diversity: A Conversation with Dana Robert on Mission, Ecumenism, and Global Christianities," *Ecumenical Trends* (June 2019): 2–15, at 4.

rooms, in other regions (time zones and bandwidth permitting), for global conversation.

Although it will be informed by literature that discusses global diversity, a program in world Christianity should be taught by a faculty that is diverse—not only disciplinarily, but also personally. It is preferable to have regional, sociocultural, and confessional diversity at least, although the potential for this will vary according to context. A diverse faculty illustrates the discipline and helps to facilitate study of the interconnections of Christian movements that are the real strength of the discipline.

Teaching world Christianity often provides opportunities to appoint people from a different continent or region. However, it cannot be assumed, on the one hand, that someone is able to teach about their own region without having studied it in its complexity, or, on the other hand, that they will necessarily understand the discipline without having studied it. World Christianity faculty are not merely from elsewhere or interested in somewhere else; they also need to have awareness of global affairs and of Christianity's contemporary cultural and social roles as well as theology and history.[72] Westerners most readily claim to have the global view that might be suggested by the nomenclature of world Christianity, but a truly global perspective in one individual is, of course, impossible. Someone who has been raised outside the West will have a significant contribution to make on history, religion, and other topics such as globalization. For example, someone from the majority world may not regard globalization positively and may challenge the "global" worldview that was presumed by those who designed the program. In the U.S. context, African Americans, Latinos, Asian Americans, and people from other minorities may also have a fertile perspective on world Christianity both as part of global diasporas and also from being on the receiving end of dominant missions.

Confessional diversity is particularly important for this discipline, and this may be more achievable in a university than in a seminary setting. Descriptions and statistics of world Christianity may vary widely according to confession, and faculty will inevitably be informed about their particular network and see the rest of Christianity through that lens. Divides may run deep, but the integrity of the subject area depends on faculty representing, or making an effort to represent, all strands of world Christianity, which could be classified as Catholic, evangelical, independent, Orthodox, pentecostal, and Protestant.[73]

---

72. Ibid., 4–5. It goes without saying that foreigners should not be confined to teaching in this area.

73. See the World Christian Database (https://worldchristiandatabase.org/). For an open-access resource that aims to bring globally diverse Christian voices into con-

Most importantly, given the scope of the field and the necessity for as comprehensive a view as possible, a world Christianity faculty must work collaboratively. Their diversity and distinct approaches are important, but without shared insights and global conversation we cannot hope to understand world Christianity.

---

versation and showcase world Christianity, see the Regnum Edinburgh Centenary Series of thirty-five volumes.

Section II

*Methodology and
Interdisciplinary Approaches*

4

Preparing and Equipping Scholars of World Christianity: Deep Understanding, Comparative Imagination, and Theological Awareness

PAUL KOLLMAN

Beginning in March 2019 and continuing through many months, protesters gathered in the streets of Hong Kong to complain about a proposed government law to extradite certain types of arrested people to mainland China. Though mentioned only rarely by international media coverage, one notable feature of the crowds was the Christian hymns they sang as they protested. In particular, "Sing Hallelujah to the Lord" emerged as their unifying anthem, at least early on. Christians only comprise about 12 percent of Hong Kong's population, yet Christians and non-Christians alike passionately sang this song, written in California in the 1970s by Linda Stassen-Benjamin, who was then involved in the Jesus People, an evangelical group that in its day was very influential.[1]

Various explanations exist for the hymn's appearance in this volatile political setting. Several suggest practical motivations. After all, religious meetings are a more protected form of assembly from police interference than gatherings overtly defined as political protests, and the hymn lends

---

1. Jessie Pang and Marius Zaharia, "'Sing Hallelujah to the Lord,' an Unlikely Anthem of Hong Kong Protests," *Reuters* (June 18, 2019), www.reuters.com. It was one of seven songs important to the protests identified in September 2019: Charley Lanyon, "Hong Kong Protest Songs: 7 Anthems of the Anti-extradition Movement—Do You Hear the People Sing?" *South China Morning Post* (September 12, 2019), www.scmp.com.

a religious air to the gatherings. It could be that the hymn was a strategic choice by the organizers to lessen the likelihood and severity of a crackdown by the authorities. Another potential strategic motivating factor might have been the well-known Christian identity of the governor, Carrie Lam, who promulgated the law. Lam sought to defuse protests at first without completely shelving the law. If this was a factor, it did not succeed, at least initially. Lam, a Catholic, for several months refused to abrogate the law or resign in response to protesters' demands, though she removed it from immediate consideration in September 2019. It was permanently shelved a month later, though some observers anticipate that it will return at a later date.

Here I want to consider the value of world Christianity as a framework to understand something like the appearance of this Christian hymn in a circumstance like the Hong Kong protests, and then to think about the right preparation for someone to embrace that framework—that is, to become a scholar of world Christianity. I bring to the case itself no special preparation for analyzing it, being neither a historian of China or its Christianity; nor a musicologist or historian of American evangelical Christianity, the source of the hymn; nor someone with expertise in religious or political protest movements, the setting in which the hymn appeared. Instead, I present this case as a thought experiment of sorts, with two goals. First, I want to use it to illustrate certain habits of thought and scholarly dispositions that identify a scholar of world Christianity, and thus to argue in favor of academic programming and curricular training that might prepare someone to participate effectively in the field of world Christianity through the development of such habits and dispositions. Second, the case, far outside of my expertise, allows me to advance the argument that such habits have particular value now, as Christianity expands and diversifies in novel ways.

I come to this discussion shaped by three experiences that have contributed to my perspective on proper preparation for engaging world Christianity. First and foremost, I have lived in eastern Africa in a variety of settings and with differing responsibilities: as a student, researcher, and professor. In addition, research in the history of Christianity in eastern Africa has been my scholarly focus, and I have sought to interpret historical materials, and especially missionary archives, in light of eastern African Christianity's various present-day manifestations. I try especially to understand the ways practices of evangelization have conduced toward various outcomes in eastern Africa. The focus of my ongoing research has been on Catholic missionary efforts undertaken by different Catholic groups and Africans' individual and collective responses to those efforts, treating both in a comparative perspective. This kind of work has drawn me into engagement with world Christianity, both because eastern Africa represents a place of growth for the world Christian movement, a common organizing motif for the field of world Christianity, and also because mission studies, a field whose academic meetings I attend, has been one common background for scholars in world Christianity.

Second, I have tried to offer reflections of a more methodological sort on historical practices that study Christianity in its immense and increasing diversity. These have led to several historiographic essays on contemporary practices in the historical study of Christianity, including engagement with perspectives linked to world Christianity.[2]

Third, I have taught for most of my career at the University of Notre Dame, a Catholic university with strong research aspirations and a concerted commitment to theological education. When I began as a faculty member in Notre Dame's theology department, I formed part of the History of Christianity area, with most of my colleagues focused on early and medieval Christianity. About a decade ago, however, the department began a new area for doctoral studies that we call World Religions/World Church (or WRWC), and this has become my primary home in the department. The WRWC concentration has served as a framework for us to welcome doctoral students who want to study another religious tradition from a Christian theological perspective *and* for students who want to study a non-Western form of Christianity. This has naturally made me consider the field of world Christianity in my research, especially as it affects the Catholic Church and engaged me in preparation of students to be scholars of world Christianity. As the department's website puts it, the goal of the WRWC program is

> to explore new ways of thinking about the study of world religions, global Catholicism, and the history of interactions between the Church and the religions of the world. Concretely, this entails providing the intellectual foundations for engaging the student with religions of the world from within a Christian theological paradigm. These foundations both enable the study of the world's religions with specific attention to their own particular historical contexts and modes of theological discourse and provide the necessary preparation for informed inter-religious dialogue. The

---

2. Paul Kollman, "Understanding the World-Christian Turn in the History of Christianity and Theology," *Theology Today* 71, no. 2 (2014): 164–77; Paul Kollman, "Analyzing Emerging Christianities: Recent Insights from the Social Sciences," *Transformation* 29 (2012): 304–14; Paul Kollman "After Church History? Writing the History of Christianity from a Global Perspective," *Horizons* 31 (2004): 322–42.

concentration also involves studying the ways in which Christianity has become inculturated in contexts shaped largely by non-Christian religious traditions.³

These experiences have suggested to me that someone properly equipped for world Christianity need not have a specific set of defined skills. Instead, I prefer to advance the claim that there are three scholarly orientations, or dispositions, that are most desirable, in some degree, for fruitful scholarship in world Christianity. One need not possess all three of these dispositions to the same degree, yet each creates a fruitful basis for world Christianity, and together I believe they reflect the developing collective wisdom of the field concerning preparation. Finally, they conform as well to my experience. Thus, for the purposes of contributions to the field and employability in academic positions linked to world Christianity, they seem desirable.

The first desideratum for world Christianity is a developed scholarly understanding of some aspect of Christianity—historical, geographic, denominational, textual, or disciplinary. Second, a scholar in world Christianity ought to possess what I will call here a comparative imagination, that is, the critical capacity to put Christian phenomena into relationship with analogous phenomena in order to advance insight. Third, such a person ought to have a certain degree of theological awareness, both to appreciate a particularly Christian perspective on what is being studied and to have appropriate empathy for Christian self-understanding more generally. Theological awareness thus allows disciplinary expertise and a comparative imagination to come together in a perspective inclined to appreciate insiders' and external viewpoints on Christian phenomena.

After discussing each of these three in loose relationship to the case of Christian hymn-singing in the Hong Kong protests, and linking them to considerations about training and preparation for world Christianity, I will offer concluding remarks about world Christianity as a discipline or field, and preparation for participation in it.

Deep Understanding

Analysis of the protests in Hong Kong has not labeled them as Christian protests for the most part. Neither am I convinced that they are Christian protests, nor am I inclined to pursue serious study about them to determine the advisability of labeling them as a Christian phenomenon in a

---

3. See https://theology.nd.edu/graduate-programs/ph-d/areas-of-concentration/world-religions-world-church/.

strict sense. The apparent prominence of the Christian hymn, however, suggests that someone engaged in the field of world Christianity could provide insight into these protests, and perhaps distinctive insight that other disciplines might not generate.

Of course, a variety of scholarly backgrounds and orientations could also provide insight into this case, including the question of its specifically Christian provenance. Examples of potentially useful scholarly backgrounds and orientations include history or political science that focuses on China, the history or sociology of Chinese Christianity, and knowledge about the denominational and religious makeup of Hong Kong's population. Also certainly valuable would be the specific history of Chinese political and religious protest, the role of political and religious protest more generally in social change movements, and the history of Christian hymnody, especially in the past half-century and with reference to its role in social change. Broader social-scientific insight into social movements more generally might also prove helpful, as might study of music in the galvanization and growth of social movements.

To bring a specifically world-Christian perspective to something like this hymn's appearance in this situation, however, requires something more: a certain kind of in-depth awareness of some particular aspect or facet of Christianity, understood broadly, that could be employed in relation to one of the aforementioned scholarly orientations (or something like them), which could then illuminate this case.

To extend the example into a generalization, I believe that to become a scholar of world Christianity, one should have developed specialized expertise in a dimension of Christianity or scholarship about Christianity. This might include one or more of the following, which are not mutually exclusive:

- a regionally linked specialization (for example, China or eastern Asia more broadly, sub-Saharan Africa, or Amazonia)
- a denominational specialization (e.g., Seventh-Day Adventists or Russian Orthodoxy)
- a historical specialization (e.g., Christianity in the Roman Empire, or Christianity in India since independence)
- a textual focus or analogous specialization in typically religious communication, which could be canonical (including but not limited to the Bible) or expertise in another communicative media (e.g., contemporary media or mythic studies); or
- a distinct disciplinary orientation (sociological or anthropological being the most likely, especially since these will likely overlap with

one or more of the preceding topics, and could include religious practices—for example, the study of rituals)

This list is not exhaustive but suggestive. Someone interested in entering the field of world Christianity, I believe, ought to know quite a bit about something that is typically linked to the study of Christianity—a place, a time, a group, a text (or para-text), a practice, or even a discipline that studies Christianity, in which one acquires that discipline's skills.

Students being trained for careers in world Christianity, therefore, ought to receive training that makes them specialists in something that is not "world Christianity." This training could take a number of forms, and could be supplemental to a primary degree that is being sought, or it could be the primary degree itself. Thus it could be in addition to the divinity-school, seminary, theological, or religious studies training that accompanies it. One might, therefore, engage contemporary media studies along with degree work in the history of Christianity, for example, or the cultural anthropology of Africa along with sacramental theology, or the history of linguistic translation along with a master of divinity, or a focus on Latin American liberation theology in the history of Christianity. Depending on the nature of the ancillary disciplinary focus, this might mean intensive language training or inculcation into a distinct methodology—like anthropological field-work methods such as participant observation or statistical reasoning. Or this specialty might be the primary field in which the student is being trained—sociology or Japanese history—in which the student then makes Christianity itself in some form or fashion the auxiliary or add-on training.

Regardless of what it might be, someone preparing for world Christianity should have some deep understanding of some Christian thing, understood broadly, and have gained the requisite skills for that study.[4]

Comparative Imagination[5]

The field of world Christianity has grown by placing particular Christian phenomena in new relationships, particularly though not exclusively

---

4. I should acknowledge here the value of serving as moderator of a panel entitled "At the Edges of Missiology: Disciplines and Practices Defining the Field," at the annual meeting of the American Society of Missiology, held at the University of Northwestern in St. Paul, Minnesota, on June 18, 2016. Presenters were Joanne Blaney, Dana Robert, Robert Priest, and Roberta King. The talks that day and subsequent email exchanges have shaped my thinking about this matter.

5. I recently learned that this term appears in a book by distinguished historian George M. Fredrickson entitled *The Comparative Imagination: On the History of Racism,*

in relationship to analogous Christian phenomena in different times and places. Ideally, the deep understanding of something Christian that orients scholars in world Christianity also serves as an invitation for them to consider it in a comparative perspective.

In the case of the Christian hymn-singing of the Hong Kong protesters, for example, productive comparisons might consider it in relation to a variety of other phenomena. For example, how does it appear in relation to previous southern Chinese or Hong Kong–based protests of the past, or to similar resistance movements by religious groups to perceived government interference elsewhere, or to other times and places where music served to mobilize and unite social protests? What is similar and what is unique about this circumstance? Have Christian features been part of Chinese or Hong Kong protests in the past? What kinds of Christian features? Has this hymn in particular been part of any protests before? Where and why? Of course, for such a study to be productive one would have to know very well the case at hand, appreciating the origins of the hymn and why it was chosen, and by whom, and when.

Comparison in scholarship need not be explicit in order to be operative and fruitful. I have come to believe, with Jonathan Z. Smith and others, that despite obvious limitations in past efforts carried out under the label "comparative religions"—often based in ethnocentric essentialisms or various forms of ahistoricism[6]—comparison is rooted in the substructure of much human thought, and certainly operates effectively, if imperfectly, in a great deal of religious studies. As Smith has long reminded scholars of religion, taxonomic operations like comparison and classification are necessary tasks in the discipline. He acknowledges that they are parasitic tasks inasmuch as they depend upon already-existing data in order to proceed, but he has made a most compelling case for their indispensability.

For Smith, conceptual categories that we use depend on comparative assumptions built into their enunciation and application to particular cases. Comparison is thus at once natural—we do it without thinking about it—yet also dangerous for a scholar, since it can lead to unhelpful

---

Nationalism, and Social Movements (Berkeley: University of California Press, 2000), with the first edition appearing in 1982. One article appearing there entitled "The Status of Comparative History" (pp. 23–36) reflects thoughtfully on the value of comparison in the discipline of history.

6. For a summary of criticisms of comparison, see David M. Freidenreich, "Comparisons Compared: A Methodological Survey of Comparisons of Religion from 'A Magic Dwells' to *A Magic Still Dwells*," *Method and Theory in the Study of Religion* 16 (2004): 80–101.

generalizations and the effacement of difference. Thus Smith has also been wary of inadequate bases for classification and comparison, warning that

> It is axiomatic that comparison is never a matter of identity. Comparison requires the acceptance of difference as the grounds of its being interesting, and a methodological manipulation of that difference to achieve some stated cognitive end. The questions of comparison are questions of judgment with respect to difference.[7]

For strong comparative analysis, he writes, "What is required is the development of a discourse of 'difference,' a complex term which invites negotiation, classification and comparison, and, at the same time, avoids too easy a discourse of the 'same.'"[8]

In world Christianity, we are just now developing the kinds of close appreciations of common and distinctive features across different Christian exempla to make explicit comparison fruitful, and the field needs to develop a self-consciously and self-critically comparative instinct. Moving ahead, I believe the sociology of religion and the anthropology of Christianity will prove particularly helpful partners in this regard. In the sociology of religion, Weberian approaches promise special value, since the methodology of ideal types conduces toward careful comparative exercises that take difference seriously while also noting commonalities.[9] The anthropology of Christianity, a more recent subfield, also probes Christianity in an implicitly comparative mode, seeking to delve deeply into particular cases for the purposes of theory- and category-building that can serve across various Christian manifestations.[10]

In their education, students who seek to contribute to world Christianity, therefore, need to develop skills and dispositions that I call here a comparative imagination. This could come through familiarity with the sociology of religion or the anthropology of Christianity, though not necessarily. They do need, however, to have an awareness of the strengths

---

7. Jonathan Z. Smith, *Relating Religion: Essays in the Study of Religion* (Chicago: University of Chicago Press, 2004), 20. He is citing *To Take Place: Toward Theory in Ritual* (Chicago: University of Chicago Press, 1987), 13–14.

8. Jonathan Z. Smith, *Drudgery Divine: On the Comparison of Early Christianities and the Religions of Late Antiquity* (London: School of Oriental and African Studies, 1990), 42.

9. Max Weber, *The Sociology of Religion* (Boston: Beacon Press, 1964 [originally 1922]). I have found the work of the late Martin Riesebrodt especially illuminating among sociologists of religion.

10. Thomas Seat II, "Similar Objects, Divergent Approaches: What Can World Christianity Learn from the Anthropology of Christianity?" *Journal of World Christianity* 9 (2019): 75–88.

and weaknesses of past efforts in comparative religion and comparative theology, as well as a reasonable grasp of Christian history and contemporary Christian diversity. This will allow them instinctively to consider Christian phenomena across time, space, denominational affiliation, and culture, and then to apply more critically self-conscious comparative methods.

Theological Awareness

Finally, would-be scholars of world Christianity ought to pursue a certain amount of theological awareness, and programs of preparation ought to impart at least some education in theology as part of their curricula. This need not mean the possession of specific faith commitments, nor does it require becoming a theologian *per se*. It does mean a capacity to appreciate theology as a human endeavor with a long history, inside and outside of Christianity, and thus an endeavor that is important for world Christianity.

I have come to believe that scholars of world Christianity are especially poised to make sense of theology as a religious practice with what might be called two distinct interrelated modes: implicit and explicit, or informal and formal. That is to say, there is theology undertaken in a deliberate manner, often by those designated to do so, usually written—that is, theology as explicit and formal. Most education in theology focuses on formal or explicit theology. Yet there is also always ongoing reflection on religious beliefs and practices undertaken by those engaged who are not designated as theologians, who comprise the majority of adherents. Such theology is rarely written and often overlooked, thus might be designated as implicit or informal. Training in world Christianity ought to invite attentiveness to both, with a particular attention to implicit theology, since it has often been overlooked.[11] This will often mean gaining an ability in research methods like oral history, ethnographic fieldwork, and interpretation of survey data—methods less commonly used in the study of formal theology.

With regard to the Christian hymns in the Hong Kong protest, the scholar of world Christianity, adopting methods similar to social sciences or social history, would seek to understand the motivations and behavior of various participants. They would focus not only on those who deliberately chose to sing those hymns but also many others, determining how variously positioned social actors reacted, and why. Did faith con-

---

11. For an example, see Paul Kollman and Cynthia Toms Smedley, *Understanding World Christianity: Eastern Africa* (Minneapolis: Fortress Press, 2018), 169–84.

victions and theological reflection motivate the choice of these hymns, and by whom? What kinds of choices did Christians and non-Christians make in the face of the hymn's appearance? Why? Were there collective discussions of the propriety of such singing? How, too, did the Hong Kong police respond to the hymns, both police authorities and the officers themselves, some of whom no doubt are Christian? Of course, not only scholars of world Christianity would ask such questions. One distinctive contribution from scholars of world Christianity, however, might be noting the specifically theological motivations present (or absent) among those engaged, either as participants or observers, partisans or police.[12]

Arguments against the study of theology for understanding something like the case of Hong Kong hymn singing are rarely made explicitly. Instead, the ways reflective faith commitments, some quite sophisticated, motivate different human actors in such a case would simply be ignored. Research might proceed with a brief reference to the Christian origins of the hymn "Sing Hallelujah to the Lord" in a onetime prominent evangelical movement, or to the religious identities of certain of the protesters. A deeper and more critical theological framework, however, can create an intuitive empathy for those involved in these kinds of circumstances. It also might elucidate other facets of the protests and reactions to them, facets that expose human realities at work in phenomena like this that someone with little theological awareness would overlook. These might include factions among the protesters and the police along the lines of differential loyalties to China and religious faith, ambivalence that exists about employing a faith-based hymn in a mixed group of Christians and non-Christians, the reasoning behind choosing that precise hymn and not some other, as well as other faith-based practices that some of the protesters undertook. In addition, various participants might well have varying theological orientations about the ways they bring their faith into political engagement, depending on their denomination, theological sophistication, or other orienting viewpoints.

Concluding Thoughts

Academic disciplines arise and disappear in response to human experience, understood broadly to include what human beings undergo and seek to comprehend, as well as what they can, in response, try to measure and investigate. Though admittedly an oversimplification, the contempo-

---

12. For a set of essays on how theology can fruitfully interact with anthropology, see Derrick Lemons, ed., *Theologically Engaged Anthropology* (Oxford: Oxford University Press, 2018).

rary field of sociology, for instance, is hard to imagine outside nineteenth-century European social changes described by terms like secularization, urbanization, and modernization, as well as tools to describe, count, and compare such historical processes. Similarly, contemporary neuroscience reflects growing sophistication in the philosophy of science, better medical diagnostics, changes in the field of psychology, and a host of other technological changes. Advances in these areas have—in scientific circles at least—replaced the once-celebrated discipline of phrenology, which assumed that cranial shape revealed important aspects of a person's character and destiny, as previous dogmas gave way to more objective approaches to human thought and behavior.

Considering the appropriate sorts of programming and curricula to prepare someone to engage the field of world Christianity means also appreciating why it has appeared as a field (or area, or subfield) in scholarly circles at this time. What kinds of human experiences have driven its appearance? The first set of such experiences are *demographic*, linked to changes in the distribution and vitality of Christians worldwide, especially in the past half-century or so. Though Christians have always had global aspirations for their message, they have not always had near-global vitality. A second set of experiential changes has to do with the world's *interconnectedness*, what the geographer David Harvey has called "time-space compression" linked to globalized communication, ease of transportation, and the mediatization of so many ways that people come to knowledge and self-expression.

The appearance of Christian hymns in Hong Kong's summer of 2019 protests reflects these kinds of experiences. Christians have long been in Hong Kong, yet they are more diverse and interconnected than ever. Thus hymn singing and other practices can spread with ease, as can strategies of protest and capacities to coordinate large crowds. Scholars equipped to engage world Christianity in all its forms can make sense of these kinds of phenomena.

Yet this case, too, raises the moral question of the stakes in something like world Christianity. As I prepared this article in September 2019, many believed the Chinese government was poised to crack down on the Hong Kong protests, with analysts recalling what happened in June 1989 at Tiananmen Square. As I submit this for publication in the summer of 2020, I am still not sure what will happen. Yet those concerned with global ethics might have a particular interest in whatever outcome unfolds, since democracy and safety, religious freedom and equality, appear to be at stake. And the presence of Christian motifs suggests that world Christianity might be a powerful tool to advance such understanding, and maybe also to develop stronger moral assessments of, and more generous human responses to, circumstances like this.

Thus I believe that a third reason why world Christianity has appeared—and a rather urgent reason for its ongoing importance—lies in the *complexity of the moral issues* that have arisen in a more diverse and interconnected world, and that are likely to be facing us in the years ahead. Scholars linked to world Christianity will be better poised to address those moral issues if they are prepared to act and think shaped by the three dispositions highlighted in this paper. Depth of knowledge will allow informed analysis; a comparative breadth will encourage broader perspectives and respect for difference; and theological awareness will generate appreciation of the richness of the Christian tradition and the scope of Christianity's moral resources.

5

World Christianity and the Challenge of Interdisciplinarity

KWOK PUI-LAN AND
GINA A. ZURLO

World Christianity emerged as an academic field in the 1980s as the result of changing social, political, and intellectual environments. The independence movements after World War II brought political independence to many nations, and the formerly colonized peoples wanted to reclaim their national heritages and assert their cultural autonomy. The widespread student movements and social protests of the 1960s and 1970s demanded radical changes to the status quo, including workers' rights, racial justice, and gender equality. Students demanded changes in academic institutions and challenged the Eurocentric biases of their educational systems. They advocated for a more inclusive curriculum, the establishment of new fields (such as ethnic studies), and an expanded canon that included the works of authors from other parts of the world and from racial and ethnic minority communities.

The notion of world Christianity can be traced to ecumenical discussions in the first half of the twentieth century about the unity and mission of the church and interdenominational collaboration in response to the world's needs.[1] The term "world Christianity" gained popularity after many former colonies became independent and Christian missions were criticized for their racism and collusion with colonialism. Joel Cabrita and David Maxwell argue that the field emerged during a "particular theological and political milieu of postcolonial anxiety."[2] As scholars grappled

---

1. Dale T. Irvin, "World Christianity: A Genealogy," *Journal of World Christianity* 9, no. 1 (2019): 5–22.
2. Joel Cabrita and David Maxwell, "Introduction: Relocating World Christian-

with the colonial legacy of Christian mission while also wanting to present a more nuanced portrayal of Christianity's interaction with diverse cultures, they began to call their field "world Christianity" instead of "mission studies." The term also became popular because of the broader turn in the humanities to the wider studies of the "world"—such as world literature and world history.³ In many fields, "world" became a coded term for "non-Western" cultures and peoples. World Christianity has often been referred to as the study of Christianity in Africa, Asian, Latin America, or the Middle East—areas outside the North Atlantic. Although this understanding still prevails in some quarters, many have tried to avoid replicating the colonial construct of "the West and the rest." World Christianity means the study of diverse local expressions of Christianity, as well as transnational and transcultural comparisons, connections, and networks across geographical, denominational, and religious boundaries.

World Christianity has focused largely on historical and theological studies. In the past, Christian scholars used to study the work of Christian missions and missionary personnel. They treated Christian history in other parts of the world as extensions of the histories of the sending countries and of their missionary enterprise. Pioneers in world Christianity, such as Andrew Walls and Lamin Sanneh, challenged this model by arguing that greater attention be paid to local institutions and the work of local agents. Walls emphasized the interaction of Christianity with local cultures, religions, and practices and the cross-cultural process of Christian history.⁴ As a scholar of African Christianity, he pointed to the importance of Africa in the understanding of Christian history and the need to "come to terms with Christianity as a non-Western religion."⁵ Sanneh lamented that Christian history has been studied following a Eurocentric plotline, which assumed that "churches everywhere are a religious expression of Europe's political reach, or else a reaction to it."⁶ As such, the vitality and agency of local women and men on the ground has often been obscured. His work pays attention to Christianity's encounter with Islam and African indigenous traditions, Christianity as a vernac-

---

ity," in Joel Cabrita, David Maxwell, and Emma Wild-Wood, eds., *Relocating World Christianity: Interdisciplinary Studies in Universal and Local Expressions of the Christian Faith* (Leiden: Brill, 2017), 4.

3. Ibid.

4. Andrew F. Walls, *The Cross-cultural Process of Christian History: Studies in the Transmission and Appropriation of Faith* (Maryknoll, NY: Orbis Books, 2002).

5. Andrew F. Walls, *The Missionary Movement in Christian History: Studies in the Transmission of Faith* (Maryknoll, NY: Orbis Books, 1996), xix.

6. Lamin Sanneh, *Whose Religion Is Christianity? The Gospel beyond the West* (Grand Rapids, MI: Eerdmans, 2003), 23.

ular movement, new ecclesial forms and practices, tension and conflict with local cultures, as well as challenges to Western Enlightenment values.[7] He argued for multiple models of interpretation that attend to specific social and cultural contexts around the world. Following the work of these scholars of African Christianity, there has been a proliferation of studies of local Christianity and actors in many different parts of world.

The second half of the twentieth century saw the blooming of many theological currents around the world. After their struggles for independence, many church leaders and theologians in the global South recognized that Western theology could no longer address their changing sociopolitical situations. Working to promote theological education at the World Council of Churches, Taiwanese scholar Shoki Coe coined the term "contextualizing theology" in the 1970s. By "contextuality" he meant that churches should better respond to emerging social, political, and cultural conditions in carrying out their mission.[8] Just as the gospel is incarnated, theology needs to dwell in a particular time and space. In Asia, various forms of contextual theologies, such as *minjung* (meaning the masses or people) theology in Korea, homeland theology in Taiwan, theology of struggle in the Philippines, and Dalit theology in India have been developed. In Africa, theologians responded to poverty and development, racism and apartheid, religious and ethnic conflicts, the HIV/AIDS pandemic, and increased gender-based violence. In the Catholic Church, the Second Vatican Council allowed the use of vernacular languages in Mass and sacraments and opened the churches to dialogue with the modern world. Following the Council, liberation theology from Latin America, with its emphasis on the preferential option for the poor, became a dominant theological current and influenced many parts of the world. Other local theologies that emphasized indigenization or enculturation also emerged that showed an increasing sensitivity to histories and cultures. Robert J. Schreiter has argued for a new Catholicity in which "universal" theology is no longer prescribed by the Vatican but is shaped instead by dialogue and interaction between the local and the global.[9]

In this chapter, we discuss the unique challenges that interdisciplinarity presents to world Christianity, paying special attention to the social sciences. "Interdisciplinarity" here refers to the use of methods

---

7. Lamin Sanneh, *Translating the Message: Missionary Impact on Culture* (Maryknoll, NY: Orbis Books, 1989), and Lamin Sanneh, *Disciples of All Nations: Pillars of World Christianity* (New York: Oxford University Press, 2008).

8. Shoki Coe, "In Search of Renewal in Theological Education," *Theological Education* 9, no. 4 (Summer 1973): 233–43.

9. Robert J. Schreiter, *The New Catholicity: Theology between the Global and the Local* (Maryknoll, NY: Orbis Books, 1997).

and theories from different academic disciplines to study phenomena and trends among Christians around the world. In order to study the complexities of the variegated expressions of local Christianity and their global connections, we need to employ the tools and insights from many disciplines. Interdisciplinarity enables us to look at social, cultural, and religious phenomena from multiple vantage points; examine and compare diverse sets of data; and employ various research methods and protocols. This approach to research has gained widespread appeal within Western academic settings upon realizing more fully the complexities of human experience and the detriments of a siloed academy. Integrative perspectives are required to make new discoveries. Using the examples of sociology of religion, gender studies, and migration studies, we discuss the ways scholars in world Christianity use these different disciplines in their work and in turn contribute to the development of these fields. World Christianity is inherently interdisciplinary and does not have a fixed methodology. Its studies are largely undertaken by scholars in Western-based institutions, even though the object of study is global.

The emphasis on interdisciplinarity also reminds us to place the study of world Christianity in the wider social and intellectual climate. For example, the second-wave women's movement beginning in the 1960s led to the establishment of women's studies and gender studies. This heightened the awareness of some scholars to pay more attention to gender analysis in world Christianity. The development of cultural studies and postcolonial studies—with their emphasis on popular culture, class structures, national formations, politics of representation, race and ethnicity, and the relation between power and knowledge—has impacted the humanities and social sciences and has bearings on the study of world Christianity.

Sociology of Religion

The relationship between Christian missions and social science has a long history, dating back several centuries. Many mainline missionaries were highly educated and represented some of the best-trained persons of their time. Their motivation for missions inspired them to study the world and the people among whom they worked, producing church-based scholarship that could now be called "social scientific" research. The production of such material was always a part of the missionary enterprise and made important contributions to the contemporary social scientific study of religion.[10]

---

10. For more on missionaries and early social science, see Gina A. Zurlo, "'A

Catholic missionaries in the sixteenth and seventeenth centuries produced social scientific data as an extension of initial encounters between the West and indigenous peoples. They saw a need to document and study new cultures and geographies and did not necessarily see data gathering explicitly as a tool for reaching people with the Christian message. They actively kept statistical records, enumerated local populations, and created maps to strengthen missionary activities overseas.[11] They produced ethnographies, which helped provide the foundation for functionalist anthropology.[12] In addition to learning local languages, they pioneered new geographical areas and kept detailed records of the people and cultures they encountered.[13] Sixteenth- and seventeenth-century Jesuits were early exemplars of the connection between mission and what would become social science.[14] While they did not necessarily set out to be social science researchers, their educational training taught them to be observant of the world around them, and they took that training directly into mission work to produce what would become critical documents for later historians, sociologists, and anthropologists.

Beginning in the late eighteenth century, most notably with the work of William Carey,[15] Protestant missionaries produced social scientific data for garnering support and resources for the evangelization and conversion of non-Christian peoples. Missionaries wanted to describe Christianity regarding its numerical relationship to other religions, their efforts to make converts, and their obligation to train and send more missionaries. The literature of the time compared global missionary statistics in surveys, atlases, encyclopedias, and dictionaries. These works contained estimates for Christian adherents, missionaries, indigenous converts, clergy, and other personnel while also documenting and describing Christian missions to evaluate their successes or failures, inform mission-

---

Miracle from Nairobi': David B. Barrett and the Quantification of World Christianity, 1957–1982" (PhD diss., Boston University, 2017), chapter 1.

11. For example, Pedro Murillo Velarde in the Philippines; Ignacio Lizasoaín in New Spain; Matteo Ricci in China; Juan Sánchez Baquero in Mexico; and Eusebio Kino in Mexico.

12. See Patrick Harries and David Maxwell, "Introduction: The Spiritual in the Secular," in Patrick Harries and David Maxwell, eds., *The Spiritual in the Secular: Missionaries and Knowledge about Africa* (Grand Rapids, MI: Eerdmans, 2012), 6.

13. Examples in Africa include Robert Hamill Nassau in present-day Equatorial Guinea, Gabon, and Cameroon; Henri Trilles in Gabon; Henri A. Junod among Tsonga peoples of southern Africa; Eugène Casalis in South Africa; and Henry Callaway and John Colenso among the Zulu.

14. See Luís Saraiva and Catherine Jami, *The Jesuits, the Padroado and East Asian Science (1552–1773)* (Singapore: World Scientific, 2008).

15. William Carey, *An Enquiry into the Obligations of Christians to Use Means for the Conversion of Heathens* (1792; repr., London: Carey Kingsgate Press, 1961).

ary deployment, and mobilize the home base for prayer and increased missionary sending.

The mainline Protestant missionary enterprise and global movements toward Christian unity and cooperation also helped shape American sociology and what would eventually become world Christianity studies. The social gospel movement during the early twentieth century was significant in the development of early sociological practice, particularly applied sociology. Adherents of the social gospel wanted to apply Christian ethics to social problems such as poverty, alcoholism, child labor, and education. They had a positive view of science and wanted to blend scientific knowledge with religious sentiments. A discourse that brought together academic and applied sociology, known as "Christian sociology," was developed and pioneered by leading researchers (many with backgrounds in missions) who produced scholarship for the church, society, and academy.[16]

From the beginning, American sociology existed in two streams: academic and applied. Two major players in academic sociology were the University of Chicago and Columbia University in New York (the latter of which developed a strong quantitative tradition). Applied sociology was pioneered by Progressive Era activists, particularly women, and honed in on key areas of study and action including the family, human relationships, politics, business, economics, urban dwellers, race relations, and women's roles. Many women, guided by Christian convictions, performed groundbreaking, empirical field research long before any of the men in the Chicago or New York schools of sociology. The Chicago school played a significant role in academically establishing and legitimizing American sociology between 1892 and 1918. It also created a dichotomy between academic and applied sociology that became even more marked in the 1920s with the professionalization of social work.[17] The academicization of sociology also led to the eventual exclusion of religious voices from the academy, leaving them without a place in the discipline's future.[18] Consequently, Christian sociology and its close relative, "Christian social ethics," were increasingly pushed into theological seminaries.

The first generation of American sociologists was cognizant of the discipline's religious roots and the common goal of applying Christian

---

16. For more on the Christian roots of American sociology, see Gina A. Zurlo, "The Social Gospel, Ecumenical Movement, and Christian Sociology: The Institute of Social and Religious Research," *American Sociologist* 46, no. 2 (June 2015): 117–93.

17. Mary Jo Deegan, *Jane Addams and the Men of the Chicago School, 1892–1918* (New Brunswick, NJ: Transaction Books, 1998), 15.

18. Anthony J. Blasi, *Sociology of Religion in America: A History of Secular Fascination with Religion* (Leiden: Brill, 2014), 3.

values and theology to society in the form of social action. By the second generation, however, the purpose of the field had shifted significantly to a secularized, "objective," scientific orientation that would have been almost completely foreign to their predecessors. Despite this change, sociology and its methods were not off-limits to individuals interested in church cooperation, social service, and mission—three defining characteristics of the thriving, global movement toward Christian unity and the beginnings of world Christianity as a discourse.

Despite a close historical connection between early social scientific work and mission studies, the two disciplines appear to have little contact today. World Christianity has grown dramatically with an increased number of doctoral programs, new university press series, regular meetings, and peer-reviewed journals. A major critique of sociology today is that the discipline has little knowledge of its religious roots and does not always take religious beliefs seriously. As a result, it often does not resonate with actual religious people.[19] Yet, the separation of the social sciences from Christianity—along with the assumption that sociologists must be "methodologically nonreligious"—is discontinuous with the discipline's past.[20]

The different ethos and training of students may explain why sociology of religion and world Christianity are not considered bedfellows. World Christianity students are not generally taught quantitative methods, which are frequently used in sociology of religion. Sociology of religion students often are not taught to think globally about their research topics. Those few who study a religion outside of Western settings are often only familiar with that particular setting and are not making connections with other contexts, unlike world Christianity students, who are required to make these global connections. Sociology of religion needs to go global to stay relevant; world Christianity needs to continue to shed its Eurocentrism and Americanness to keep relevance as well.

There have been many discussions concerning the methods for studying world Christianity and the training of future students. In 2013, Boston University School of Theology, in conjunction with Gordon-Conwell Theological Seminary, held a conference on world Christianity. Its purpose was to bring together, for the first time, leaders of research centers in world Christianity to discuss the state of the field. Its two main con-

---

19. See Christian Smith et al., "Roundtable on the Sociology of Religion: Twenty-Three Theses on the Status of Religion in American Sociology—A Mellon Working-Group Reflection," *Journal of the American Academy of Religion* 81, no. 4 (December 2013): 903–38.

20. Michael A. Cantrell, "Must a Scholar of Religion Be Methodologically Atheist or Agnostic?" *Journal of the American Academy of Religion* 84, no. 2 (June 2016): 373–400.

cerns were defining the study of world Christianity and how new scholars and doctoral students were prepared for the field. The presenters and participants raised questions about the methods of the study of world Christianity: What is the method that makes this field distinctive? Is world Christianity emerging as a distinctive Western initiative in terms of centers and discipline and is it therefore preoccupied with questions of the Western academy? How can we go beyond asking questions in an American way, shaped by the priorities and interests of our own training? How can scholars bring the global and the local together? Can we do more than local studies? What kind of methods do we need? How can we listen better to the questions others are asking? What are the priorities of Christians in other parts of the world?[21]

The consultation prompted us to consider a pointed question: does world Christianity *need* a fixed methodology to be a field? The uniqueness of world Christianity demands that scholars be creative and innovative in their methods. What makes the methods of world Christianity special is that scholars can have many tools in their toolbox. But the siloed nature of the academy does not always allow students to be trained in multiple methods. World Christianity programs are in religious studies departments and other areas of universities or in schools of theology and seminaries that have their own methods to pass on to the next generation of scholars. It appears that the onus is on students to think creatively when it comes to breaking out of methodological boxes to do research in a way that makes sense to them while remaining relevant to their interests and their subjects. They are fully aware that Christianity is not a Western religion, so it cannot be studied as such. It makes more sense for a student of African Christianity, for example, to conduct research in African ways and students of Asian Christianity to approach it from Asian perspectives. Are focus groups and in-depth interviews followed by hours of transcribing, translation, coding, and analysis the best way to do research on Christianity in Africa? This may be so in some cases, and in other cases it may not be. It will also be advantageous to test out methodologies developed in one part of the global South in another region. In the same vein, are there different sources of information that world Christianity scholars could be using? Given the ubiquity of smartphones and social media, are there digital sources that could be used and what methods are needed to analyze these data?

World Christianity is also a peculiar field because of the local/global dynamic. Scholars have different expertise, such as area (e.g., African Christianity), country (e.g., Kenyan Christianity), tradition (e.g., Catho-

---

21. Scholars who raised these questions included Bryan Froehle, Jehu Hanciles, Michael McClymond, and Xi Lian.

lics), and topic (e.g., gender). However, while one can make poignant discoveries about Kenyan Catholic women religious in the 1890s, a study such as this might have little light to shed on Peruvian pentecostal male pastors in the 1960s. What makes world Christianity hang together as "world Christianity" and not dissolve into "world Christianities"? This is where tapping into sociological methods could be helpful because they can handle large data sets and make generalizations based on representative samples. Some sociological methods lend themselves better to large-scale discoveries that help us better understand global trends and realities.

World Christianity needs robust methods that take into consideration both the local and the global, lest we lose the rainforest for a piece of bark on a single tree. The mission and social science researchers of the past appeared to move seamlessly between worlds—Western/non-Western; applied/academic; church/society—but this close connection seems to have been lost today. For example, a leading quantitative demographer of religion and his colleague presented a paper at the International Society for the Sociology of Religion in July 2019 about religion and income distribution.[22] The authors provided a fascinating global picture of how income by religion has shifted over a forty-year period—in 1970 the highest absolute poverty was among the unaffiliated (atheists, agnostics) but today it is among Christians. That is, Christians overall are becoming poorer. In their analysis, however, they did not mention that Christianity has demographically shifted to the global South, that it is no longer a Western religion, and that there are more Christians in Africa, Asia, and Latin American than there are in Europe and North America. In many ways, this kind of study could have represented a resounding effort to tie sociology of religion and world Christianity back together but stopped short. Likewise, studies in world Christianity could benefit from some of the approaches and emphases of the sociology of religion, such as how Christian communities function and develop in relation to religion and gender, religion and social change, and religion and migration.

Gender Studies

The establishment of women's studies and gender studies in the academy has challenged mission studies and world Christianity to include gender analysis in their investigation. Women's studies challenges the androcentric nature of educational institutions and knowledge production by

---

22. Vegard Skirbekk and Jose Navarro, "Poor Man's Religion: Poverty and Religious Affiliation Worldwide, 1970–2010" (paper presented at the International Society for the Sociology of Religion, Barcelona, Spain, July 2019).

focusing on women's agency, experiences, and their roles in both the private and public realms. Women's studies does not simply add women's voices or stories, in what has been called an "add and stir" approach, but challenges the conceptual foundations of the disciplines and the categories of analyses. Gender studies argues that "gender," which is different from biological sex, is socially constructed. It studies "the social organization of the relationship between the sexes,"[23] as well as gender identity and gender representation. Both women's studies and gender studies are interdisciplinary fields, using a variety of methods and approaches.

In the past, the study of Christian missions was focused on the work of male missionaries and has not paid sufficient attention to female missionaries. Women missionaries were needed because in some traditional societies, such as China, India, and the Middle East, there was segregation between the sexes. At first, married women accompanied their husbands to the mission fields, and later single female missionaries, who played important roles in the expansion of mission work, were sent. In addition to carrying out evangelistic work, female missionaries opened schools for girls and women, established health clinics and dispensaries, promoted hygiene, and were involved in social reforms. These missionaries carried out "woman's work for woman" and developed gender-based mission theories because of their identity as women.[24] In some cases, when mission work met strong resistance from local people, female missionaries were sent instead of male missionaries because they were seen as less threatening. Although female missionaries may have been subordinate to male leaders in the mission societies, they carved out a sphere of influence for themselves. For those working in a colonial situation, the mission field accorded them privileges they did not enjoy back home because of gender discrimination.

The participation of women in Christian missions must be seen in the context of changing gender relationships within the social and religious institutions of Europe and North America. In the last decades of the nineteenth century, more women gained access to higher education but, because of their gender, some of the professions were closed to them. Mission work enabled educated women to develop a career and express their religious zeal. As the demand for female missionaries grew, women's overseas mission boards were formed for recruiting women and sending them out. For example, the Church of England Zenana Missionary Society was established in 1880 to spread Anglicanism among Indian women

---

23. Joan W. Scott, "Gender: A Useful Category of Historical Analysis," *American Historical Review* 91, no. 5 (1986): 1053.

24. Dana L. Robert, *American Women in Mission: The Social History of Their Thought and Practice* (Macon, GA: Mercer University Press, 1996).

and later expanded its work to women in China and Japan.[25] In the United States, the women's departments in mainline denominations raised funds to support women's work, which had become an integral part of Christian mission. The support for mission strengthened Christian women's organizing efforts, connected them with women far away, and inculcated a sense that they belonged to a worldwide community. Pamphlets and bulletins promoting mission work were published to galvanize support. Some of these literatures propagated the pitiful condition of "heathen" women and the inferiority of their cultures, thus contributing to cultural ethnocentrism. But many female missionaries devoted their lives to mission work and formed strong bonds and life-long friendships with the women they served.[26]

While we can study female missionaries and their activities by consulting mission archives and their personal papers and correspondence, it is far more difficult to study the lives and work of local Christian women. Many of the early converts were illiterate, and local Christian women did not leave behind many writings or records for study. We have to carefully piece together information from a wide variety of sources: missionary reports, Christian women's journals, YWCA magazines, church bulletins, autobiographies, and even obituaries. Other important resources that help to place their lives and activities in context include sermons, church catechisms, religious tracts, hymns, church yearbooks, and national church surveys. We have to borrow tools from historical, sociological, and anthropological disciplines to recover their agency and their contribution to the spread of Christianity. They served as local evangelists and assistants to Western missionaries, taught children in Sunday schools, visited women in their homes, and tended to the sick. After they had received an education, they became teachers and administrators of mission schools and community leaders. Some of them were social reformers and involved in movements such as literacy campaigns, education and health reform, temperance movements, and anti-footbinding and anti-concubinage movements. International networks, such as the YWCA and the Women's Christian Temperance Union, provided opportunities for leadership training and involvement in society.[27] The Mothers' Union in the Anglican Church was established in 1876 to promote the sanctity

---

25. A. D., *Until the Shadow Flee Away: The Story of the C.E.Z.M.S. Work in India and Ceylon* (London: Church of England Zenana Missionary Society, 1912).

26. See, for example, Jane Hunter, *The Gospel of Gentility: American Women Missionaries in Turn-of-the-Century China*, rev. ed. (New Haven, CT: Yale University Press, 1989).

27. For the Chinese case, see Kwok Pui-lan, *Chinese Women and Christianity, 1860–1927* (Atlanta, GA: Scholars Press, 1992).

of marriage and strong motherhood. It spread to many countries and is especially strong in Africa today.[28] These organizations facilitated transnational linkage and enabled local Christian women to learn from women outside their countries.

Local "Bible women" played crucial roles in the church and community at the grassroots level. They were female evangelists trained and employed by the missionaries to assist in mission work. The origin of the term is debatable and can be traced to the establishment of training schools for girls in the Middle East in the 1840s. For example, the graduates of a female seminary in Constantinople were employed by an American mission board as Bible women to preach the gospel to local women. The number of training schools dramatically increased with forty training schools in China by 1900 and more than thirty such schools in India.[29] In her study of Bible women in nineteenth-century China, Zhou Yun describes their various roles, including interpretation for Western missionaries, teaching the Bible and prayers, itineration and visiting girls' day schools, and house visitation. In rural China, where many people were illiterate, they served as important role models and community leaders.[30] Zhou concludes that "they were local evangelistic agents contributing to the global development of Christianity,"[31] as they were intermediaries both in the transnational exchanges between Chinese women and Western missionaries as well as between Chinese culture and Christian ideals.

The study of gender and world Christianity is interdisciplinary for it has to take into consideration additional factors such as class, caste, race, ethnicity, and religious backgrounds. In colonial India, for example, gender intersects with class and caste in determining women's responses to Christianity. Because it was harder for Christianity to convert rich and high-caste women, Christian missionaries turned their attention to low-caste and Dalit women, who found opportunities for social mobility in the foreign religion. Eliza F. Kent points out that when the Tamil-speaking Dalit women in southern India became Christians, they negotiated new gender norms and developed a "discourse of respectability." To validate their new and higher social status, they adopted new sartorial styles and

---

28. Cordelia Moyse, *A History of the Mothers' Union: Women, Anglicanism, and Globalisation, 1876–2008* (Woodbridge, UK: Boydell and Brewer, 2009).

29. Ruth A. Tucker, "The Role of Bible Women in World Evangelism," *Missiology* 8, no. 2 (April 1985): 135.

30. Zhou Yun, "The Making of Bible Women in the Fujian Zenana Mission from the 1880s to the 1950s," in Wai Ching Angela Wong and Patricia P. K. Chiu, eds., *Christian Women in Chinese Society: The Anglican Story* (Hong Kong: Hong Kong University Press, 2018), 70–74.

31. Ibid., 73.

appropriated Christian notions of femininity and domesticity selectively informed by upper-caste Hindu women's notions of "respectable" womanhood. As a result, the new gender norms regarding marriage and divorce were more restrictive than those in the Dalit community.[32] In Africa, the study of women's participation in the rapidly growing African Initiated Churches needs to consider gender, race, class, and African traditional religions. Unlike the mainline Protestant denominations, these African Initiated Churches were founded by Africans without foreign control and represent an indigenous form of African Christianity. They retain certain elements of African cultural forms and often work among the poor and low-class people and rely on local leadership. Women can be founders of these churches, enjoying the same status and respect as male founders. In traditional African religions, women can serve as healers and diviners. They carry over their healing roles to the African Initiated Churches and, in a continent in which many people suffer from physical and social illnesses, they are sought after and respected by people.[33]

The critique of gender oppression led to the development of Christian feminism in many parts of the world. Mary Daly published her pioneering book *The Church and Second Sex*, in which she criticized the Catholic Church for treating women as second-class citizens.[34] Since then, Western Christian women have argued for the inclusion of women's experience in theology, the use of inclusive language, women's ordination, and women's participation in decision-making bodies of the churches. Feminist scholars have exposed deep-seated patriarchal and misogynistic concepts and practices in the Christian tradition and have also developed feminist theology that affirms the humanity and dignity of women. However, Western Christian women's worldviews and theology are often limited by their white, middle-class experiences. Although they are discriminated against because of their gender, they enjoy racial and class privileges along with the legacies of Western hegemony. Because women in their contexts suffer from multiple oppressions, feminist theologians from racial and ethnic minority communities from within and without the global South use an intersectional approach in their social analyses.

The study of feminist theology from a world Christianity perspective needs to attend to the colonial legacy and the complex interactions between

---

32. Eliza F. Kent, *Converting Women: Gender and Protestant Christianity in Colonial South India* (New York: Oxford University Press, 2004). See also Chad M. Bauman, "Redeeming Indian 'Christian' Womanhood: Missionaries, Dalits, and Agency in Colonial India," *Journal of Feminist Studies in Religion* 24, no. 2 (2008): 5–27.

33. Chammah J. Kaunda and Isabel A. Phiri, "African Initiated Churches Pneumatology and Gender Justice in the Work of GC Oosthuizen," *Scriptura* 115 (2016): 1–12.

34. Mary Daly, *The Church and the Second Sex* (New York: Harper & Row, 1968).

Christianity and local cultures in shaping women's lives. Kenyan theologian Musimbi Kanyoro points to the need to develop an "engendered cultural hermeneutics" that examines critically the relation between gospel and culture while also bringing a gender and feminist perspective to the inculturation of theology.[35] As feminist theology becomes more global, intercultural, and ecumenical, we need to explore the commonalities and differences within the field as well as the ways feminist theology addresses crucial issues such as globalization, poverty, militarism, war and violence, climate change, migration, and human trafficking.

Since gender studies explores the relationship between the sexes, it includes men and men's studies in its purview. Gender and feminist studies of Christianity have prompted scholars to explore the construction of masculinity in different periods and contexts within Christian history. These studies are not meant to reinforce androcentrism and misogyny but rather to scrutinize critically the positions of men in church and society, male religious authority and power, and the ideals of masculinity engendered in Christian discourse. The anthology *Men and Masculinities in Christianity and Judaism: A Critical Reader* examines issues such as Jesus and masculinity studies, Christian manliness, circumcision and patriarchy, ideals of male beauty, the discovery of sodomy, Christian machismo, gay sexuality, and the sanctity of male desire. Much of these discussions have taken place in Europe and North America in dialogue with continental philosophy with an emphasis on male sexuality.[36] A very different discourse on redemptive or transformative masculinity has arisen in Africa in the last decade as a response to HIV/AIDS, male domination, and gender-based violence. African scholars have produced Bible studies and study guides to overcome biased views of manhood such as male superiority, the need to be in control, the lack of respect for women's human rights, and the refusal to accept women's leadership. They want to encourage the development of redemptive masculinity modeled after Jesus, who took women seriously, broke cultural taboos, and advocated for social justice.[37]

---

35. Musimbi Kanyoro, "Engendered Communal Theology: African Women's Contribution to Theology in the Twenty-First Century," *Feminist Theology* 27 (2001): 36–56.

36. Björn Krondorfer, ed., *Men and Masculinities in Christianity and Judaism: A Critical Reader* (London: SCM, 2009).

37. Ezra Chitando and Sophie Chirongoma, eds., *Redemptive Masculinities: Men, HIV and Religion* (Geneva: World Council of Churches, 2012); and Ezra Chitando and Nyambura J. Njoroge, eds., *Contextual Bible Study Manual on Transformative Manhood* (Harare, Zimbabwe: Ecumenical HIV and AIDS Initiative in Africa, 2013).

Human sexuality has been a contentious issue in Christian mission and world Christianity because sexuality is related to discourses on cultural difference, racial stereotypes, and gendered hierarchy. In the nineteenth century, missionaries debated about polygamy and whether or not to allow polygamous persons to be baptized. In the first half of the twentieth century, churches debated about divorce and birth control.[38] In our contemporary period, lesbian, gay, bisexual, transgender, and queer (LGBTQ) issues have threatened schisms in several denominations such as the Anglican communion and the United Methodist Church.[39] Those who study world Christianity need to pay attention to shifting dynamics shaping the relationship between churches in the global North and South. In the past, it was the Western churches that condemned polygamy and sexual practices in the global South. Today, African church leaders accuse Western churches of deviating from Christian norms. As the Christian demographic has shifted to the global South, some of the southern leaders want to assert more power and moral authority in the worldwide church. There is a new alignment between conservative churches in the United States with churches in the global South.[40] In the past, much of LGBTQ activism has been carried out in Europe and North America while today LGBTQ Christians in other parts of the world have become more vocal in pushing for their rights and recognition in the church.[41]

In the past several decades, organizations such as the Circle of Concerned African Women Theologians, Ecclesia of Women in Asia (Catholic), and the Asian Women's Resource Centre for Culture and Theology (Protestant) have organized meetings and published volumes on biblical studies, theology, and women's ministries. It will be very fruitful to develop analytical frameworks for cross-cultural comparison and linkages. Specifically, this will contribute to the study of the relationship between gender

---

38. See, for example, the discussion in the Anglican Communion in Jane Shaw, "Bonds of Affection: Debates about Sexuality," in Kwok Pui-lan, Judith Berling, and Jenny Plane Te Paa, eds., *Anglican Women on Church and Mission* (Harrisburg, PA: Morehouse Publishing, 2012), 37–53.

39. William L. Sachs, *Homosexuality and the Crisis of Anglicanism* (Cambridge: Cambridge University Press, 2008); Alex Joyner et al., *Living Faithfully: Human Sexuality and the United Methodist Church*, rev. and updated (Nashville, TN: Abingdon Press, 2019).

40. Miranda K. Hassett, *Anglican Communion in Crisis: How Episcopal Dissidents and Their African Allies Are Reshaping Anglicanism* (Princeton, NJ: Princeton University Press, 2007).

41. Terry Brown, ed., *Other Voices, Other Worlds: The Global Church Speaks Out on Homosexuality* (New York: Church Publishing, 2006); "Voices of Witness Africa," film, directed by Cynthia Black and Katie Sherrod (Claiming the Blessing, 2009); and Sharon A. Bong, *Becoming Queer and Religious in Malaysia and Singapore* (London: Bloomsbury Academic, 2020).

and global modernity. Just as the missionary movement has been an element in a globalizing modernity, a comparative study will illumine how gender factors into the process of modern cultural globalization. Such an approach will be dynamic and interactive—emphasizing the receptors and not the transmitters, by going beyond the binary construct of imposition and resistance to look for multiple possibilities in cultural interactions.[42] Interdisciplinary collaboration will be necessary for these kinds of innovative inquiries. In particular, quantitative research in mission and world Christianity today has lagged in its consideration of gender, even though master statistician James Dennis produced estimates for both male and female missionaries in his substantial quantitative assessment of the Western missionary movement at the turn of the twentieth century.[43] Despite this historical precedent, many churches, denominations, and mission agencies today fail to report on the gender makeup of their congregations and organizations. This lack of data is an opportunity for researchers to do the necessary creative interdisciplinary research to report on this fundamental demographic of Christians worldwide.

Migration Studies

Migration has become a global phenomenon, and the plight of migrants, refugees, asylum seekers, and internally displaced persons demands the church's critical attention. According to the United Nations, the number of international migrants was over 271 million in 2019, about 3.5 percent of the world's population.[44] More than half of these international migrants (141 million) live in Europe and North America. The top destination remains the United States, at nearly 51 million. Even though the South-to-North flow is significant, the majority of migrants from Asia and Africa live in their region of origin. An estimated 52 percent of the migrants are male, and two-thirds of the migrants are looking for work. The widening gap between the rich and the poor coupled with environmental devastation due to climate disasters has driven many migrants to seek better living conditions elsewhere. In addition, war, violence, and conflict have led to massive internal displacement in places such as the Central African Republic, Congo, Myanmar, South Sudan, Syria, and Yemen. There

---

42. For a discussion on global modernity and the role of Christian mission in it, see Ryan Dunch, "Beyond Cultural Imperialism: Cultural Theory, Christian Missions, and Global Modernity," *History and Theory* 41 (2002): 301–25.

43. James S. Dennis, *Christian Missions and Social Progress: A Sociological Study of Foreign Missions* (New York: Fleming H. Revell, 1897–1906).

44. World Migration Report 2020 (Geneva: International Organization for Migration, 2019), 21.

were about 41.3 million internally displaced people at the end of 2018 and nearly 26 million refugees.[45] Migrants and refugees bring traits of their religious and cultural identities with them, and they have to reorganize and reconstruct their religion in their host countries. Given that our time has been dubbed "the Age of Migration," scholars have to examine the changing landscape of world Christianity with respect to the characteristics of migrant churches, religion in diaspora, and new Christian networks between sending and hosting countries.

Peter C. Phan, a Catholic theologian, argues that migration has played a central role in the expansion of Christianity and calls the church an "institutional migrant." He writes, "My contention is that without migration as a whole, [. . .] Christianity as such, would not have existed as a *world religion*" and a catholic (meaning worldwide) institution.[46] He outlines different migrations or migratory movements in the history of Christianity that have led Christianity to encounter other peoples and cultures, resulting in the changing demographics and face of the church. Following the destruction of the Second Temple in 70 CE, the migration of Christians out of Jerusalem and Palestine transformed Christianity from a Jewish sect into a worldwide migrant institution. Constantine's relocation of the capital from Rome to Byzantium (Constantinople) not only shifted the political center but also led to the development of "Orthodox Christianity." Later, the sack of Rome and the migration of German tribes, such as the Vandals and the Goths, into Europe resulted in the establishment of churches in northern Europe. Between the fifteenth and seventeenth century, the expansion of Christendom into the New World and parts of Asia during the so-called "Age of Discovery" contributed to the spread of the Roman Catholic Church. From 1650 to World War I, colonization and industrialization of the world economy brought millions of Europeans to live outside Europe while missionary movements established churches around the world. At the same time, ten to twelve million slaves were forced to migrate from Africa, thereby changing the face of American Christianity.

After World War II and decolonization, many former colonized persons migrated to Europe and North America, forming migrant churches in diaspora. In our contemporary world, war, poverty, violence, and conflicts cause mass migration and displacement. Concurrently, globalization and the ease of travel have made transnational and transcontinental connections more possible.[47] As a result of these waves of migration, Phan

---

45. Ibid., 3.
46. Peter C. Phan, "*Deus Migrator*—God the Migrant: Migration of Theology and Theology of Migration," *Theological Studies* 77 (2016): 848 (emphasis in original).
47. Ibid., 850–53.

argues that "Christianity itself is now 'World Christianity,' a world religion that has always been but is becoming more than ever diverse, multiple, transnational, transcultural, and polycentric in all aspects of its life."[48]

Migration has changed the configuration of Christianity and contributed to religious diversity and plurality in Europe and North America. In the United States, the Immigration and Nationality Act of 1965 opened the doors to migrants from Africa, Asia, Latin America, and southern Europe and changed the mosaic of the American people. The influx of migrants from Central and Latin America, both documented and undocumented, has transformed the American Catholic Church. Hispanic and Latino Christians make up 52 percent of Catholics under thirty.[49] Migrants from different continents and nations worship together in Catholic churches in metropolitan areas, making congregational lives more diverse and pluralistic. These new immigrants brought with them a new type of Catholicism—such as devotion to Our Lady of Guadalupe, among other saints; that is quite different from the Catholicism of early migrants from Europe. In the evangelical churches, it is racial minority and immigrant churches that are showing vitality and growth. Soong-Chan Rah argues that, while white evangelical churches remain captive to Western cultural trappings, immigrant, ethnic, and multi-ethnic churches are flourishing because they can better respond to a changing, multicultural America. He says that while the U.S. Census projects that racial and ethnic minorities will become the majority around 2040, the trend of a nonwhite majority in America will be found in churches faster than in the general population. This is because of the large influx of new immigrants, many of whom are Christians revitalizing the churches.[50] These changes have prompted some world Christianity scholars, such as Jehu Hanciles, to argue that what we are seeing is not a decline of Christianity in America but the de-Europeanization of American Christianity.[51]

Migration studies is an interdisciplinary field that draws on anthropology, sociology, economics, law, postcolonial studies, and so forth. Scholars who study world Christianity contribute to the field by using a variety of methods like interview, case studies, participatory observation, qualitative research, and ethnography in their research. They have studied the trajectories, narratives, and patterns of migration and Christianity

---

48. Ibid., 853.

49. Michael J. O'Loughlin, "The U.S. Catholic Experience Is Increasingly Hispanic and Southwestern," *America: The Jesuit Review,* September 6, 2017, https://www.americamagazine.org.

50. Soong-Chan Rah, *The Next Evangelicalism: Freeing the Church from Western Cultural Captivity* (Downers Grove, IL: IVP Books, 2009), 14.

51. Jehu J. Hanciles, *Beyond Christendom: Globalization, African Migration, and the Transformation of the West* (Maryknoll, NY: Orbis Books, 2008), 293–95.

in diasporas. They discuss the development, social composition, membership, leadership, and modes of operation of immigrant churches on different continents.[52] These churches serve not only the migrants' spiritual needs but also foster a sense of belonging and identity whereas migration often brings alienation, uprootedness, and discrimination. They provide social support and practical assistance for migrants to adjust to the social and cultural environments of their host country. Religious communities act as buffer zones against social alienation, racism, and hostility that exist in some host countries. In the United States, many immigrants become more religious after coming to the United States, with many Asian immigrants converting to Christianity after immigration. For example, more than 70 percent of Korean Americans are Christians (Protestant and Catholic),[53] though Christians constitute only about 30 percent of South Korea's population. While the immigrant churches want to preserve their cultural identities, they have to adjust to the host country's social, political, and economic milieu, especially in multigenerational churches. At the same time, many immigrants maintain contact with their communities and churches in their home countries since migration is no longer a one-way street in our globalized age. The age of migration heightens the need to study multidirectional and global-local linkages in world Christianity.

The global migratory movement from the South to the North is tied to the process of what has been called "reverse mission." The global South, once on the receiving end of Western mission, has become the center for reverse and multidirectional missions. Of the world's 425,000 cross-cultural missionaries in 2020, 224,000 come from the global North and 201,000 from the global South.[54] Some immigrant Christians have found Western societies to be very secularized and their churches lacking in vitality. They have founded immigrant churches and taken upon themselves the responsibility to re-evangelize or re-Christianize the West. Some churches and church-related ministries, especially from pentecostal/charismatic backgrounds in Africa, have sent missionaries to Europe, North America, and other parts of the world. Hanciles notes that this African migrant-missionary movement is different from the earlier missionary movement, which was associated with colonialism and pater-

---

52. Hanciles, *Beyond Christendom*; Afe Adogame, *The African Christian Diaspora: New Currents and Emerging Trends in World Christianity* (London: Bloomsbury, 2013); Karen I. Leonard, Alex Stepick, Manuel A. Vasquez, and Jennifer Holdaway, eds., *Immigrant Faiths: Transforming Religious Life in America* (New York: Altamira Press, 2006).

53. Pew Research Center, "Asian Americans: A Mosaic of Faiths," July 19, 2012, 16, https://www.pewresearch.org.

54. Todd M. Johnson and Gina A. Zurlo, *World Christian Encyclopedia*, 3rd ed. (Edinburgh: Edinburgh University Press, 2019), 32.

nalism. Without backing from the state or substantial funding, this new missionary movement has to acclimate to the host countries and become self-reliant by depending on local resources. There is no strict distinction between sending and receiving countries since each nation sends and receives missionaries. Indeed, over half of all missionaries in the world serve in countries that are more than 80 percent Christian.[55] Thus, the whole world is the mission field. This movement exemplifies New Testament models of mission by emphasizing evangelistic zeal and spiritual power, the use of house churches, tent-making ministries, and reliance on lay leadership.[56] Afe Adogame, who has studied African Christian diaspora, says that reverse mission has brought a shift in mission understanding and a better appreciation of the multicultural character of Christianity. He writes, "Missionary work has changed to become multi-lateral rather than unilateral, itinerant missionaries have grown, while mission understanding has moved from cultural transplantation to contextualization. This reverse trend in missions offers the old heartlands of Christianity a model for renewal and a call for structural reform of the Church in order to grapple with the challenges of migration."[57]

The study of migration and world Christianity could benefit from gender studies, as the experiences of female migrants have often been overlooked. An important trend in global migration is its increasing feminization. According to the United Nations report, women comprise 48 percent of international migrants. This trend shows divergence from the past, which was dominated by men. Women are often assigned the role of guardians of culture, and they are responsible for passing the cultural traits from one generation to another. In some of the immigrant communities and churches, the preservation of cultural and religious identity often entails the perpetuation of gender roles in the home churches and society. For example, in her sociological study of first-generation Korean women in immigrant churches, Ai Ra Kim shows how Korean Christianity perpetuates institutional sexism at home, in the church, and in the immigrant community.[58] She argues that Korean women's traditional role as "self-sacrificial warriorlike caretaker" has been perpetuated and

---

55. Gina A. Zurlo, Todd M. Johnson, and Peter F. Crossing, "World Christianity and Mission 2021: Questions about the Future," *International Bulletin of Mission Research* 45, no. 1 (2021): 15–25.

56. Jehu J. Hanciles, "Beyond Christendom: African Migration and Transformations of Global Christianity," *Studies in World Christianity* 10, no. 1 (2004): 107–10.

57. Afe Adogame, "Transnational Migration and Pentecostalism in Europe," *PentecoStudies* 9, no. 1 (2010): 70.

58. Ai Ra Kim, *Women Struggling for a New Life: The Role of Religion in the Cultural Passage from Korea to America* (Albany: State University of New York Press, 1996).

reconfirmed as "appendix self" and "second-class persons" in Korean immigrant Christianity. Many of the immigrant churches have male leadership, sometimes hired from the home countries, while women have been marginalized in decision-making processes. Women's relationships with immigrant churches are more complex and ambivalent than men's because churches can be sources of social support, but at the same time marginalize them.

Inequality in the global economy, growing unemployment, and the burden of family survival have led many female migrant workers to work as domestic helpers, nurses, and laborers in other countries only to remit their hard-earned foreign currencies home. Many migrant women work under unfavorable working conditions, and some suffer from abuses and discrimination. Gemma Tulud Cruz offers insights on gender and religion in global migration by studying Filipina migrant workers in Hong Kong using interdisciplinary approaches. She shows that these migrant female workers' Catholic faith is important in sustaining them through the travails of living in a foreign place. Their Sunday and cultural rituals and other Catholic observances provide them a sense of communal belonging and solidarity. She calls on the church to develop a theology of migration by learning from the migrants.[59] As a pilgrim people, she argues, the migrants have recreated a sense of home based on relationality and an understanding of church that is flexible, improvisational, and less tied to a clerical model.[60]

Conclusion

The study of world Christianity has grown in the past several decades to become an interdisciplinary, transcultural, transnational, and interreligious field. It is an opportune time to strengthen South-to-South comparative studies because previous studies have focused on comparing Christianity in the metropolitan centers and the former colonies. The focus on South-to-South connections and comparative studies will generate new research agendas, questions, and methodologies. In the past, the study of Christianity around the world was shaped by missionaries interested in propagating the faith, followed by scholars studying African Christianity, such as Walls and Sanneh. Comparative studies in other parts of the world will bring out other issues and develop new inquiries.

---

59. Gemma Tulud Cruz, *Toward a Theology of Migration: Social Justice and Religious Experience* (New York: Palgrave Macmillan, 2014).

60. Gemma Tulud Cruz, "Between Identity and Security: Theological Implications of Migration in the Context of Globalization," *Theological Studies* 69 (2008): 369.

For example, a comparative study of Christianity along the Silk Road will offer fresh perspectives on Christianity's encounter with Buddhism and Islam, religious appropriation, and interreligious dialogue in multiscriptural and multireligious contexts.

Currently, most of the centers and scholars in the study of world Christianity are located in Europe and North America. As we look toward the future, we welcome the contributions of scholars from other parts of the world so that we can better understand the polycentric nature of world Christianity. The research centers of world Christianity can strengthen their collaboration and partnership with scholars in the global South. An important step is the gathering and publication of primary resources to make material scattered in libraries and research centers more accessible.[61] In addition, the digitalization of archives and collections in some major universities, such as Harvard University,[62] and the development of digital projects at the Center for Global Christianity and Mission at Boston University will make resources more available to scholars worldwide.[63]

The study of world Christianity will also be affected by the development of digital humanities, which include the systematic use of digital resources and apply computing and digital technologies in data analysis. These new applications and techniques allow scholars in world Christianity to use large-scale quantitative studies and data-mine large digital archives to investigate macro-level cultural and religious trends. Training in the use of digital tools and methods opens world Christianity to a wider breadth of resources besides the printed word, such as audio-visual material and digital media. For example, the Chinese Christian Posters Project at Boston University makes hundreds of images of Christian posters circulated in China between 1927 and 1951 freely accessible and searchable for the first time.[64] Digital technologies will greatly expand and perhaps revolutionize our understanding of world Christianity in the future.

---

61. For example, Klaus Koschorke, Adrian Hermann, E. Phuti Mogase, and Ciprian Burlacioiu, eds., *Discourses of Indigenous Christian Elites in Colonial Societies in Asia and Africa around 1900: A Documentary Sourcebook from Selected Journals* (Wiesbaden: Harrassowitz Verlag, 2016).

62. The Digital Collections at Harvard University provides free, public access to six million objects from the library's collection. It has a rich collection of primary resources for the study of Chinese Protestant Christianity; see "Digital Collections," Harvard University, https://library.harvard.edu/digital-collections.

63. "Digital Projects," Boston University School of Theology, Center for Global Christianity and Mission, http://www.bu.edu/cgcm/digital-projects/.

64. "Chinese Christian Posters," Boston University School of Theology, Center for Global Christianity and Mission, https://ccposters.com/pg/home/.

6

"Worlding" Christianity: Approaches to the Making and Breaking of Confessional Boundaries

Shobana Shankar

Of the two concepts in the field of "world Christianity," Christianity arguably gets more attention. The church's presence in all corners of the globe and the modalities of the gospel's movement—through missions, media, and migrants—and its theological imperatives, such as Pauline missions and the moving Spirit's centrality in pentecostalism, have inspired rich extensive discussion and debate that seem to explain easily how "worldness" exists within Christianity. Many scholars have argued that, as a religion, it has been made to move. Andrew F. Walls describes how Christian theology "springs out of practical situations" and has been occasional, local, and a form of "explanation of faith to outsiders."[1] Walls captures these productive tensions between the universal and the local—the pilgrim's principle and indigenous principles—that have held together diverse Christians in a far-reaching communion.

"World" may seem clearly definable as signifying an expanded and expansive geography, yet, recently, Joel Cabrita and David Maxwell point out in their call for a critical reappraisal of world Christianity that the idea of "world" is not so simple; they argue that, in the context of Christianity, it is "normative," emphasizing cultural specificity at the expense of larger-scale connectivities.[2] Lamin Sanneh's preference for "world"

---

1. Andrew F. Walls, *Missionary Movement in Christian History: Studies in the Transmission of Faith* (Maryknoll, NY: Orbis Books, 2015), chapter 1. Tim Tennent, *Theology in the Context of World Christianity: How the Global Church Is Influencing the Way We Think about and Discuss Theology* (Grand Rapids, MI: Zondervan, 2009).

2. Joel Cabrita and David Maxwell, "Introduction: Relocating World Christian-

instead of "global" relates precisely to this distinction, calling attention to how "worldwide Christian resurgence" is "disturbing the public peace" in the cities of the secular global North.³ In other words, world Christianity has pushed open the doors of the West, forcing many new considerations, perhaps most remarkably a reappraisal of what modernity and liberal universalism mean. Yet the contentions over "world" are hardly resolved; indeed, they are fruitful for challenging world Christianity studies to continue to map out new research agenda and for challenging the wider academic study of religions. Even beyond academia the decentering of the West in Christianity has filtered into popular media in wealthy countries of the West, which cannot help but acknowledge the presence and even influence of non-Western Christians. Reportage on Nigerian evangelicals' support for American president Donald Trump, the persecution of Chinese Christians, and the Bolivian evangelical forces mobilized against the indigenous ex-president Evo Morales reveals the political interest in world Christianity, even if it is implicitly or explicitly filtered through political interests like pro-Israel lobbies, Islamophobia, fear of China's economic power, and capitalist control in Latin America.⁴

The purpose of this essay is examine what we can learn about the "worlding" of Christianity as a method, particularly as religious studies overlaps with other disciplines. While history is the discipline of focus here, a survey across several disciplines reveals a similar conceptualization that "to world" is an active verb. Like Cabrita and Maxwell, historians of Christianity in Africa, religious studies scholar Dorottya Nagy argues that "world-mindedness" "as an approach starts with the recognition that knowledge construction is always purposeful action."⁵ The similarity in perspective of Pheng Cheah, a scholar of rhetoric, is striking; he agrees that "world" is not neutral, writing in very similar language to Cabrita

---

ity," in Joel Cabrita, David Maxwell, and Emma Wild-Wood, eds., *Relocating World Christianity: Interdisciplinary Studies in Universal and Local Expressions of the Christian Faith* (Leiden: Brill, 2017), 4.

3. Lamin Sanneh, *Whose Religion Is Christianity: The Gospel beyond the West* (Grand Rapids, MI: Eerdmans, 2003), 3–4.

4. See the following articles for a small sample: Yomi Kazeem, "Nigerians Have Been Targeted by Trump's Immigration Policies but He's Still Popular," *Quartz Africa*, October 16, 2020, https://qz.com/africa; Francis X. Rocca and Chun Han Wong, "Vatican, Beijing Renew Deal on Bishop Appointments, as Catholics Remain Divided," *Wall Street Journal*, October 22, 2020, https://www.wsj.com; Tom Philips, "'Satan Be Gone!' Bolivian Christians Claim Credit for Ousting Evo Morales," *The Guardian*, January 27, 2020, https://www.theguardian.com.

5. Dorottya Nagy, "Recalling the Term 'World Christianity': Excursions into Worldings of Literature, Philosophy, and History," in Martha Frederiks and Dorottya Nagy, eds., *World Christianity: Methodological Considerations* (Leiden: Brill, 2020), 40–64, 60.

and Maxwell that the world is "a normative basis for a radical rethinking," in his case, about "world literature."[6] He sees this normativity as a reorientation in premises underlying world literature as understood by modern European, particularly German, philosophers. Scholars have vigorously challenged the conflation of world with globalization, read in economic terms of markets and circulation, by drawing attention to cultural understandings and processes of world making. Referring to Erich Auerbach and Johann Wolfgang von Goethe, Cheah notes that Auerbach, writing in 1952, did not merely consider world literature to be about what is common and human: "Humanity was not something naturally given but a telos to be achieved through intercourse across the existential plurality and diversity of human traditions and cultures whose individuality must be maintained and whose unique historical development must be respected."[7]

Auerbach drew on Goethe's writing to insist that "Weltliteratur has an irreducible temporal dimension." The connection of world is to past and future, to causality as "a form of action that actualizes or brings something into actuality."[8] Contemporary scholars of world literature should not ignore the spiritual connectivities Goethe envisioned in world literature, Cheah argues, which were the embodiment of an ethical search for universal humanity, someday, somewhere and everywhere. Cheah unearths Goethe's likening of world literature authors to prophets and their works to the transmission of the sacred word to show how in Goethe's "sacralization of world literature," "the world transcends mere geography" and "opens a new universal horizon by pointing to humanity's spiritual unity."[9]

Cheah makes a powerful critique of the secularist biases of global and globalization studies. These same biases have also been called into question by historians who are working in a discipline that has turned increasingly toward world or global foci but with an insistence on the justification that such a wide-angle lens is not reproducing imperial, top-down, or dominant perspectives of the "victors," as it were. The debates about world versus global history reveal many important distinctions and, perhaps, more importantly, convergences with the arguments made in other disciplines—the rejection of (1) the Eurocentric models of the past imposed onto all others; (2) the primacy of the nation-state; and (3) the telos of Euro-American cultural, economic, and political hegemony. If we

---

6. Pheng Cheah, "World against Globe: Toward a Normative Concept of World Literature," *New Literary History* 45, no. 3 (Summer 2014): 303–29, at 303.
7. Ibid., 305.
8. Ibid., 306.
9. Ibid., 318.

simply accept these premises, are we studying the world, be it world politics, world Christianity, or world economy, if we simply transcend boundaries of geographical, disciplinary, and other academic conventions? Historian Sebastian Conrad addresses this very real question many of us ask ourselves, saying, "everything can become global history. This is less absurd than it seems."[10] Different ways of doing global history are available, but the key point he emphasizes is that "worlding" is an approach—a method—that ultimately focuses on how people have engaged in "world-making," that is, a particular perspective and desire not merely a reflexive response to being involved in wider-scale interactions.[11] Constructing the world, in the far past and in more recent times, has involved the conceptualization of self and other in terms of who and what mattered at a given moment, not in terms of a "planetary totality."[12]

The challenge of what world is and is not gives scholars of world Christianity a critical framework to reimagine their field in ways that are remarkably similar to what historians must confront. In a collection of essays titled *Religions on the Move! New Dynamics of Religious Expansion in a Globalizing World*, edited by myself and Afe Adogame,[13] the introduction lays out how the model of reverse missions, developed from the Christian evangelization of the wealthy West by those who had been the targets of traditional foreign or overseas Christian missions, especially during the era of European colonization, can be applied to explore cases of more recent Christian and non-Christian transnational and even local growing religious movements. Many of the cases relate to Africa and the African diaspora, as Africanist scholars have most fully articulated the reverse mission model. The conceptual idea behind such missions—of a desire, to use Conrad's word from world history—to remake the world clearly comes through.

For one critic of the model, however, "there is a limit to analytical clarity when every transnational network is loosely conceptualized as global. Not every instance of 'religious expansion' . . . can be fruitfully conceptualised as global, not every instance of African migrant religious outposts in Europe or America qualifies as reverse mission."[14] He also

---

10. Sebastian Conrad, *What Is Global History?* (Princeton, NJ: Princeton University Press, 2016), 8.
11. Ibid., 17.
12. Ibid., 20.
13. Shobana Shankar and Afe Adogame, eds., *Religions on the Move! New Dynamics of Religious Expansion in a Globalizing World* (Leiden: Brill, 2013).
14. Asonzeh Ukah, "Review of *Religions on the Move! New Dynamics of Religious Expansion in a Globalizing World* (Leiden: Brill, 2013)," *Journal of Religion in Africa* 45, no. 2 (2015): 228–31, at 229.

objects to the periodicity of the late twentieth century as new, as "colonial subjects mediated data and information on religion from their positions on the periphery,"[15] and argues that the book does not fully explore the conceptual utility of reverse mission since it does not include case studies of Buddhism or African indigenous religions.

In these critiques, it is possible to discern a question about what boundaries the study of global religions imposes. They also reveal the challenge of meeting expectations that readers of world or global religious studies hold, for a totality of time, space, and case, which, as Conrad suggests, miss the point about world- or global-making. Indeed, what these critiques miss but give us an opportunity to address is that the world is constituted by religious practitioners and scholars alike, through the breaking and remaking of boundaries. Indeed, the very call to more fully investigate the dividing lines, say between what makes one Christian movement more local and another "world," should draw our attention to that unstable borderland that itself shapes the redefinition of local and global centers.

This is the essence of what historians of borderlands have been attempting to do by "assign[ing] an active historical role to borderlands and their populations."[16] Borderlands histories have challenged centrist models of states while also exposing the "incoherence," unfinished, and "unclosed" nature of power.[17] Therefore, we do not have to view borderlands only as physical spaces or zones where nations or cultural communities meet; they are ideological terrains. What borderlands research does—which is to break down center–periphery relations and "false dichotomies"—bears many resemblances to the work of world Christianity scholars, who challenge the bifurcation of the secular and religious and "taken-for-granted separations of religion from other spheres."[18] Defining what counts as Christian and what does not is a process that occurs at the edges, which have been calibrated since the founding of the Christian faith, from Jesus's own life onward to the establishment of Christendom and its movement to the non-West, with the ongoing encounters between non-Christian and Christian communities. World Christianity studies has mapped moving centers, and as the field has challenged Western

---

15. Ibid., 231.
16. Michiel Baud and Willem Van Schendel, "Toward a Comparative History of Borderlands," *Journal of World History* 8, no. 2 (1997): 211–42, 235.
17. Pekka Hämäläinen and Samuel Truett, "On Borderlands," *The Journal of American History* 98, no. 2 (2011): 338–61.
18. Cole Carnesecca, "Religious Borderlands: Sociology of Religion in Conversation with Disciplinary Neighbors," *Sociology of Religion: A Quarterly Review* 77, no. 3 (2016): 225–40.

Christianity's self-perception as exceptional and extraordinary, it is "far more than the sum of its local parts," like borderlands history.[19] Here I focus on how religious experiences on the frontiers or margins, specifically in the missionary struggle to demarcate a widening Christian world in West Africa, reveal new methodological possibilities.

Beliefs, Bodies, and Bandits in Between

The rest of this essay offers illustrations of religious experience "in between," to suggest how "worlding" reshapes our understanding of Christianity as a protean but powerful force. My focus is on Christianity in Northern Nigeria, which was a significant field of Christian evangelization by European, American, and Afro-Caribbean missionaries during the era of British colonization (1900–1960), and Southern Nigerian Christians thereafter.[20] But it is perhaps somewhat surprising and overlooked that this region has a Christian history because history and politics place it in the Muslim world, albeit even as a "periphery" because of conflicted and sometimes isolationist Islamic interpretations and practices. Christians in Northern Nigeria, when considered at all, have been cast as "non-indigenous" migrants from Southern Nigeria.[21] The sizeable local Christian populations are often obscured in this map of South and North, creating a cultural borderland in between, in the so-called Middle Belt. Indeed, it is impossible to understand how this border region saw the rise of its own movement for recognition, both in political and Christian terms, apart from its disentanglement from its domineering neighbors.[22]

What has pushed the coming of age of the Nigerian Middle Belt into the Christian world is arguably its instability between two regions that

---

19. Hämäläinen and Truett, "On Borderlands," 361.

20. Barbara MacGowan Cooper, Gary Corwin, Tibebe Eshete, Musa AB Gaiya, Timothy W. Geysbeek, and Shobana Shankar, eds., *Transforming Africa's Religious Landscapes: The Sudan Interior Mission (SIM), Past and Present* (Trenton, NJ: Africa World Press, 2018); Andrew E. Barnes, *Making Headway: The Introduction of Western Civilization in Colonial Northern Nigeria* (Rochester, NY: University of Rochester Press, 2009); Waibinte E. Wariboko, "'I Really Cannot Make Africa My Home: West Indian Missionaries as 'Outsiders' in the Church Missionary Society Civilizing Mission to Southern Nigeria, 1898–1925," *Journal of African History* 45, no. 2 (2004): 221–36.

21. Shobana Shankar, *Who Shall Enter Paradise? Christian Origins in Muslim Northern Nigeria, c. 1890–1975* (Athens: Ohio University Press, 2014); Olufemi Vaughan, *Religion and the Making of Nigeria* (Durham, NC: Duke University Press, 2016); Mukhtar Umar Bunza, "Challenges of Muslim-Christian Relations in Nigeria," in Edmund Kee-Fook Chia, ed., *Interfaith Dialogue: Global Perspectives* (New York: Palgrave Macmillan, 2016), 59–72.

22. Andrew Barnes, "The Middle Belt Movement and the Formation of Christian Consciousness in Colonial Northern Nigeria," *Church History* 76, no. 3 (2007): 591–610.

have, in turn, destabilized the very idea of a single Nigerian nation. This uncertainty has produced a sense of religious identity seeking that is, among other forms of security, a search for freedom from discrimination in a region beset by great ethnic and religious diversity, economic and political insecurity, and corruption in which groups in power favor their own.[23] The worlding of Northern Nigerian Christianity resembles processes in Asian and African cities that social scientists Aihwa Ong and AbdouMaliq Simone say "put forth questions, initiatives, and procedures in the midst of uncertainty, without guarantees of successful outcomes.[24] Their concern is with a certain kind of temporality, notably flux and shifts in "forms and norms" that give these non-Western cities a "buoyant sense of being on the cusp of an urban revolution."[25] Simone calls it a "permanent state of change."[26]

Christianity in Northern Nigeria has not only been an answer to instability but has also itself been a catalyst for instability and the questioning and destabilizing of accepted truths, thereby creating dynamic exchanges of ideas and practices on the part of religious seekers. "Worlding" is therefore not a physical expansion but an ideological and intellectual sojourn that takes religious seekers outside established truths into uncertain reaches.

Beliefs

While there is no doubt that Muslims and Christians see the lines between their beliefs as very clear, in some moments of history the lines might not have been so stark and sure. This gray area between theologies may appear more obvious or alluring to the young, students, new converts from indigenous religions (who often saw "religions of the book" in the same way), and the skeptical. Some of the first converts to Christianity from Islam in Northern Nigeria were young men who considered themselves to be pious protestors, terribly disillusioned that their religious leaders had failed to deliver on promises of protection during the French and British conquests of the Sudanic region. The biography of an early

---

23. Abdul Raufu Mustapha, Adam Higazi, Jimam Lar, and Karel Chromy, "Jos: Fear and Violence in Central Nigeria," in A. R. Raufu and David Earhardt, eds., *Creed and Grievance: Muslim-Christian Relations and Conflict Resolution in Northern Nigeria* (Woodbridge, UK: Boydell and Brewer, 2014).

24. Aihwa Ong, "Worlding Cities, or the Art of Being Global," in Ananya Roy and Aihwa Ong, eds., *Worlding Cities: Asian Experiments and the Art of Being Global* (Malden, MA: Wiley-Blackwell, 2011), 4.

25. Ibid.

26. AbdouMaliq Simone, "On the Worlding of African Cities," *African Studies Review* (2001): 15–41, 18.

Christian named Inusa Samuila, a Zarma man from Dosso, in French Niger, reveals how the centrality of Jesus in revolutionary millennialist Islam—in the form of Mahdism—engendered a radical questioning. From this place of uncertainty of belief, Christianity took root in Northern Nigeria as a dissident Muslim sect.[27]

Inusa left for British Northern Nigeria, seeking to make a new life after the Mahdist (millennial Muslim uprising) revolt in 1905–1906 in Dosso, French Niger, which nearly crushed the French and the British colonial governments in the region. The cleric leading the uprising was a blind man claiming to be the Mahdi, a redeemer, who would lead the faithful in the end times. The military struck very forcefully against the Mahdists, who had settled in an enclave where they hoped to isolate themselves from nonbelievers. Inusa fled south along the Niger River, ending up in Pategi, where he met a white Christian missionary in a market where he had gone looking for work. Inusa became a servant to a Nupe *malam* who had a Qur'anic school. He agreed that if Inusa served him as a manservant, he would resume Inusa's Qur'anic studies from the fourth chapter, where he had left off in Dosso.[28] Inusa at first resisted invitations to hear the white people's preaching because he was sure that whites did not believe in God.[29] Yet when Inusa eventually did visit the S.I.M. (Sudan Interior Mission) station, he was struck by the white man's knowledge. Though he could understand very little because the missionary in charge spoke only Nupe, Paul, a Laka man from Adamawa, far to the east, spoke Hausa and showed Inusa a map. "He pointed out to me the name of many towns in my own country. I was amazed and asked him whether he had been to my country, but he answered, no. I said, how can you know all these places, even Dosso, without ever going to my country?" Inusa wrote in his diary.[30] He was captivated by the idea that the whites also believed in Jesus (Isa) and decided that studying with these teachers was a good idea. Inusa left the Muslim teacher to become a student of the Christian mission.

Mahdism did not die out in the following decades but instead lived on in the Christian anticipation of Christ's second coming and in Islamic reli-

---

27. Shankar, *Who Shall Enter Paradise*; and Shobana Shankar, "A Fifty-Year Muslim Conversion to Christianity: Religious Ambiguities and Colonial Boundaries in Northern Nigeria, c. 1910–1963," in Benjamin Soares, ed., *Muslim/Christian Encounters in Africa, Islam in Africa Series* (Leiden: E. J. Brill, 2006).

28. Inusa Samuila, "To God Be the Glory," written in Hausa and translated by Rev. Albert Diamond, SIM International Archives (hereafter SIMIA), Evangelical Churches of West Africa Biographical Sketches L-S, Fort Mill, South Carolina.

29. Yarima Inusa Samuila, unpublished Hausa diary, 1910, in author's possession, 1.

30. Samuila, "To God Be the Glory," 6.

gious movements in Nigeria and West Africa more broadly. For instance, many Mahdists and their descendants converted to the Tijaniyya sufi tariqa, as documented in research about the migration of Mahdists from Northern Nigeria to Cameroon in the 1940s.[31] Their attraction to this path was shaped by the transethnic alliances it offered and its rejection of hereditary leadership in favor of religious election and blessedness (*baraka*).

The roots of Mahdism have been traced to more recent Islamic movements, such as the radical and violent reformist Islamists in the Boko Haram group, which has wreaked violence in Nigeria, Chad, Niger, and Cameroon since the 2010s. Some experts on Islam in the region have argued that Boko Haram is not a novel movement but one emerging from a "tradition of dissidence" that developed during the Sokoto jihad in the early 1800s.[32] The writings of the murdered leader of Boko Haram, Muhammad Yusuf, suggest that non-Muslims' casual claims to the prophet Isa were perceived as an insult to Muslims. He referred to Nigerian news media stories about the prophet Isa (Jesus) and, not surprisingly, the prophet Muhammad as profane encouragements for further blasphemies that reveal the social decay and corruption in Nigeria that Boko Haram claims to fight.[33]

Jesus's divinity has been, of course, a key difference between Christians and Muslims. A method that examines the uncertainty surrounding this fundamental difference over the nature of divinity, as a productive border space, shows how the coming of Christianity into an Islamic region imbued changes in religious and social identification, intellectual output, and politics. A borderlands approach to world Christianity attends to the multiplicity of beliefs in the same revered figure and to the redrawing of religious boundaries through the processes of these believers' social and cultural interaction. This example does not mean to deny real differences of belief but instead draws attention to Andrew Walls's reminder that our understanding of theology should be rooted in understanding of practice, people's actions, and popular intellectual history. Missions, schools, and

---

31. Harmony O'Rourke and Mohammed Bashir Salau, "The Life and Experiences of Said Ibn Hayatu, a Mahdist Leader: New Findings from the Buea Archive," *Journal of West African History* 2, no. 2 (2016): 51–78.

32. Murray Last, "From Dissent to Dissidence: The Genesis and Development of Reformist Islamic Groups in Northern Nigeria," in Abdul Raufu Mustafa, ed., *Sects and Social Disorder: Muslim Identities and Conflict in Northern Nigeria* (Woodbridge, Suffolk, UK: James Currey, 2014), 18–53.

33. Abdulbassit Kassim and Michael Nwankpa, eds., *The Boko Haram Reader: From Nigerian Preachers to the Islamic State* (Oxford: Oxford University Press, 2018).

print are not merely tools of Christian evangelism but rather mediations in the struggle over boundaries.

Bodies

Bodily comportment has also served as a frontier for drawing lines between religions; women's bodies have often been a veritable battleground. Strikingly, in Northern Nigeria, Christian women have been relatively invisible and ignored, in contrast to the extensive focus on Muslim women in the region. In her study of a Christian mission in southern Niger, with historical ties to Northern Nigeria, Barbara Cooper discusses the conversion of *arna* ("pagan") Hausa women in the late 1920s as a key part of the creation of a Christian minority community that remained largely separate from the Muslim majority. Cooper tells the story of one ex-slave woman, Tashibka, who was considered one of the strongest Christian believers yet also something of an embarrassment to Nigerian men—"a former slave, a medium of sorts, a 'traditional' illiterate person, a poverty-stricken dependent of the mission."[34] Tashibka's story makes clear the forgetting of women that helped build the modern respectability of a religious minority in a Muslim region, as well as the alternative streams of history-making among white women missionaries as compared to male missionaries. In some sense, Boko Haram's violence against Christian women in Northern Nigeria, particularly the kidnapping of 276 girls from their school in Chibok in 2014, made these believers visible. And it is no stretch to emphasize the identifiable piety of the Christian Chibok abductees, as I have written in another essay; the reminiscences among Christian Chibok survivors and their communities' attachment to these girls emphasize the Christian stalwartness of girls who resisted forced conversion to Islam and marriage to Boko Haram "husbands." These girls wrote diaries as acts of faith, depicting their prayers. They continue to speak about the miraculous strength God gave them in times of indescribable suffering.[35]

Christian women's respectability in Northern Nigeria and other predominantly Muslim lands has been shaped by the norms and expectations of Muslim and non-Muslim women. A critical point in the longer history of gendered religious norms came when the British colonial authorities abolished slavery in Northern Nigeria in 1900, an act that opened a flood

---

34. Barbara Cooper, *Evangelical Christians in the Muslim Sahel* (Bloomington: Indiana University Press, 2006), 190–91.

35. Shobana Shankar, "Notes on Women's Evangelical Revolutions in Northern Nigeria," in Jacob Olupona, ed., *Evangelical Christianity and the Transformation of Africa* (in progress).

of girls and women escaping the bonds of the domestic slavery practiced in Muslim households. Fearing that these "loose" females would fall into prostitution, the British allowed Christian missionaries to establish homes for freed slaves, believing that the association of freed slave girls with Christianity, and their eventual conversion, would not contradict the colonialists' pledge of noninterference in the practice of Islam. What we can discern from the perspectives of these female "freed slaves" is that they had to weigh Christian conversion against Islamic practices and pathways to mobility. What Islam offered in many cases was the "pretense of free marriage." Malam Koki, a respected Kano judge, noted in his memoirs that the British allowed the local Muslim authorities to deal with freed slaves according to custom, and women slaves were sent to different homes in the town.[36] His family took in two girls, an older one who had already been married and a second girl of eleven or twelve years old. Such girls could become Muslim and be absorbed into the social and religious fabric by the fact of their familial networks.

While that kind of religious assimilation was available in Islam, women who took a route outside Islam had to contend with the precolonial reputations of slave women as adherents of indigenous African religions. Thus conversion to Christianity required a marked separation from indigenous customs. White Christian missionaries often saw non-Muslim peoples in very derogatory ways, even in the context of the freed slaves' homes, where they were to make new people out of these wards. J. Lowry Maxwell of the Sudan United Mission, who led the freed slave work on the Benue River from 1909, had little hope about the prospects for Christianity among freed slave girls, who numbered well over half of the town's population. He believed that they did not work hard enough and were easily seduced by town life.[37] He refuted the claim of his mission's founder, Karl Kumm, and others that Islam endangered African women, citing their recourse to justice in *shari'a* courts and the Islamic prohibition on drinking, which kept Muslim men in check while "pagan" men were drunkards. Maxwell implied that Islam in Northern Nigeria was a better option than "paganism" or even Christianity. Maxwell also believed that running away from slavery did not mean that girls did not want to marry Muslim men. "Islam is the system of the country. Pagans hate it first but grow to appreciate the order, trade goods. And so the pagan is patient with the stranger and his pack, and the first missionary to many a pagan community may have taken

---

36. Alexander Neil Skinner, *Alhaji Mahmudu Koki, Kano Malam* (Zaria: Ahmadu Bello University Press, 1977), 18–19.

37. J. Lowry Maxwell, diary entry, June 26, 1911, Rhodes House Library, Oxford, UK, MS.AFr.S.1112, vol. 5.

the impersonal form of a sack of salt."[38] He complained of his male wards who "do not realize that they are not by their accepting Christ emancipated from their position as inferiors, boys, ex-slaves. They must be taught firmly (and forcibly, if necessary) that they must accord proper respect and proper courtesy to native elders and *dattibai* [gentlemen]."[39] He worried about making unions between these "useless" young men and "uncontrollable" girls. "The girls can't marry trees, rocks, equally they can't marry the Basa heathen or the Igbirra or Hausa Muslim; whom shall they meet at Umaisha [the location of the Home]?"[40]

Christian missionaries, thus ceding to Islam's power in Northern Nigeria, took a heavy hand in shaping Christian culture as unthreatening. Marriages were highly controlled, in order to keep young women and men in line. Owing both to doubts of the fidelity of new Northern Nigerian Christians and to the fear of losing their converts to Islam or backsliding to "paganism," Christian missionaries drew out the process of marriage. The promise of marriage to a girl was often an incentive for male converts to remain within the ambit of missions for many years—thus betrothals were prolonged over many years. In the case of one of the earliest Muslim Fulani converts to Christianity, a boy named Audu at the Zaria Church Missionary Society station did not become betrothed until eight years after his baptism, until he was in his twenties. The Christian Fulani bride-to-be was named Hawa'u.[41] The missionary who arranged their marriage insisted that she reach the age of twenty before marriage, and the couple waited nearly three more years to wed. This was well out of the norm in the area, where Muslim girls, especially from elite families, married at a younger age.

In some sense, to be a Christian, for a girl or woman in Northern Nigeria in the 1900s, meant a loss of social value and power by virtue of physical and social mobility, if she went outside the bounds of Islamic domestic spheres. In Northern Nigeria, as in much of colonial Africa, Christian missions expected African girls to bear the norms of respectability of the new religion,[42] but a contradiction existed since missionaries held doubts

---

38. Maxwell diary entry, June 3, 1911.
39. Maxwell diary entry, September 8, 1911, 92. He uses *dattibai*, which is the same as *dattijo*.
40. Maxwell diary entry, April 18, 1911.
41. Ethel Miller to friends, December 2, 1912, BSC CMS/ACC237 F1: 2, University of Birmingham Library Special Collections.
42. Karen Tranberg Hanson, ed., *African Encounters with Domesticity* (New Brunswick, NJ: Rutgers University Press, 1992); Elizabeth Prevost, *The Communion of Women: Missions and Gender in Colonial Africa and the British Metropole* (New York: Oxford University Press, 2010).

as to the value of Christianity in these girls' lives. In the early 1900s, to run away or to become a Christian reflected, in some measure, women's conscious refusal of marriage into Muslim homes, or removal from marriage, for whatever reason. Had these girls stayed with Muslim slave masters, they belonged as wealth to the household. In the missions, the girls were clearly marked as a financial burden and a challenge to marry. It is also noteworthy that the popularity of the seclusion of women in Muslim households increased in Northern Nigeria in nonelite Muslim households over the twentieth century,[43] a phenomenon not seen in other parts of Islamic West Africa (even more Islamic societies, such as in Senegal). It is arguably the interreligious dynamics of Northern Nigeria that heightened the distinctiveness of seclusion, which brought formerly slave and free women into a shared position and demarcated lines between Muslim and non-Muslim women. This kind of grounded explanation is an intriguing possibility to chart the rise of "conservatism" in interpretations of Islamic norms in the midst of Christianity's growth.

Furthermore, polygamy looked more appealing in contrast to the monogamy imposed by Christian missionaries. Christian women missionaries, like the Anglican evangelist Ethel Miller, appreciated that Christian monogamy actually alienated and disempowered Nigerian women, compared to the situations they could find in Muslim marriages. She told the story of an African Christian male convert who struggled to choose one of his two wives. The abandoned wife became a divorcée, a status looked down upon in Christian missions and often led back to Islamic marriage. The wife he kept was "very spiteful because she knows he is half a Christian and won't divorce her or get another."[44] No longer a full Muslim herself, she had no one to share the work of managing a household, raising children, and keeping a husband happy. She showed her anger toward the Christian missionaries whom she blamed for her husband's conversion.

The politics of marriage were also tied to other institutions, such as the predominance of Islamic law courts in Northern Nigeria. As Christian missionaries competed with Muslims to convert non-Muslims, village heads arranged Muslim marriages for non-Muslim women, which allowed them to marry wealthier men and use the courts where non-Muslim men did not feel they could get their cases fairly heard: "These husbands have not attempted to recover the bride price as they are consid-

---

43. Catherine M. Coles and Beverly Mack, eds., *Hausa Women in the Twentieth Century* (Madison: University of Wisconsin Press, 1991).

44. Extracts from letter of Ethel Miller, November 26, 1907, University of Birmingham Library Special Collections, CMS/ACC237 F10, Papers, etc., of WRS Miller.

ered that they were wasting their time if they brought the matter before the Alkali [Muslim judge]."[45] This worked against Christians and practitioners of indigenous religions alike.

A multireligious history of women in Northern Nigeria reveals a growing reformist zeal in both Islamic and Christian norms, practiced in no small way in women's lives. The struggles on the margins, on marginalized women's bodies and in their spheres beyond the public realm, allowed the members of each community to make competing claims to cultural and moral respectability and economic power. A confessional isolationist approach—treating Christian missions on the one hand and Islamization on the other—does not reveal the same kinds of cross-cultural fertilization or the increasingly more insistent claims of difference and delineation.

Women's conversion stories in Northern Nigeria do more than fill in a gap about a new group that emerged over the twentieth century. They expose the gendered negotiations and realignments that produced changes in discourses of religious difference. Indeed, gender relations—not just between men and women, but equally between women and women—have historically undergirded momentous religious transformations. As Leila Ahmed, Hanna Papanek, and others have shown, religiously sanctioned practices such as seclusion acted simultaneously as expressions of class and religious difference in the eras of Islam's growth among non-Muslims.

Studying moments and spaces where religions meet, their rough edges, provides elements for a framework for making more processes and actors visible in world Christianity. For one, the co-construction of Christianity and Islam in Nigeria shows "distinctive visions of the global that exist without essential reference to the West."[46] Moreover, attending to women who belonged to neither Islam nor Christianity for some time allows us to see how these two world religions became stronger, as being in-between or outside them was socially, culturally, and materially alienating. For them, "worlding" was a state of being "cast out" into the world.[47] This kind of approach acknowledges the material realities and exclusions in which world religions are produced and defined.

Bandits

Marauding figures living on frontiers between established states and settled communities are a commonplace of frontier and borderlands his-

---

45. Report on Pagans in Kano Province [1–9], Kano History and Culture Bureau, Kano, Nigeria, File name KANO PROF. HIS/5/1936.
46. Ong, "Worlding Cities, or the Art of Being Global," 4.
47. Simone, "On the Worlding of African Cities," 17.

tory, and their disregard for established norms and conventions reveal the limits of power and control—military, social, and cultural. We do not often think about such characters in studies of religion, yet stories of encroachment, theft, and scofflaws do reveal glimpses of vigilantism and iconoclasm that have embedded within these acts real moral, ethical, and utopian idealism.[48]

In archival sources of Christian mission, bandits appear, that is to say, people who seem to have gotten their hands on that which did not belong to them or Christian goods that they perhaps acquired undeservedly. In missionary discourses about indigenous believers, conversion was a critical zone, navigated between old and new faiths. Many meandered across this zone, while others practiced concealment and secrecy. "Backsliders," for J. D. Y. Peel, were those who could not say "no" to their old ways,[49] while David Lindenfeld calls them compartmentalizers who did not simply "line cultural traits up on either side of an equation."[50] However one measured the transformation, missionaries saw backsliders as social disrupters within their Christian realm. For indigenous communities, however, these converts with new skills and status were often recognized more for their more prominent social roles as mediators rather than as exiles.[51]

In Northern Nigeria, missionaries added another meaning to this conversion journey. They wrote about "secret believers," like the Pharisee Nicodemus, fervently believing that Christianity's march went beyond its visible and public disempowerment vis-à-vis Islam. Albert Ter Meer, an American missionary serving with the Sudan Interior Mission in Northern Nigeria, reported on the unusual profession for Christ by a young man, a student at the Kano School of Hygiene. In 1951 he happened to come to a youth meeting and explained that he was a Muslim of the Ahmadiyya sect, founded in India in the 1880s, but that he had attended Christian schools in Lagos. His father, who had passed away, had encour-

---

48. British historian Eric Hobsbawm's examination of social banditry in peasant societies spawned a serious interest in social protest outside the bounds of accepted political norms and channels, and was particularly influential in the study of uprisings of colonized peoples whose struggles did not necessarily line up with established anti-colonial resistance. K. C. Hanson, "Jesus and Social Bandits," in Wolfgang Stegemann, Bruce J. Malina, and Gerd Theissen, eds., *The Social Setting of Jesus and Gospels* (Minneapolis: Fortress Press, 2002), 283–300.

49. See J. D. Y. Peel, *Aladura: A Religious Movement among the Yoruba* (London: Oxford University Press, 1968).

50. David Lindenfeld, "Indigenous Encounters with Christian Missionaries in China and West Africa, 1800–1920: A Comparative Study," *Journal of World History* (2005): 327–69, 331.

51. Shankar, "A Fifty-Year Muslim Conversion to Christianity."

aged his education and given him religious texts, including an American Standard Version Bible. Ter Meer asked how the father had acquired it. The young man did not say specifically, only revealing that his father had used it in Muslim missionary work.[52] Ter Meer noted that this young man, like others, including a Muslim leader, "dropped in like Nicodemus," even "dressed in dirty ragged clothes so that he would not be known as he entered the compound."[53]

Added to these concealed figures was the uncontrollability of religious media—tracts and books that missionaries had to recognize. Though unpredictability in the flow of texts and ideas was hardly new, scholars of media and religion have tended to be short-sighted in their approaches to mediated Muslim-Christian competition in Nigeria and elsewhere.[54] This media uncontrollability and unpredictability richly illustrate how the worlding of Christianity has occurred on the ground, outside the reach of authorities like missionaries who lost the ability to know how their goods had been acquired by others and what was being done with them. The violation of rightful ownership was a boundary transgression and a check on Christian mission power. This loss of control is as much about the presumed hierarchy of white missionaries and Africans as it is about the ability of Africans to remain in-between and not choose to join the Christian fold but instead define conversion as an ambiguous and uncertain process. The Ahmadiyya, as a new Islamic sect deeply inspired by Christian missionaries and other new religious movements, challenges the fixity that Western missionaries and reformers in recent times have tried to impose.[55]

In Northern Nigeria, Christian missionaries also found their spaces invaded by interlopers, causing them alarm and prompting them to shore up their spiritual bulwarks and believers. Sudan Interior Mission doctor Marion Hursh reported on a number of disturbing incidents at the SIM Kano Eye Hospital, serving a predominantly Muslim population in the 1940s, such as strange occurrences after he had performed cataract surgeries:

---

52. SIM Kano Station Reports, April–June 1951, SIM International Archives, Fort Mill, South Carolina.

53. SIM Kano Station Reports, July–September 1953, SIM Archives, Fort Mill, South Carolina.

54. See, for example, Brian Larkin and Birgit Meyer, "Pentecostalism, Islam & Culture," in Emmanuel Kwaku Akyeampong, ed., *Themes in West Africa's History* (Athens, OH: Ohio University Press, 2006), 286–312; Birgit Meyer and Annelise Moors, eds., *Religion, Media, and the Public Sphere* (Bloomington: Indiana University Press, 2005).

55. Garth N. Jones, "The Ahmadis of Islam: A Mormon Encounter and Perspective," *Dialogue: A Journal of Mormon Thought* 19, no. 2 (1986): 39–54.

The women who we had operated . . . their eyes were covered and so forth. And they would start, in their own language, of course, start talking in a way . . . you see, they never stopped, just go on and on, and that's very unusual for them. . . . And more than once I had people that I knew had no contact with white people before, talking to me in English, not even knowing what they were saying. . . . So I would call the church elders. This is early days, but we had some Nigerian Christians then. And they said, "Oh, this is the devil, this is evil spirits, no question about it."[56]

In such cases, a group of Christian workers in the hospital would assemble around the patients' beds, praying, invoking Christ's power over Satan, over possessed people, over their power to speak the white man's tongue spontaneously. Hursh had no choice but to accept his African underlings' explanations of *iskoki*, spirits, and their leadership in exorcism. The relations of power at the mission hospital had been inverted—the world had collapsed or been scrambled with Hausa Muslim women uttering English, and biomedical procedures were now causes of spiritual disease and catalysts for prayer healing.

Religious interlopers were part and parcel of foreign missionary encounters precisely because of the rigid lines Christians tried to draw between their belief system and those of others. In the worlding of Christianity, it is possible to trace archival fragments alluding to this kind of intrusion and its effect on Christianity's self-construction. What is also striking is the inability of Hursh to explain these encounters. It was only within the worldview of Northern Nigerians—reflecting the encounter of different religions and a particular understanding of religious difference—that makes this Christian missionary encounter knowable as part of a longer history. This brief scene at the hospital encapsulates many layers of meaning that a multilingual and intercultural methodology exposes, much like the African Christians themselves had to use to translate the devil for the missionary. World Christianity studies must grapple with these multiple and vernacular logics to become a richer field of study.

Conclusion

As Adogame and I wrote in the introduction to *Religions on the Move!*, "religious capital" might outweigh material power in instances of missions, including traditional Christian evangelism and phenomena such as

---

56. Dr. Marion Douglas Hursh, interview conducted by Galen Wilson, June 29, 1982, transcript 2, p. 1. Billy Graham Center Archives, Wheaton, Illinois.

reverse missions and those of Islam, Hinduism, and other religions whose modern activists include missionaries. This statement should not be misconstrued as an attempt to "ignore the insidious and ongoing ravages of neo-imperialist, neocolonialist ethos."[57] Rather, the reappraisals of colonial history, through fields like world Christianity studies as method, are precisely what have allowed us to better appreciate how colonized subjects were unruly, especially in religious encounters that were not separable from politics, economy, or medical power. Borderlands show that power is not predictable and assured. The image of African women in their hospital beds confounding and terrifying an American doctor at a mission hospital illustrates well how world Christianity concerns itself with the unruly and unregulated power of religious actors.

Even in this preliminary analysis, it is clear that world Christianity is connected to cutting-edge scholarly concerns in allied fields like history, anthropology, sociology, media studies, and urban studies. Indeed, world Christianity studies, as a field, has helped expose the hypersecularist biases of these fields and turn them, even without acknowledgment, to new nonmaterial directions. It is important for world Christianity scholars to force the acknowledgment of their contributions in fields beyond their own.

Yet these fields also challenge scholars of world Christianity to not take the "world" part of their work lightly. Conscious critical engagement with how Christians envision and actualize world as a temporal, spatial, and intellectual imperative could advance the frontiers of this field in exciting new directions. At the very least, we have to insist that worlding is not simply proffering views of non-Western Christianity but instead a set of approaches to understand dynamic and revolutionary configurations and reconfigurations of power.

Postscript: Which World Are We Talking About?

Cabrita and Maxwell ask what world Christianity studies would be like if its foundational scholarship had been drawn from Asia, "with the vast world religions of Hinduism and Buddhism that cut across language groups and huge geographical areas," instead of from Africa, which has generated scholarship "highly amenable to culturalist analyses"?[58] Yet, West Africa, as a region where Islam cuts across language groups and vast distances, and where other examples like *vodun* or *candomblé* have been ably demonstrated to cut clear across the Atlantic with porous

---

57. Ukah, "Review of *Religions on the Move*," 228.
58. Cabrita and Maxwell, "Relocating World Christianity," 23–24.

boundaries between African religions and different Christian traditions,[59] weakens the query. African religions like *zar* spirit possession have to be fully mapped precisely because migration and cultural flows have new directions.[60] Moreover, Asian religions should not be viewed necessarily as a uniform ecosystem, given that, for instance, Hinduism may not be recognizable as one travels from one region to the next, in any direction, within India and beyond to Bali and other locations.

One senses that African studies of Christianity could generate theories and conceptual frameworks for the study of religions and globalization more broadly. I am struck by the fact that in the study of religions in Asia and Asian religions around the world, including Christianity, the culturalist turn was badly needed because of the overemphasis on textual traditions in Hinduism and Buddhism. Ethnography, oral history, ritual performance—scholars working on Asia and religions appear to be employing these methods more, perhaps precisely because scholarship on African Christianity has inspired them.

Christianity as a non-Western intellectual paradigm must also be given more notice. Studies like Valentin Mudimbe's *The Invention of Africa* acknowledge African Christian historicism—such as Samuel Johnson's *History of the Yorubas* (1921)—as a part of making Africa a subject of modern knowledge systems; that is to say, the historiography of Africa would not look the same without the experience of Christian missionary education that Johnson had. Scholars of Asian Christianity, like Sanal Mohan, have relied on Mudimbe, Matthew Engelke, and other Africanists to reexamine Christian forms such as Dalit Christianity far beyond a response to Hindu oppression and instead as a reorientation of self and community in past, present, and future.[61] "Worlding" is not just finding commonalities from Dalit Christianity in India across Africa to African-American slave religion, for example, as an exercise in comparative studies but rather as a radical practice of methodological expertise drawn from outside Eurocentric models and ultimately the political choice of citation of intellectuals around the world.

---

59. J. Lorand Matory, *Black Atlantic Religion: Tradition, Transnationalism, and Matriarchy in the Afro-Brazilian Candomblé* (Princeton, NJ: Princeton University Press, 2005). Paul Christopher Johnson, *Diaspora Conversions: Black Carib Religion and the Recovery of Africa* (Berkeley: University of California Press, 2007).

60. Don Seeman, "Coffee and the Moral Order: Ethiopian Jews and Pentecostals against Culture," *American Ethnologist* 42, no. 4 (2015): 734–48.

61. Sanal Mohan, "Creation of Social Space through Prayers among Dalits in Kerala, India," *Journal of Religious and Political Practice* 2, no. 1 (2016): 40–57.

Section III
Expanding Horizons

7

Taking More Seriously the Asian Faces of World Christianity

Gemma Tulud Cruz

Asia could be regarded as a continent of superlatives. First and foremost, it is the world's largest continent. It encompasses one-third of the land area of the whole world, spanning Turkey in the west to Japan and Indonesia in the east. In addition, Asia is the world's most populated continent. It is home to almost 60 percent of humanity, many of whom live in about twenty megacities,[1] which have populations of around five to forty million. Asia is also impressive when it comes to cultural and religious diversity. It has seven major linguistic zones, the highest that any continent can boast of,[2] and an array of dialects or local languages. Further, it is the birthplace of the world's major religions. On the economic front, the picture seems to be largely rosy for Asia, as well. In 2019 three of the five largest economies in the world were countries from Asia (China, Japan, and India). The four so-called tiger economies, Hong Kong, Singapore, South Korea, and Taiwan, have also enjoyed half a century of success[3] with their relatively robust economic conditions. Pundits on the global economy even regard the twenty-first century to be the Asian century.[4] While the pandemic may very well alter this economic

---

1. A megacity is typically characterized as a metropolitan territory with an aggregate populace of at least ten million individuals. A megacity can be a single metropolitan territory or at least two metropolitan ranges that focalize.
2. Aloysius Pieris SJ, *Asian Theology of Liberation* (Maryknoll, NY: Orbis Books, 1988), 70.
3. Simon Rabinovitch and Simon Cox, "Special Report: After Half a Century of Success the Asian Tigers Must Reinvent Themselves," *The Economist* (December 5, 2019).
4. Michael Berry and Benno Engels, *Global Prospects: The Asian Century?* (Oxford: Oxford University Press, 2018).

outlook, the rise and status of Asia as a global economic force is without dispute.

Asia, however, is also a continent of contradictions. While it is home to some of the world's prosperous economies it is also home to a large number of the world's poor. It is the birthplace of Christianity yet, to this day, Christianity remains a minority religion despite centuries of Christian missionary activities. Christians predominate in only two countries, namely, the Philippines and East Timor. Today, in Asia, the vast majority of people are Hindus, Buddhists, Taoists or Confucianists, and Muslims. Adding insult to injury is the misleading description of Christianity as a foreign import to Asia. Take, for example, the following account of the history of Christianity in Asia: "Christianity's first recorded *arrival* in Asia is still visible in China even today. Christians first appeared in Xian in 635. . . . They were Nestorians who came to Asia when their leader Nestorius was condemned as heretic at the Council of Ephesus (431 AD)."[5] As Edmund Chia rightly points out, "like other religions, Christianity also had its birth in Asia, specifically in West Asia more commonly known as the Middle East. So, by right, it should be considered an Asian religion."[6] This is an assertion shared by most contemporary historians and theologians on Christianity, especially those of Asian descent.

One could argue that the above-mentioned anomalous historical account has more to do with a Eurocentric outlook on the history of Christianity and less to do with geographic ignorance. Unfortunately, the above-mentioned framing of Nestorian Christians' history in China as the "arrival" rather than the resurgence of Christianity in Asia, reinforces the notion of Christianity as a Western religion—or, more explicitly, a "white man's religion" by most people in Asia, both Christians and non-Christians. Chia observes that the Asian perception of Christianity as a Western religion could probably be attributed to the fact that "it moved westward from its birthplace in Palestine and found a new home in Rome and other parts of Europe, from where it spread to the rest of the world, including *back to Asia*. But, for the first four centuries of Christian history, it was more present in Asia and Africa than elsewhere. . . ."[7] The twentieth century, when missionaries who were mostly from the global North took the gospel to the "ends of the earth," lit the spark that abetted the rise of Christianity not just as a worldwide phenomenon but also as a Western

---

5. Emphasis mine. Michael Kelly, "The Many Faces of Religious Persecution in Asia," *Journal of the Australian Catholic Historical Society* 36 (2015): 274–84, at 275.

6. Emphasis mine. Edmund Chia, *World Christianity Encounters World Religions: A Summa of Interfaith Dialogue* (Collegeville, MN: Liturgical Press, 2019), 132–33.

7. Italics mine. Chia, *World Christianity Encounters World Religions*, 133.

religion. Christianity was imposed on other cultures, giving the impression that Christianity, despite its translatability, was a Western religion.

Indian theologian Stanley Samartha uses the metaphor of the "helicopter versus bullock cart"[8] to describe how this phase and process of Christianity's expansion through Western missionary activity impoverished and continues to cast a shadow on Asian Christianity, especially in terms of Christology. For Samartha, "helicopter Christology," which represents the Christology brought by Western missionaries in colonial times, makes a lot of missiological noise (in a pluralistic context of Asia) and kicks up so much theological dust that people nearby are prevented from hearing the voice and seeing the vision of the descending divinity. A "bullock-cart Christology," which embodies inculturated (Asian) Christologies, has its wheels always touching the unpaved roads, for without the continual friction with the ground, the cart cannot move forward at all.[9] Korean missiologist Moon-jang Lee points to how the "subsequent globalization of the image of Western Christianity poses a problem for non-Western Christianity" because "though we talk about a post-Christian West and a post-Western Christianity, the prevailing forms of Christianity in most parts of the non-Western world are still dominated by Western influences."[10] This continuing domination of Western influences highlights the need for the full incorporation of perspectives, religious histories, and debates from non-Western regions. Part and parcel of addressing this need is the critical engagement of such Western influences and, alongside it, the (re)discovery and (re)engagement of the indigenous histories, facets, and faces of Christianity among Asians in Asia and, to a certain extent, those in the diaspora.

James Strasburg deftly discusses the shifts in the understanding and practice of world Christianity from world evangelization to ecumenism to the current focus on indigenous contexts.[11] In what follows I explore the ways in which the perspectives, religious histories, and debates from diverse regions, particularly Asia, can be fully incorporated into the teaching, practice, and scholarship on world Christianity to truly do justice to the

---

8. Stanley Samartha, *One Christ, Many Religions: Toward a Revised Christology* (Bangalore: SATHRI, 2000), 131–33.

9. Ibid., 132.

10. Moon-jang Lee, "Future of Global Christianity," in Todd Johnson and Kenneth Ross, eds., *Atlas of Global Christianity* (Edinburgh: Edinburgh University Press, 2009), 104.

11. See James Strasburg, "Creating, Practicing, and Researching a Global Faith: Conceptualizations of World Christianity in the American Protestant Pastorate and Seminary Classroom, 1893 to the Present," *Journal of World Christianity* 6, no. 2 (2016): 217–36.

"world" in world Christianity, in general, and in order for world Christianity to take more seriously its Asian roots and faces. The chapter does this through a critical discussion of issues around politics of epistemology and politics of identity that are at play in the teaching, practice, and scholarship on (world) Christianity in/on Asia and, to a certain extent, in connection with the West and other regions, particularly the global South. More specifically, the chapter examines issues surrounding methodology and *orthoproxy* (representation) that impinge on the task of taking more seriously the Asian faces of world Christianity inside as well as outside of Asia.

Digging Deep

It could be argued that the task for the full incorporation of the perspectives, religious histories, priorities, and debates from diverse or non-Western regions, notably Asia, is twofold. The first revolves around the critical engagement of Western influences in Christianity. Vietnamese-American theologian Peter Phan reckons that accomplishing this "old task" requires "new ways" in utilizing the six sources for doing theology in contemporary times: experience, Bible, revelation, reason, tradition, and culture.[12] The above-mentioned work by Samartha, for instance, shows how the Christ received by many Christians in the global South, from Western missionaries, was too Eurocentric and became less relevant in their new indigenization and social movements.

The other side of the task is a (re)discovery as well as critical and creative (re)engagement of Asian Christian histories, contexts, and practices. The Federation of Asian Bishops' Conferences (hereafter FABC) lays out the implications of this task: "The decisive new phenomenon for Christianity in Asia will be the emergence of genuine Christian communities in Asia—Asian in their way of thinking, praying, living, communicating their own Christ-experience to others. . . . If the Asian Churches do not discover their own identity, they will have no future."[13] Malaysian Methodist bishop Hwa Yung reinforces FABC's assertion by pointing out that as the Asian church grows rapidly it needs to self-theologize, developing a theology for itself that is rooted in one's culture, history, and context.[14] This section explores two key areas that play an important role in

---

12. Peter Phan, *Asian Christianities: History, Theology, Practice* (Maryknoll, NY: Orbis Books, 2018), 103–8.

13. Gaudencio Rosales and Catalino Arevalo, eds., *For All the Peoples of Asia: Federation of Asian Bishops' Conferences*, vol. 1. *Documents from 1970 to 1991* (Maryknoll, NY: Orbis Books, 1992), 70 (see no. 14, ii).

14. See Hwa Yung, *Mangoes or Bananas: The Quest for an Authentic Asian Christian Theology* (Oxford: Regnum, 1997).

accomplishing the twofold task, and the concrete ways in which a full incorporation of the Asian Christian perspectives, religious histories, priorities, and debates might be achieved.

Methodology

A full incorporation of Asian perspectives, religious histories, priorities, and debates on Christianity entails, first and foremost, a closer scrutiny of the production, dissemination, and reception of Christian knowledge, in general, and in relation to Asian Christians, in particular. More specifically, how is Christian history and theology in/on Asia done, taught, and received inside and outside of the continent? Which Christianity? Whose Christianity?

The contextual and contemporary situation in Asia is fluid, as there is a great variety and complexity of backgrounds and situations in the countries in Asia. These diverse and changing contexts constitute what the late Japanese theologian Kosuke Koyama considered important "raw materials" for doing Christian theology in Asia, which, according to Koyama, "begins by raising [Asian] issues, not by digesting Augustine, Barth, and Rahner."[15] Writing on the contextualization of Asian theology, Bong Rin Ro echoes Koyama's sentiment by lamenting how theological ideas that are developed by Euro-Americans are "crammed into Asia" and that such "shoving [of] the 'Westerner's Christianity' upon other nationals is no longer acceptable."[16]

The contextual content and method of doing Asian theology and, at the same time, a more critical approach to Western theology, are nothing new among Asian Christians in the twenty-first century. However, for forerunners and pioneers, like Koyama,[17] paving the way toward the development, articulation, and recognition of Asian Christian theologies has not been easy. The struggle of Asian theologians who engage in contextual theologies could be glimpsed in the preface of Franklyn Balasundaram's book distilling the works of notable Asian Christian theologians of the late twentieth century. Balasundaram implores readers,

---

15. Kosuke Koyama, "Theological Situations in Asia and the Mission of the Church," in Douglas Elwood, ed., *What Asian Christians Are Thinking: A Theological Sourcebook* (Quezon City: New Day Publishers, 1976), 16–40, at 16.

16. Bong Rin Ro, "Contextualization: Asian Theology," in Elwood, ed., *What Asian Christians Are Thinking*, 47–58, at 47.

17. Koyama's key contributions include *Water Buffalo Theology*, 25th Anniversary ed. (Maryknoll, NY: Orbis Books, 1999), and *Mount Fuji and Mount Sinai* (Maryknoll, NY: Orbis Books, 1985).

Please do not underestimate and misunderstand these thinkers for their faith-articulations. If they are critical of their Christian heritage, traditional/classical Western theology, Western Missionary Movement, etc. it is not because they want to get away from or dilute or disown their "Christian" heritage. Contrary. Asian thinkers today are moving towards not only which is "Asian" but also "Global" and truly "Christian."[18]

It goes without saying that having the opportunity and platform to (re)discover and (re)engage the Asian contexts and faces of Christianity in critical dialogue with its Western influences is not sufficient. Recognition and ongoing support for the widest possible range of scholarship are equally important. This is particularly true for Catholic theologians, some of whom have suffered from investigations by religious authorities in Asia and the Vatican's Congregation for the Doctrine of the Faith.[19] A full incorporation of Asian Christian experiences and perspectives is not possible if (academic) freedom and diversity in theological scholarship and formation are severely stifled, particularly for pastoral and/or scholarly works that genuinely broaden and enrich the understanding as well as practice of Christianity with an Asian face.

Achieving full incorporation of Asian Christians' perspectives, religious histories, priorities, and debates necessitates full respect and recognition of Asian epistemologies. Epistemology asks the hard questions: What is knowledge? How is knowledge acquired? What do people know? How do we know what we know? Different cultures arguably vary in the perception and production of knowledge and in analyzing its relationship with concepts like truth, belief, and justification. Asian theologians, for example, talk of the yin-yang way of thinking in Asia.[20] In a number of countries in Asia, notably India, China, and Japan, there are centuries-old and well-developed philosophies. Further, for the majority

---

18. Franklyn Balasundaram, *Contemporary Asian Christian Theology* (Delhi: ISPCK, 1998), ii.

19. These include Sri Lankan theologian Tissa Balasuriya OMI, who was even excommunicated for his book *Mary and Human Liberation*, and Peter Phan. See Helen Stanton, ed., *Mary and Human Liberation: The Story and the Text—Fr. Tissa Balasuriya* (Harrisburg, PA: Trinity Press International, 1997), for the original text as well as correspondence between the Vatican and Balasuriya; and Peter Phan, *The Joy of Religious Pluralism: A Personal Journey* (Maryknoll, NY: Orbis Books, 2017), for the story on Phan's run-in with Vatican authorities regarding the alleged errors and ambiguities in his book *Being Religious Interreligiously: Asian Perspectives on Interfaith Dialogue* (Maryknoll, NY: Orbis Books, 2004).

20. See, for instance, Jung Young Lee, "The Yin-Yang Way of Thinking," in Elwood, ed., *What Asian Christians Are Thinking*, 59–67.

of Asians where orality is predominant, philosophical worldviews are expressed not in philosophical texts but in myths, stories, proverbs, songs, dance, rituals, festivals, and dramas. Then there are the "small traditions" embodied in popular religiosity or popular devotions that predominate among Catholics, especially in Vietnam and the Philippines.[21] One can also throw into the mix what *Ecclesia in Asia* refers to as cultural and religious values that ostensibly constitute the "Asian soul" or "being Asian" (Asianness, in itself, is admittedly a slippery concept): "love of silence and contemplation, simplicity, harmony, detachment, non-violence, discipline, frugal living, the thirst for learning and philosophical inquiry . . . respect for life, compassion for all beings, closeness to nature, filial piety toward parents, elders, and ancestors, and a highly-developed sense of community."[22]

To be sure, differences in intellectual styles and the cultural value accorded to these intellectual styles will have an impact when it comes to determining the nature and scope of what constitutes sound scholarship. Arguably, there is no apolitical scholarship. Scholarly practices are inscribed in power relations. Indian American academic Chandra Talpade Mohanty points to this discursive nature of scholarship, particularly in relation to feminist literature. Mohanty posits that there is a certain mode of appropriation and codification of "scholarship" and "knowledge" about women in the Third World by particular analytic categories that take, as their referent, feminist interests as they have been articulated in the United States and Western Europe.[23] She goes on to say that this is one of the effects of the implicit assumption of "the West" (in all its complexities and contradictions) as the primary referent in theory and praxis.[24]

Dutch theologian Frans Wijsen echoes Mohanty's argument by pointing out that theological hermeneutics, indeed, largely remains a Western enterprise or that it is chiefly dominated by the Western philosophical tradition. At the same time, Wijsen says this tradition is increasingly challenged by non-Western philosophers. He summarizes this "North-South dialogue" toward intercultural hermeneutics in four points. First, in classical hermeneutics the aim is ultimately to understand oneself. It is an individualistic enterprise. The non-Western hermeneutics has a communitarian approach. Second, classical hermeneutics is focused on harmoni-

---

21. Phan, *Asian Christianities*, 107–8.
22. John Paul II, *Ecclesia in Asia*, no. 6, http://www.vatican.va.
23. Chandra Talpade Mohanty, "Under Western Eyes: Feminist Scholarship in Colonial Discourses," in Chandra Talpade Mohanty, Ann Russo, and Lourdes Torres, eds., *Third World Women and the Politics of Feminism* (Indianapolis: Indiana University Press, 1991), 333–58, at 333.
24. Ibid., 334.

zation. Intercultural hermeneutics recognizes differentiation. The other, as a stranger, is to be done justice. Third, classical hermeneutics is seen as instrumental: the reader takes possession of the text, makes the text his/her own property. Intercultural hermeneutics is relational. Last but not least, classical hermeneutics is based on a propositional understanding of truth; intercultural hermeneutics is based on an existential understanding of truth.[25] For example, Walter Hollenweger contends that if Koyama, whom the former describes as one of the most creative theologians from Asia, were to present one of his books to any of the European universities, "he would surely have failed because *his* understanding of scholarship and consistency clashes with that of the European-American."[26] While Hollenweger's observation is more than two decades old and non-Western scholarship is accorded better respect these days in the West, lament about having to work harder to prove themselves is not uncommon among postgraduate students in theology and religious studies from the global South who are studying in Western contexts.

Such marginalization of non-Western contexts and epistemology occurs not only at the individual level but also at the institutional level. The reaction of the Japanese bishops to the questions they needed to respond to as part of the *Lineamenta* prepared by the Vatican for the Asian Synod reflects this. Since the questions of the *Lineamenta* were composed in the context of Western Christianity, they are not suitable. Among the questions are some concerning whether the work of evangelization is going well or not; but what is the standard of evaluation? If it is the number of baptisms, etc., it is very dangerous. The judgment should not be made from a European framework, but must be seen on the spiritual level of the people who live in Asia.[27]

In contemporary times, dialogue is the mode of being an Asian Christian—thus, a full incorporation of the perspectives, religious histories, priorities, and debates in and from Asia inevitably entails the engagement of dialogue as both content and method in the teaching, practice, and scholarship on Asian Christianity. More specifically, to be an Asian Christian is to engage in what the FABC and notable theologians of Asian descent refer to as the triple dialogue: dialogue with poverty (liberation), dialogue with cultures (inculturation), and dialogue with religions (interreligious

---

25. Frans Wijsen, "Intercultural Theology and the Mission of the Church," *Exchange* 30, no. 3 (2001): 218–28, at 224.

26. Italics in original text. Walter Hollenweger, "Intercultural Theology," *Theology Today* 43, no. 1 (1986): 28–35, at 34–35.

27. "Japan's Response," *UCAN* (July 30, 1997), as quoted in Edmund Chia, *Towards a Theology of Dialogue* (Bangkok: E. Chia, 2003), 80. A *lineamenta* is a preparatory document.

dialogue).²⁸ While this vision of triple dialogue is Roman Catholic in its roots, it is neither sectarian nor denominational. Most Christian churches can readily subscribe to its basic orientations.²⁹ Thus, it is no coincidence that the six volumes containing the compilation of FABC documents are titled "For All the Peoples of Asia."

I have seen, first-hand, these three key expressions of dialogue as fundamental feature and character of Asian Christianity not only in the predominantly Christian Philippines, where I lived for about three decades, but also in various Asian countries I have spent some time in more than once in the past two decades. I have encountered these, too, in my involvement as a consultant to the Sub-Committee on Asian and Pacific Affairs for the Secretariat on Cultural Diversity in the Church for the American Catholic bishops' conference when I was still living and working in the United States. In a formation seminar for Asian American pastoral leaders, for instance, a participant asked, "On Sundays when I go home after the Eucharist I honor my ancestors, does this make me less Catholic?"

The missionary experiences of Matteo Ricci in China, Roberto de Nobili in India, and Alexander de Rhodes in Vietnam illustrate the positive effects of openness to, as well as respect and recognition of, a different context and its epistemologies.³⁰ In more recent times Carrie Pemberton's reflections on her three-year experience in the Congo as a British scholar doing field research for her doctoral dissertation at Cambridge³¹ shed light on the challenges and gifts of an attitude of full respect and recognition for a different context and its epistemologies. Like all field research-

---

28. Chia, *World Christianity Encounters World Religions*, 141–44. Peter Phan has an impressive body of work on this topic. See, for example, *Mission and Catechesis: Alexander de Rhodes and Inculturation in Seventeenth-Century Vietnam* (Maryknoll, NY: Orbis Books, 2015); *Being Religious Interreligiously* (2004); *In Our Own Tongues: Perspectives from Asia on Mission and Inculturation* (Maryknoll, NY: Orbis Books, 2003); and *Christianity with an Asian Face: Asian-American Theology in the Making* (Maryknoll, NY: Orbis Books, 2003).

29. Peter Phan, "Conclusion: Wither Asian Christianities?" in Peter Phan, ed., *Christianities in Asia* (Malden, MA: Wiley-Blackwell, 2011), 255–62, at 259. For an incisive treatment of Protestant contributions to Asian Christian identity that contains resonances to the Roman Catholic concept of triple dialogue, see David Thompson, "Introduction: Mapping Asian Christianity in the Context of World Christianity," in Sebastian Kim, ed., *Christian Theology in Asia* (Cambridge: Cambridge University Press, 2008), 3–21.

30. See Chia, *World Christianity Encounters World Religions*, 139; Chia regards these missionaries' efforts simply as a first step because the critical issues of the Catholic Church's identity, especially how it relates with its surrounding contexts and cultures, were not adequately addressed by these missionaries.

31. Titled "Feminism, Inculturation and the Search for a Global Christianity: An African Example—The Circle of Concerned African Women Theologians."

ers with human subjects, Pemberton had fears of desubjectifying those whom she was researching, especially given her supervisor's mandate to research, chronicle, and abstract theological themes and concerns in the work of certain African women theologians. Her social location, Pemberton says, complicated her encounters with members of the Circle due to what she perceives as the misunderstanding, dis-ease, and mistrust that faces any Northerner who dares to research and reflect on the gathered material in contemporary Africa. She was told by certain lead members of the Circle that African women cook alone in their kitchens and that her presence around the theological cooking pot would be unwelcome. Others in the group, however, felt that the presence of someone outside the Circle would help in the group's critical reflection, and that contact with a researcher and theologian from the West was part of the process of interdependence that was needed for both churches and academic maturity.[32]

Pemberton especially notes what she learned regarding the primacy of praxis in African women's theologies. She writes:

> After all, my quintessential experience of African women in the face of multiplicity of struggles they encountered, had been one of movement and self-authoring. Against what was perceived as our western academic economy of analysis, drawing and quartering—duly noted, appendixed, referenced, refereed and, finally, entombed in print—African women theologians had constantly reminded me that the praxis of their theology, the actual doing of it, and the song, dance, laughter and tears in the making of it in the company of others was what was essential. . . .[33]

While scholars from the West, especially those who do field research in Asia, Africa, and Latin America, are legitimate sources and interlocutors for the full incorporation of the perspectives, religious histories, priorities, and debates from the said regions, there is a great need for developing and nurturing a critical mass of ethnic scholars of non-Western Christianity who are from, as well as lifelong residents in, these regions.[34] For

---

32. Carrie Pemberton, "Whose Face in the Mirror?: Personal and Postcolonial Obstacles in Researching Africa's Contemporary Women's Theological Voices," in Tina Beattie, ed., *Gender, Religion, and Diversity: Cross Cultural Perspectives* (London: Continuum, 2004), 250–61, at 258.

33. Ibid., 251–52.

34. A recent initiative in the case of Asia is the creation of the India-based *International Journal of Asian Christianity*, which was spearheaded by Felix Wilfred, an Indian theologian. The journal is dedicated to the scholarly examination of Christianity in

example, a cursory look at the authors of a book on Christianity in Asia has twelve (out of fifteen) authors with Western-sounding names.[35] Creating and nurturing possibilities for Asian scholars, especially those living in Asia, to have contributions in publications on Christianity in/on the region and facilitating the widest possible circulation and access to these publications, e.g., through translation, are essential.

It is equally important for established scholars of Asian descent, both in Asia and overseas, to assist in the dissemination of Asian works and ideas by supporting the introduction and/or mainstreaming of reputable works of other Asian scholars, especially those scholars from the region who do not get well-deserved exposure and recognition, by citing these other scholars' works in their (established scholars') own publications. I refer here specifically to those established scholars whose publications not only have gravitas but also wide circulation and readership in the academic world inside and outside of Asia. There is, it seems to me, what may be called "footnote politics," which could impoverish the vision of fully incorporating Asian histories and perspectives. For example, at a gathering of women theologians of Asian descent there was a suggestion to try to cite or quote relevant works of colleagues for purposes of better exposure and mainstreaming, especially in the academic world. On more than one occasion I received a copy of the work of a couple of theologians of Asian descent with a request to cite their text in my future publications.

In the area of teaching, a full incorporation of Asian Christian experiences and perspectives will mean a shift in understanding and teaching world Christianity from "church history" to "history of Christianity." Phan posits that implicit in the common practice in seminary curriculum and academic scholarship of separating church history and missiology is the colonialist understanding of Christianity, with the church as the West and mission as the rest. Such practice, Phan says, has church history dealing with the Western churches (dubbed as "historic churches") and missiology with the "mission lands," with their presumably immature

---

Asia and of Asian Christian diaspora in the West and elsewhere. In a similar and broader initiative in 2018, two theologians of African descent in the United States tried to spearhead the creation of a journal called *LaFricAsia: The Journal of World Christianity* to serve, though not exclusively, the needs of theologians from Africa, Asia, and Latin America.

35. See Richard Fox Young and Jonathan Seitz, *Asia in the Making of Christianity: Conversion, Agency, Indigeneity, 1600s to the Present* (Leiden: Brill, 2013). More encouraging examples include the above-mentioned *Christianities in Asia*, ed. Peter Phan; and Felix Wilfred et al., eds., *Oxford Handbook on Christianity in Asia* (New York: Oxford University Press, 2014), in which the overwhelming majority of contributors are scholars of Asian descent.

"younger churches" beholden in every way, not least financially, to the historic churches.

Phan argues that such a shift would mean beginning the history of mission by adding another narrative, that is, the mission of the apostle Thomas to India in 57 CE, to the hallowed Eurocentric history of mission. For the historical purists who may object to the suggestion, Phan proposes the incontrovertibly historical story of the missionaries of the Church of the East, misnamed Nestorian, led by the monk Alopen, who came to Chang-an (modern Xi-An) in 635 during the Tang dynasty. This alternative history of mission, Phan contends,

> has the advantage of introducing our often historically and culturally-challenged students to a different non-Western land, language, culture, people, and church tradition. This knowledge will disabuse them of the common notion that Christian mission began from Rome or Canterbury or Geneva or the United States. Furthermore, the text inscribed on the Xi'-an Stele offers an unparalleled example of contextualizing the Christian faith into a non-Semitic and non-Western context, with an extraordinarily bold employment of Buddhist, Confucian, and Daoist concepts and terms to express Christian beliefs.[36]

The use of texts and other nontraditional sources such as stories and art, especially those that challenge or provide alternative perspectives to (neo)colonial Western mainstream accounts and perspectives, are equally important.[37] The choice of textbooks and reading lists, as well as who teaches relevant classes or courses, is also critical.[38] At an international conference on intercultural communication, for instance, a Hispanic-American participant who was then a doctoral student in theology at a renowned American university shared how he and his fellow students from minority groups complained that, with the exception of a book by Peruvian liberation theologian Gustavo Gutiérrez, the reading list was composed of the works of "dead white dudes" (read: Euro-American male scholars).

---

36. Peter Phan, "Teaching Missiology in and for World Christianity: Content and Method," *International Bulletin of Mission Research* 42, no. 4 (2018): 358–69, at 367.

37. David Tonghou Ngong, "The Ethics of Identity and World Christianity," *Missionalia: Southern African Journal of Missiology* 45, no. 3 (2017): 250–62, at 254.

38. Aside from the publications on Asia cited in this essay, other valuable sources include the three volumes edited by John England and others, *Asian Christian Theologies: A Research Guide to Authors, Movements and Sources*, vol. 1. *Asia Region, South Asia, Austral Asia* (Maryknoll, NY: Orbis Books, 2002); vol. 2. *Southeast Asia* (Maryknoll, NY: Orbis Books, 2003); and vol. 3. *Northeast Asia* (Maryknoll, NY: Orbis Books, 2004).

In order not to run the risk of a myopic approach it is beneficial, as well, not to engage Asian Christianity in complete isolation from Christianities in other regions. Such an intersectional approach is needed in relation to Western Christianity, which is forever linked with Asian Christianity, at the very least, in terms of history. An intersectional approach in relation to Christianities in the global South, which have shared experiences with Asian Christians such as colonialism and marginalization, is helpful, too. The reading list for a class on Asian liberation theology, for example, can be enriched by books on liberation theology from Latin America, Africa, and the Caribbean. Such an approach avoids ecclesial apartheid[39] and provides potential for broader and richer understanding as well as paths for mutual solidarity, particularly a "solidarity of others."[40] An excellent candidate for the reading list in this regard is Ahn Tran's essay "Jesus beyond the West: Christological Conversations in the Age of World Christianity," which pays tribute to the triple dialogue by presenting Jesus Christ from the three perspectives of liberation, inculturation, and interreligious, and, where relevant and appropriate, discusses shared interests, cross-conversations, and mutual influences between Christologies generated from Latin America, Africa, and Asia that have reach beyond their geographic origin[41] and are significant to understanding world Christianity today.

Last, but not least, of what may be regarded as necessary methodological steps is the need for more serious engagement of an interdisciplinary approach in both teaching and scholarship. Such an approach ensures that narratives and perspectives that have been previously missed, marginalized, suppressed, or buried are brought to the fore and enrich, clarify, or rectify prevailing thinking. As has already been proven in contemporary scholarship, such as biblical scholarship, critically engaging other disciplines, e.g., history, literature, linguistics, archaeology, social psychology, cultural anthropology, sociology, ethnography, gender studies, cartography, demography, art, architecture, etc., provides fertile ground for a more substantive and comprehensive engagement of diverse experiences and perspectives. The current indigenous focus in world Christianity itself is partly a result of creating theoretical frameworks within which the demographic (Southern) shift of Christianity may be understood. In other words, it is partly because scholars of Christianity have taken seriously

---

39. Ngong, "The Ethics of Identity and World Christianity," 260.

40. For a helpful treatment on the solidarity of those who are different, see Anselm Min, *The Solidarity of Others in a Divided World: A Postmodern Theology after Postmodernism* (New York: T & T Clark, 2004).

41. Ahn Tran, "Jesus beyond the West: Christological Conversations in the Age of World Christianity," in Jonathan Tan and Anh Tran, eds., *World Christianity: Perspectives and Insights* (Maryknoll, NY: Orbis Books, 2016), 182–203.

the reality and implications of this demographic shift that there is better attention to Christianity's indigenous contexts.

*Ortho*proxy

Fully incorporating Asian Christian perspectives, religious histories, priorities, and debates also means attending not only to the *how* (methodology) and *what* (content) but also *who* (identity) is engaged in the teaching, scholarship, or practice of Asian Christianity. In other words, who might be considered to be in the best position to offer an Asian perspective? Needless to say, authenticity and integrity of the messenger are essential. This litmus test applies not only to non-Asian scholars but also to those with Asian ethnic roots or background. As it is, the term "Asian" itself does not really refer to a single homogenous enclave but a panethnic category that includes persons, cultures, and languages from a vast geographical area, which includes close to fifty countries. The ethnolinguistic diversity that characterizes Asian peoples themselves is staggering. It is hard to see, for example, what a Korean and an Indonesian may have in common. There is not even a common language that could bind diverse peoples from Asia, as is the case for those coming from Latin America.

Filipino-American theologian Tito Cruz argues that whenever we use panethnic categories such as Asian, Pacific, Latino, Anglo, or Black we take the risk of naming people in ways that they do not use themselves. Cruz notes that just as most "Latinos" identify themselves by using their specific national or regional name, persons from Asia generally do the same. It is, therefore, important not to sideline specific ethnic identities, asserts Cruz, as these "represent distinct narratives that connect us to our myths, symbols, and rituals. They call us to examine critically our colonial history, teach us to embrace persons who call themselves by other names, impel us to work for peace and justice, and encourage us in faith to strive toward a more abundant life in a new land."[42] While it is desirable, a pan-Asian perspective is, most likely, improbable since this involves amalgamating the close to fifty diverse national identities in Asia, which contain diversities within themselves, e.g., the Hmong and Montagnards from Vietnam, into a single "Asian" classification.[43]

---

42. Tito Cruz and Rosanna Ella, "To Live Church More Authentically: Ministry with Asian and Pacific Catholics in the United States," *Pastoral Music* 27, no. 4 (April 2003): 19–21, at 19.

43. Robert Schreiter, "Spaces for Religion and Migrant Religious Identity," in Josef Meili, Ernstpeter Heiniger, and Paul Stadler, eds., *Migration: Challenge to Religious Identity II. Forum Mission*, vol. 5 (Luzern: Verein zur Förderung der Missionswissenschaft, 2009), 155–70, at 162–63.

Indeed, such diversity within the region and among Asians in diaspora has serious implications on what may be called *ortho*proxy, a term loosely used here to refer to who might qualify or count as the right (or best) representative of a specific Asian country, much less the continent, to write or speak on Asian Christianity.[44] In scholarship, as well as centers of learning and formation, practicing *ortho*proxy means taking care not to consider or, worse, make students from minority groups, in this case Asians, as "representatives" or "experts" of their ancestral religious history and culture, especially when it comes to those who have little or no contact with their (or their parents') homelands. *Ortho*proxy also implies not automatically assuming, or making, international students from Asia, especially those studying in the West, as the experts or spokespersons of their region's, or country's, or ethnic group's theologies. The following recollection by M. T. Dávila illustrates this cultural trap:

> As a Puerto Rican woman doing a Master in Theological Studies at the Boston University School of Theology, I was asked repeatedly what I thought of liberation theology. I was both resentful and jealous that my white male colleagues were more versed in Latin American theologies than I was. Second, I found it offensive that they assumed that the Puerto Rican feminist would, of course, be well acquainted with the liberation movement. I did not want anyone else telling me what field I was supposed to be good at or interested in or, worse yet, that I owed it to "my people" to become their theological spokesperson.[45]

I had a similar experience when, in my early years as a theologian in the United States, the immediate response of a white male theologian whom I was introduced to was "So you're doing Asian theology?" It appears that just because I look Asian my research specialization or, at the very least, research interest would be Asian theology.

Attending to questions and concerns regarding *ortho*proxy requires judicious transpositional and transvaluational relationality vis-à-vis ethnicity. This entails sensitivity to the complexity of people's different stories, worldviews, and interests, which may not be directly linked to or aligned with their ethnic background. Theologians in/from Asia are not always, or necessarily, experts or interested in Asian theologies, so a well-informed

---

44. A term originated by Carmen Nanko-Fernández in her book *Theologizing en Espanglish: Context, Community, and Ministry* (Maryknoll, NY: Orbis Books, 2010), 39.
45. M. T. Dávila, "Catholic Hispanic Theology in the U.S.: Dimensiones dela Opcíon Preferencial por los Pobres en el Norte," *CTSA Proceedings* 63 (2008): 28–48, at 28.

and cautious approach is needed when it comes to identifying and choosing who could provide deeper or more authentic Asian perspectives.

*Ortho*proxy, therefore, involves resisting insensitive and uncritical value-coding of ethnicity. In the case of Asian Christianity this applies not just to non-Asian scholars but to/among Asian scholars, too. Such a stance avoids the risk of Asians themselves automatically assuming that everyone who looks and speaks like them are experts or, at the very least, interested in Asian theologies or theologies from a particular Asian country. A possible problematic side effect of prioritizing or absolutizing shared identity when it comes to *ortho*proxy is that the group, in this case Asians, may limit access, or constrain validity and authority, in the teaching and scholarship on Asian Christianity only and exclusively to/among "pure" Asian members of the group and/or those mixed-race Asians who live in Asia. Such perspective poses a daunting challenge for Asian scholars, especially those in the diaspora who maintain close personal and academic links with their homeland, or with Asia in general, but are still seen by Asians in Asia and those in the diaspora as well as Western society as the "not quite" or "half-baked" Westerner and Asian, particularly because they are not citizens or residents of Asia. Some Asian scholars living in the West even end up being unkindly, if not unfairly, regarded as "bananas," "coconuts," or "mangosteen," that is, yellow, brown, or black outside but white inside. Asian American scholars, for example, talk about the "perpetual foreigner" syndrome.[46] Biblical scholar Gale Yee's experience as a visiting professor in Hong Kong shows how such alienation extends to one's ethnic origins or ancestral homeland: "I am also an outsider in a Chinese context. . . . People realized that I was not a 'real' Chinese as soon as I opened my mouth."[47] Yee's experience is instructive as her social location as a perpetual foreigner, that is, as an Asian American, is "further marginalized by being a female who had to endure both the patriarchal attitudes of her Chinese ethnicity and those of her U.S. context."[48]

---

46. See Mia Tuan, *Forever Foreigners or Honorary Whites: The Asian Ethnic Experience Today* (New Brunswick, NJ: Rutgers University Press, 1998); Peter Phan and Jung Young Lee, eds., *Journeys at the Margin: Toward an Autobiographical Theology in Asian Perspective* (Collegeville, MN: Liturgical Press, 1999); and Frank Wu, *Yellow: Race in America beyond Black and White* (New York: Basic Books, 2002), 79–129. This is echoed by the American Catholic bishops in *Encountering Christ in Harmony: A Pastoral Response to Our Asian and Pacific Island Brothers and Sisters* (Washington, DC: USCCB, 2018), 18.

47. Gale Yee, "Where Are You Really From?: An Asian American Feminist Biblical Scholar Reflects on Her Guild," in Mary Hunt and Diann Neu, eds., *New Feminist Christianity: Many Voices, Many Views* (Woodstock, VT: Skylight Paths Publishing, 2010), 79–85, at 80.

48. Ibid.

The patriarchy that continues to characterize many Asian countries, including Christian institutions, organizations, and scholarship, means that care must be taken to ensure a balance of, as well as critical approach to, gender experiences and perspectives in determining *ortho*proxy when it comes to scholars, teachers, and sources on Asian Christianity. Korean American feminist theologian Namsoon Kang, for instance, laments the continuing deployment of the naturalized and essentialized category of Asian women, whose dangers and problems lie in its mode of seeing which is fixed, homogenized, and unchanging.[49] Kang also points to her experience of ethnic cultural essentialism, deployed both ways (East and West), as an unchallenged dominant rhetoric whenever she goes to conferences where theologians from the West and the East gather together. Kang explains that both groups—the Westerners and the Easterners—tend to presuppose that the East is and should be completely different from the West and that native Asians should claim their essential difference as a unique virtue that Westerners do not possess. For non-native Westerners, Kang reveals, respect and encouragement for the presumably unique virtues of the East seem to function as nonimperialist sentiments in engaging with the non-West. For the native Easterners, on the other hand, their ethnic essentialist position often functions as a form of survival technique that makes their voice heard in a world of neo-imperialism where the West (especially Western Europe and the United States) still dominates every sector of reality.[50]

Such cultural essentialism often functions as a "culturalist alibi" that works "within a basically elitist culture industry, insisting on the continuity of a native tradition untouched by a Westernization,"[51] which some Asians might use to block any criticism on patriarchal and hierarchal aspects of Asian culture and tradition. Kang explains what is lost in this ethnic cultural essentialism:

> The adoption of an ethnic essentialist rhetoric, by both natives and non-natives, keeps the West at the universal center of knowledge and the discursive norm, whereas the non-West remains as the particularized, ethnicized, often exoticized, and idealized margin in the world of knowledge production, archiving, and dissemination. Here both natives and non-natives, regardless of

---

49. Namsoon Kang, *Diasporic Feminist Theology: Asia and Theopolitical Imagination* (Minneapolis, MN: Fortress, 2014), 74.
50. Ibid., 75.
51. Gayatri Chakravorty Spivak, "Who Claims Alterity?" in Barbara Kruger and Phil Mariani, eds., *Remaking History* (Discussions in Contemporary Culture; Seattle, WA: Bay Press, 1989), 269–92, at 281.

their intentionality, end up homogenizing the heterogeneity of the East and suppressing the critical difference within the East and among its people in different nation-states based on their respective geopolitical power, economic status, social class, religion, gender, or other axis of oppression and discrimination.[52]

The reverse may also be true. By this I refer to Christian scholars of Asian descent who study, or have studied, in the West and exhibit lower regard for Asian theologies (especially when compared to Western theologies) for various reasons, e.g., lack of exposure to Asian texts and theologians in their studies. At an annual informal gathering of theologians of Asian descent at a convention, for example, one new member who lives in Asia and was, at that time, doing doctoral studies in the United States said he was glad to hear about Asian theology and to attend the convention session on Asian and Asian American theology, given that he has been studying "pure theology" (read: Western theology) all this time, even in the seminary in his home country in Asia. Indeed, in Catholic (especially diocesan) seminaries in Asia a good number, if not a majority, of the required readings are written by Western authors. In the case of a small seminary in Southeast Asia that I visited, all of the required readings have Western authors, and all the textbooks were published in the West. How can we talk about the full incorporation of genuine Asian perspectives when theological studies and formation are still dominated, or heavily colored, by Western thinking and knowledge?

What is worse is when Asian scholars who studied in the West uncritically subscribe to Western scholarship and use Western epistemologies as a yardstick to criticize their region's, their country's, and all other non-Western methods and perspectives. Muriel Orevillo-Montenegro, for example, talks about a Western-educated Filipino male theologian who did not recognize *In God's Image* (IGI)—the first and only feminist theological journal in Asia—as a "scholarly" journal because its format resembles that of a magazine (each issue usually contains women's essays, poetry, and art illustrations of Asian women). What he failed to see, according to Orevillo-Montenegro, is that (1) the creativity of Asian feminist theologizing is expressed in the journal; (2) it popularizes theology through a variety of forms of expressions; and (3) it is not wedded to the traditional format of dense words and high language that is not accessible to the ordinary person.[53] Other Western-educated Asians, in

---

52. Kang, *Diasporic Feminist Theology*, 76.
53. Muriel Orevillo-Montenegro, "My Search for Asian Women's Voices," *In God's Image* 26, no. 4 (December 2007): 21–24, at 23.

the meantime, try to literally and uncritically import or transfer what they learned in their studies overseas to their home countries without regard for cultural sensibilities or sensitivities.[54] This has problematic implications to efforts toward inculturation.

Hence, *ortho*proxy also requires that Asians who, from the perspective of position and value, are well placed to be agents in the full incorporation of Asian perspectives, religious histories, priorities, and debates in world Christianity are respectful toward, as well as well versed in, indigenous scholarship and sources on Christianity in Asia. This is especially true in centers of learning and formation, such as seminaries, whose students often become the leaders as well as the faces and agents of Asian Christianity not only in the academies, both inside and outside of Asia, but also in the trenches in Asia itself.

Conclusion

To take seriously the "world" in "world Christianity," in this case the Asian faces of Christianity, means understanding and engaging the contemporary multifaceted, as well as profoundly complex, expressions of the politics of identity (*ortho*proxy) and politics of epistemology (methodology) that are at work in the teaching, practice, and scholarship on Asian Christianity with a special attention to the triple dialogue. It means fully embracing the reality that there are unique and, at the same time, extremely diverse and cross-cultural contexts for understanding and practicing Christianity among Asian Christians, and that insisting on, or imposing, particular ways and perspectives is tantamount to a form of control of memory, history, and identity not just of Asian Christians but Christianity itself as a world religion that originated from Asia. Taking more seriously the Asian faces of world Christianity, in other words, is about the challenge of not being afraid of the potential scandal, or struggle, in carving a space for theorizing and making affirmations on cultural stories, worldviews, or practices that are devalued by, or contradict, the dominant consciousness. It does more than pay lip service to diversity. It celebrates otherness with a steadfast refusal to conflate diverse experiences into a false synthesis. In doing so one reveals not only Christianity *in* Asia but, more importantly, Christianities *of* Asia.

---

54. Florentino Hornedo, for example, points to the problem with theologians who form their theology in Europe and come to rural Philippines and try to make the Philippines into Europe. Hornedo regards this as imperial theology. As quoted in Leonardo Mercado, *Filipino Popular Devotions: The Interior Dialogue between Traditional Religion and Christianity* (Manila: Logos Publications, 2000), 71.

8

Granting Full Citizenship to Latin American Christianities in World Christianity

RAIMUNDO C. BARRETO

What is the place of Latin America in world Christianity discourse? What contributions can Latin American religious studies make to world Christianity as a burgeoning field of study? Why hasn't the field of world Christianity engaged Latin American studies more extensively? These are some of the questions this essay addresses, while arguing for the importance of the sustained inclusion of Latin America in the study of world Christianity. Such an argument considers not only the variety of Christian experiences, stories, discourses, and networks in Latin America but, more specifically, Latin American scholarship on religion coming out of the numerous departments of religious studies in Latin American universities and produced by Latin American scholars spread throughout the world.

Despite the growing interest in Latin America among world Christianity scholars, guilds, and networks, the engagement with Latin American scholarship in this field of study remains timid. This limited interaction, among other things, reflects the bias of a field that emerged mostly among Anglophone scholars studying sub-Saharan African Christianities. To be clear, there is nothing detrimental about the fact that the study of African Christianities has played a prominent role in the development of world Christianity. This is not the point. In fact, the attention paid to Africa and African Christianities in this still-expanding field should be appreciated as an important correction to a long oversight in the historiography of modern Christianity. That said, the acknowledgment of an Afrocentric emphasis in Anglophone perspective in this field is important for the argument of this essay as one considers the social history of the field and explores the next steps in the expansion of its horizons. My emphasis on the Anglophone element also implies that other traditions in the study of African religion have not been sufficiently considered by world Christianity scholars, including Francophone and Lusophone transatlantic African researchers, whose knowledge is important, among other things, to the deepening of the understanding of South–South religious networks such as the ongoing partnerships between African scholars and their counterparts in the African diaspora in Latin America and the Caribbean.[1]

Despite its emphasis on the Christianities of the global South, the field of world Christianity has developed mostly through chairs, departments, and centers located in the West and the global North.[2] And yet most of the movements and histories studied in the field originate in the postcolonial world.[3] In this chapter, I look at the field of world Christianity as a Latin American scholar currently living in the global North. This is also the backdrop against which I examine the Anglophone Protestant "bias" of the field. Such discussion is intended to strengthen the case for the fuller

---

1. While some scholars identified with the field of world Christianity have turned their attention to such South–South relations, there is literature in Portuguese, Spanish, French, and other languages that remains largely untapped in the Anglophone studies of world Christianity. A recent example of a gathering that predominantly focused on South–South relations was the international and interdisciplinary conference gathered around the theme of "Global African Indigenous and Derived Religions," in Juiz de Fora, Brazil, on October 22–25, 2018. Despite the richness of the multilingual and transcontinental conversations that took place during that event, it remains unknown to most of the Anglophone academy of religion, since its papers were published in a Brazilian journal that is not widely read by Anglophone scholars in the North Atlantic. See *Numen—Revista de Estudos e Pesquisa da Religião*. Special Issue, "Religiões Africanas e Afrodiaspóricas," ed. Afe Adogame, Raimundo C. Barreto, Sonia R. Lages, Felipe F. Rodrigues, and Humberto A. Quaglio de Souza, 22, no. 1 (2019).

2. Jacob K. Olupona has sharply criticized the continued protagonist role of the global North in the field. In his own words, "the West and the Global North continue to be the financial epicenter and the intellectual and academic hub of world Christianity. He who pays the piper dictates the tune." Jacob K. Olupona, "World Christianity: An Agenda for the Twenty-First Century," *Journal of World Christianity* 9, no. 1 (2019): 23–33, at 25.

3. The postcolonial world includes both "the world born in the aftermath of Western colonialism and imperialism" and the persistence of imperial and colonial structures after the colonial era properly considered, impacting life and relations in both the global North and the global South. See Jyotsna G. Syngh, "Introduction: The Postcolonial World," in Jyotsna G. Syngh and David D. Kim, eds., *The Postcolonial World* (New York: Routledge, 2017), 3. With regard to these persisting conditions in the Puerto Rican context, see Luis Rivera-Pagan, "The Plight of Puerto Rico: Coloniality, Diaspora, and Decolonial Resistance." Paper delivered at the Herencia Lecture, Princeton Theological Seminary, April 13, 2018.

inclusion of Latin America—its languages and its religious, cultural, and intellectual histories—as critical for the future of this still-evolving field of study.

Every discourse—whether their enunciators admit it or not—is socially, culturally, and epistemologically located. In my case, I speak from a hybrid location, a liminal space. I have lived in the United States for the past eleven years. Prior to that, I was a pastor and a professor in Brazil, the country where I have spent more than half of my life. Although I hold a doctoral degree from a renowned North American seminary, most of my education took place before I ever set a foot outside of Brazil.

The Christianity that I experienced in my early life was for the most part evangelical and, in many ways, experientially pentecostal. Both my parents were first-generation Baptist converts from Catholicism. My father, a former Catholic who also practiced Kardecist Spiritism and Candomblé, had a dramatic conversion experience, after which he became a lay preacher, with little formal education. Raised in such a religious environment, in my early twenties I went to seminary, got a degree in theology, and was ordained a Baptist minister in Brazil. I served in that capacity for ten years in multiple congregations. This kind of Christianity loomed prominently in my early life. Although I've been removed from it in the past decade, that kind of spirituality left indelible marks in my formation, having put me in a privileged position to interact with many religious actors in my current study of Latin American Christianities.

Along with the charismatic Christianity I experienced in my early years, I also grew up in an environment of economic impoverishment, under an authoritarian regime supported by the United States. This, more than any theological or philosophical language I came to learn later as a graduate student, has placed an interest in how faith operates in environments profoundly marked by social injustice at the center of my concerns.[4]

For many Latin American intellectual traditions, praxis is at the root of theorizing. Some of the first generation of liberation theologians had been pastors or priests in impoverished communities. Such a pastoral praxis informed their theological perspectives. But while many in that first generation did not themselves come from among the poor and oppressed,

---

4. I use social injustice to refer broadly to varied forms of structural injustices based on class, race, gender, and sexuality. Nancy Fraser talks about two kinds of social justice claims, one based on redistributive criteria, focusing on the distribution of resources and goods, and the other based on the "politics of recognition." Both dimensions are part of my use of the term here. See Nancy Fraser, "Social Justice in the Age of Identity Politics: Redistribution, Recognition, and Participation," in Larry Ray and Andrew Sayer, eds., *Culture and Economy after the Cultural Turn* (London: Sage Publications, 1999), 25–52.

subsequent generations who have expanded the horizons of Latin American liberation theology, adding new frameworks for theologizing in Latin America, are replete with voices that represent the "irruption of the poor," which Gustavo Gutiérrez prophesized about more thoroughly.[5] These are women, queer, black, brown, mestiza, migrant thinkers, many of whom are originally from economically impoverished communities and from a variety of Christian traditions, who are at the cutting edge of Latin American scholarship on religion and theology.

Writing as an immigrant in the United States who remains umbilically connected to his origins in an impoverished neighborhood of Salvador, Bahia, the "black Rome"—the city's nickname owing to the centrality of Afro-Brazilian culture and religion in its life—I deeply relate to the words of Edmund Chia when he says, "My bias, therefore, is toward those on the margins."[6]

World Christianity and the Postcolonial World

World Christianity, as a field of study, has helped in the past few decades to move the study of Christianity beyond the captivity of Eurocentric modernity/coloniality. It portrays Christianity as a world religion that has taken root in six continents and as a religion shaped by diverse local cultures and multidirectional, transnational interactions. Such a portrait allows world Christianity scholars to make the claim that "Christianity is as African as it is European, as Asian as it is North American and so on."[7] This field of study aggregates a number of disciplines and approaches. In its initial years, much emphasis was placed on the popularized image of the shift in the epicenter of world Christianity from the global North to the global South. Lately, thanks to the work of historians such as Klaus Koschorke, many in the field have shifted their attention to the polycentric structures and transcontinental links in the world Christian movement.[8] This transnational historiography advanced primarily by the Munich School emphasizes the need to take both transnational and transcontinental connections seriously in the development of a global history of

---

5. Gustavo Gutiérrez, *A Theology of Liberation*, 15th Anniversary Edition (Maryknoll, NY: Orbis Books, 1988), xxi.
6. Edmund Kee-Fook Chia, "Ecumenical Pilgrimage toward World Christianity," *Theological Studies* 76, no. 3 (2015): 503–30, at 504.
7. Sebastian Kim and Kirsteen Kim, *Christianity as a World Religion: An Introduction*, 2nd ed. (London: Bloomsbury Academic, 2016), Kindle edition.
8. Klaus Koschorke, "Transcontinental Links, Enlarged Maps, and Polycentric Structures in the History of World Christianity," *Journal of World Christianity* 6, no. 1 (2016): 28–56.

Christianity and the imperative of situating distinctive regional, cultural, and denominational structures into the broader narrative of a Christianity that has been a polycentric movement from its inception.

The turn to Christianity's transnational links and polycentric structures is undoubtedly a welcome counterpart to the initial emphasis on the indigeneity of world Christianity in the field. In his keynote address to the first World Christianity Conference at Princeton Theological Seminary,[9] Dale Irvin rightly pointed out that "the study of world Christianity needs to be more than the study of various local expressions of Christianity around the world."[10] World Christianity, he argued, must also be concerned with comparisons, connections, "networks of exchanges," and the "'panlocal' dimensions of our world."[11] While such an expanded approach seems crucial for the advance of the field, it should not take place at the expense of the persistent need to continue excavating hidden and buried local Christian experiences, since the task of retrieving local agency is still far from complete. In other words, concerns with broader network exchanges, connections, and links should not be turned into "the next phase" in the development of the field at the expense of a continuous concern with indigeneity and indigenous agency, considering the long oversight of the latter in Western scholarship of Christianity. There is room and need for both elements, and in our way forward these tasks should go hand in hand, rather than represent sequential stages in the development of the field. Moreover, priority must still be given to marginalized, long-ignored, and suppressed voices, narratives, and experiences in the history of the world Christian movement.

One of the existing tensions in the label "world Christianity," as scholars such as Dale Irvin, Jacob Olupona, and Thomas Thangaraj have noted, resides exactly in the way one defines "world."[12] While there is a catho-

---

9. "Currents, Perspectives, and Methodologies in World Christianity," An International, Interdisciplinary Conference organized by The World Christianity and History of Religions Program, Department of History & Ecumenics, Princeton Theological Seminary, NJ, January 18–20, 2018.

10. Dale T. Irvin, "World Christianity: A Genealogy," *Journal of World Christianity* 9, no. 1 (2019): 5–22, at 5–6.

11. Ibid., 6. Irvin's reference to the "'panlocal' dimensions of our world" is borrowed from Roland Robertson. See Roland Robertson, "The Conceptual Promise of Glocalization: Commonality and Diversity," *Art-e-fact* 4 (2004), http://artefact.mi2.hr/_a04/lang_en/theory_robertson_en.htm.

12. See Thomas Thangaraj, "What in the World Is World Christianity?," http://www.bu.edu/cgcm/annual-theme/what-in-the-world-is-world-christianity/ (cited in Irvin, *World Christianity: A Genealogy*, 6); and Jacob Olupona, "World Christianity: An Agenda for the Twenty-First Century," *Journal of World Christianity* 9, no. 1 (2019): 23–33, at 24. Further discussion of the expression can be found in Paul Kollman,

licity implied in the term "world Christianity," the inclusivity meant by the use of the word "world" has often existed in tension with hegemonic Christian attempts to limit the scope and extent of the Christian community. As Olupona notes, a similar debate has taken place in connection with the use of the expression "world religions." In that debate, the term "world" does not actually imply inclusivity. It has rather been turned into a selective and hierarchical qualifier, applied to a higher class of religions in a way that stigmatizes or infers a level of inferiority to African and other non-Western indigenous religions.[13] Greater awareness about who is defining "world" in world Christianity and how it is defined is of critical importance. Thus, while the need to pay attention to transnational and transregional networks is warranted, the insistence on hearing voices that have been silenced for too long must persist.

To illustrate this point, let us consider the assertion of the African credentials of Christianity and the African emphasis on Christianity's indigeneity. The conversation about the "indigenous principle" in world Christianity is often traced back to Andrew Walls's essays in the late 1970s and early 1980s—and he indeed deserves considerable credit for the key role he played in the creation of a vocabulary that became crucial for the development of world Christianity studies. However, when one digs a little deeper to understand the origins of the emphasis on the indigeneity of African Christianity, one realizes that debates about the indigenous credentials of African Christianity have been taking place at least since the 1950s.[14]

In one of his essays on the translatability of the Christian faith, Kwame Bediako recalled how such conversations loomed over a 1965 conference in Accra, Ghana, convened under the auspices of the International African Institute.[15] As Bediako notes, that conference still privileged the emphasis on missionary transmission that made Christianity a foreign

---

"Understanding the World-Christian Turn in the History of Christianity and Theology," *Theology Today* 71, no. 2 (2014): 164–77.

13. Olupona, "World Christianity: An Agenda." See also Jacob K. Olupona and Terry Rey, eds., *Òrìṣà Devotion as World Religion: The Globalization of Yorùbá Religious Culture* (Madison, WI: University of Wisconsin Press, 2008). In this collection of essays, the editors subvert the hierarchization of the concept of "world religions," applying it to describe a border-crossing indigenous tradition, which, given its worldwide presence, should be understood as a "world religion."

14. Kwame Bediako, *Christianity in Africa: The Renewal of a Non-Western Religion* (Maryknoll, NY: Orbis Books, 1995), 110ff.

15. Ibid., 110. The proceedings of the conference appeared later in the edited volume *Christianity in Tropical Africa: Studies Presented and Discussed at the Seventh International African Seminar, University of Ghana, April 1965*, ed. C. G. Baeta (London: Oxford University Press, 1968).

element in Africa, thus reflecting the "general hesitancy [on the part of the Western missionary movement] about ascribing to Africa's pre-Christian religious traditions and socio-cultural forms of life any substantial theological status."[16] However, in that same essay, Bediako situates the conference in the golden age of African nationalism, a time when, in his own words, "African Christian intellectuals were themselves beginning to make serious efforts to come to terms with the Christian presence in African life."[17] This is an important fact that cannot be overlooked. At least part of the backdrop that led African Christian scholars to turn their attention to the indigeneity of African Christianity was a broader conversation taking place in postcolonial Africa, in which African intellectuals and political leaders pondered Africa's place and identity in a new world order—a postcolonial world order still in the making. The issue of nationality and the place of African Christianity in the growing self-affirmation of the new African nations vis-à-vis the former colonizing powers and a neocolonizing world order was of enormous significance. Similar conversations took place among Asian and Latin American Christians.[18]

These conversations help us understand, for instance, the importance of examining the broader social history of postcolonial Africa, Asia, and Latin America when interrogating the formation of the field of study we came to call world Christianity. Likewise, the rise of world Christianity as a field of studies cannot be fully considered without reference to the rise of the postcolonial world and the diverse local and regional experiences that formed it. The roots of this field, therefore, can only be fully understood if examined in relation to the broader context of the *Zeitgeist* that impacted other sectors of society and scholarship in Africa, Asia,

---

16. Bediako, *Christianity in Africa*, 111.
17. Ibid., 113.
18. The same kind of sentiment seen among African Christians could also be found among young Brazilian Protestants who in the mid-1950s started reflecting on the place of the Brazilian churches in the construction of the nation. As I have shown elsewhere, this interest in affirming the Protestant participation in nation-building processes in Latin America arose from a growing concern with establishing the "Latin-Americaness" of the Protestant churches. See Raimundo C. Barreto, "Pistas Sobre o Pensamento Ético-Social Protestante Latino-Americano," *Reflexus: Revista de Teologia e Ciências da Religião* 9, no. 18 (2017): 307–36. Similar concerns were also found among Asian Christians during the struggle for independence and nation-formation in Asia. As he reflected on the fiftieth anniversary of the 1938 World Missionary Conference in Tambaram, M. M. Thomas affirmed: "Tambaram 1938 took place at a time when the churches of Asia were awakening to the need of a selfhood oriented to witnessing to Jesus Christ among Asian peoples who were themselves struggling for self-identity and for the renaissance of their nations in the world of nations." See M. M. Thomas, "An Assessment of Tambaram's Contribution to the Search of the Asian Churches for an Authentic Selfhood," *International Review of Mission* 77, no. 307 (1988): 390–97, at 390.

and Latin America. As I have discussed elsewhere, some of the concerns that led to the formation of the field of world Christianity have parallels with ideas that also influenced the formation of the Third World movement.[19] Among those influences, one must include the "cultural turn" in the humanities and the social sciences,[20] and, more recently, what Boaventura de Sousa Santos has called "the coming of age of epistemologies of the South."[21] Locating world Christianity discourse in conversation with the backdrop of the postcolonial world and these other social, economic, political, and philosophical movements of the time, particularly in what became known as "the Third World," and later "the global South,"[22] is critical for understanding why a fuller engagement of Latin American scholarship on Christianity and, more broadly, on religion, is so urgently needed in the field of world Christianity.

Engaging Latin American History, Experiences, and Scholarship in World Christianity

Much of the recent work in world Christianity highlights the exponential growth of literature, degree programs, departments, chairs, and centers with a world Christian focus. In fact, world Christianity has become an academic home for an increasing number of scholars from different disciplines—history, theology, Bible, and the social sciences. Such expansion of the field, though, is not uniformly distributed. With a few exceptions,

---

19. See Raimundo Barreto, "The Epistemological Turn in World Christianity: Engaging Decoloniality in Latin American and Caribbean Christian Discourses," *Journal of World Christianity* 9, no. 1 (2019): 48–60.

20. See, for instance, Kate Nash, "The 'Cultural Turn' in Social Theory: Towards a Theory of Cultural Politics," *Sociology* 35, no. 1 (2001): 77–92. Stephanie Lawson has defined the cultural turn as "a diffuse intellectual movement within the humanities and social sciences challenging orthodoxies concerning the possibility of objective, universal knowledge." The continuous influence of this movement, as she states, "is evident in the extent to which many contemporary studies are described not merely in terms of conventional disciplines such as history, geography, sociology or politics, but cultural history, cultural geography, cultural sociology and cultural politics, along with 'cultural' studies and the closely related field of 'cultural theory.'" See Stephanie Lawson, *Culture and Context in World Politics* (London: Palgrave Macmillan, 2006), 18. For the impact of this cultural turn upon the area of Latin American studies, see Catherine Walsh, "The Politics of Naming: (Inter)Cultural Studies in De-colonial Code," *Cultural Studies* 26, no. 1 (2012): 108–25. The impact of the cultural turn on Latin American studies has been felt in both the study of Latin American Christianity and Latin American theology.

21. Boaventura de Sousa Santos, *The End of the Cognitive Empire: The Coming of Age of Epistemologies of the South* (Durham, NC: Duke University Press, 2018).

22. For a history and connection of these two terms, see Vinay Prashad, *The Poorer Nations: A Possible History of the Global South* (New York: Verso, 2014).

much of this growth is concentrated in the North Atlantic. To the best of my knowledge, there is no chair, department, or center of world Christianity in Latin America. The absolute majority of Latin American scholars who identify world Christianity as their academic home are based in North American or European educational or research institutions.

This disconnect is exacerbated when one considers the language barrier. Many scholars in Latin America have never come across the methodological and theoretical discussions in this burgeoning world Christianity literature—mostly available in English and German (usually sold at prohibitive prices), with very few existing translations into Spanish and Portuguese. Speaking as a Lusophone Brazilian, I am not aware, for example, that any of the books written by Andrew Walls, Lamin Sanneh, and Kwame Bediako—just to mention three of the founding scholars of the field—have ever been translated into Portuguese.[23] Similarly, considering that most studies of local Christian experiences in Latin America are written in Spanish or Portuguese—many of which are never translated into English—a large number of scholars who identify world Christianity as their academic home and use English as their main research language are not aware of much of the research on Christianity (and, more broadly, on religion) done in Latin America.

A few initiatives have tried to remedy the problem. The best known are the translations of (1) the volume *A History of Christianity in Asia, Africa, and Latin America, 1450–1900: A Documentary Sourcebook*, edited by Klaus Koschorke, Frieder Ludwig, and Mariano Delgado, into Spanish; and (2) the first volume of Dale Irvin and Scott Sunquist's *History of the World Christian Movement* into Portuguese.[24] I myself am involved in a couple of incipient initiatives aimed at closing this gap. The first one is a six-volume bilingual series on world Christianity and public religion published in English by Fortress Press and in Portuguese by Editora Unida. One of the goals of this series is to create a joint publishing space for scholars who work primarily in Portuguese and Spanish to publish their work alongside world Christianity scholars from other regions of the world who pri-

---

23. To the best of my knowledge, on top of a couple of articles written by Klaus Koschorke, only the first volume of *History of the World Christian Movement*, written by Dale Irvin and Scott Sunquist, is available in Portuguese, from among all the foundational literature in the field of world Christianity.

24. Klaus Koschorke, Frieder Ludwig, and Mariano Delgado, eds., *A History of Christianity in Asia, Africa, and Latin America, 1450–1900: A Documentary Sourcebook* (Grand Rapids, MI: Eerdmans, 2007); and Dale T. Irvin and Scott W. Sunquist, *History of the World Christian Movement, Volume 1: Earliest Christianity to 1453* (Maryknoll, NY: Orbis Books, 2001).

marily publish in English and other languages.[25] The Portuguese versions of these volume are, to my knowledge, the first book-length literature in Portuguese whose titles include the phrase "cristianismo mundial"—world Christianity.

Another initiative underway, still in negotiation with publishers, is the translation into English of select works on Brazilian Christianity currently available only in Portuguese. The language challenges I just described, which can also be applied to other parts of the world, show how significant are the efforts to connect the guilds of world Christianity in the Anglophone academy and the equally booming scholarship on religion—and more particularly on Christianity—taking place in Latin American universities, seminaries, and research centers.

Latin America was Christianized in the context of a violent conquest.[26] After more than five centuries of troubled and creative intercultural interactions, the South American continent remains the home to the largest contingent of Catholic Christians in the world. It is also the birthplace of Latin American liberation theology, one of the most influential theological developments in the last quarter of the twentieth century, and a fertile soil for a rapidly growing pentecostalism. One of the results of its religious effervescency is the substantial expansion in the number of religious studies departments and theological schools in the region. The scholarship coming out of those religious studies departments and theological programs is significant, as is the profusion of associations of scholars of religion, research centers, scholarly events, and journals.[27] In Brazil alone, there are at least twenty-seven research-oriented religious studies pro-

---

25. The series also includes scholars who primarily work in other languages besides English, Portuguese, and Spanish. The first volume of the series featured the work of a scholar who publishes mostly in German. The second volume not only includes scholarship that involves research done in African native languages but also scholars whose primary working languages are Portuguese, Spanish, and Italian. The third volume includes the work of a Chinese scholar who has primarily published in Chinese. All these volumes are simultaneously published in English and Portuguese. See Raimundo Barreto, Ronaldo Cavalcante, and Wanderley P. da Rosa, eds., *World Christianity as Public Religion* (World Christianity and Public Religion; Minneapolis, MN: Augsburg Fortress Press, 2017); Afe Adogame, Raimundo Barreto, and Wanderley P. da Rosa, eds., *Migration as Public Discourse in World Christianity* (Minneapolis, MN: Fortress Press, 2019), and Raimundo Barreto, Moses Biney, and Kenneth Ngwa, eds., *World Christianity, Urbanization, and Identity* (Minneapolis, MN: Fortress Press, 2021).

26. See Luis Rivera-Pagan, *A Violent Evangelism: The Political and Religious Conquest of the Americas* (Louisville, KY: Westminster/John Knox Press, 1992).

27. For example, the Latin American collection of the Princeton Theological Seminary library has more than 1,400 of those Latin American journals, most of which are in Spanish and Portuguese. Yet, very few Anglophone scholars make use of it.

grams accredited by the Brazilian Ministry of Education.[28] On top of that, a vast array of academic books on religion in Portuguese and Spanish has flooded Latin American bookstores in recent years. Most publishers and libraries in the Anglophone world have not kept up with this emerging literature on religion and theology in Spanish and Portuguese.[29] In short, scholarship on religion in Latin America today is more widespread and decentralized than ever before. This recent flourishing of research and publication on religion and theology in Portuguese and Spanish has widened the gap I mentioned earlier between the scholarship on religion done in Latin America and the Anglophone world Christianity guilds.

Such a gap causes a qualitative loss to those who do not have access to more recent productions in the region. For example, it is common for courses on Latin American theologies in North Atlantic schools not to engage with second- and third-generation liberation theologies, or with the most recent turns in Latin American theological thinking. Likewise, descriptions of Latin American Christianity in introductory world Christianity textbooks tend to focus only on the shift from the religious monopoly of Catholic Christianity, which just a century ago represented 98.5 percent of the Latin American population, to a newly discovered reli-

---

28. This number does not include departments of history, anthropology, and sociology at different universities throughout the country that are also known for their research on religion; neither does it include a number of denominational seminaries and schools of theology around the country. Religious studies, or the "sciences of religion," is a sub-area of the social sciences. In such departments and programs—the equivalent to U.S.-based universities' departments of religious studies—religion is often studied vis-à-vis its "interrelations with the social, cultural, economic and political fabric." See Ana María Bidegain and Juan Jennis Sánchez Soler, "Religion in Latin America," *Hemisphere* 19, no. 1 (2010): 5–7, at 5. The academic study of religion in Latin America is highly interdisciplinary.

29. Here is a short list of recent books published in Brazil that could be of interest to students of world Christianity, and which are basically unknown to most of them: Angélica Tostes and Claudio Ribeiro, eds., *Religião, Diálogo e Múltiplas Pertenças* (São Paulo: Editora Annablume, 2019); Wanderley P. da Rosa and Reginaldo P. Braga Jr., eds., *Religião, Gênero, Violência e Direitos Humanos* (Vitória, Brazil: Editora Unida, 2019); Odja Barros and Paulo Nascimento, eds., *Vocação para a Igualdade: Fé e Diversidade Sexual na Igreja Batista do Pinheiro* (Brasília: Selo Novos Diálogos, 2019); Nelson Lellis, ed., *Política e Religião à Brasileira: Ensaios sobre Trajetórias Políticas de uma Sociedade Bravamente Religiosa* (São Paulo: Terceira Via, 2017); Ronaldo Cavalcante, *As Relações Entre Protestantismo e Modernidade: História e Memória* (São Paulo: Ed. Paulinas, 2017); Flavio Conrado and Clemir Fernandes, eds., *Reimaginar a Igreja no Brasil: 40 Vozes Evangélicas* (Rio de Janeiro, RJ: Novos Diálogos, 2017); and Wanderley P. Da Rosa and Oswaldo L. Ribeiro, eds., *Religião e Sociedade (Pós) Secular* (Santo Andre, SP: Editora Unida/Editora Academia Cristã, 2014). This short list represents just a drop in the ocean of publications of interest for world Christianity scholars recently made available in Portuguese (comprised of works I had the opportunity to be involved with in some capacity), which are basically unknown in English-speaking circles.

gious plurality in the region, exemplified by the exponential growth of Latin American evangelical and pentecostal churches.[30] Much less can be found in those resources, for instance, on indigenous and African-derived religions and their impact on Christianity or in terms of a more thorough history of the region's religious plurality. Students being introduced to Latin American Christianity through world Christianity introductory books in English, therefore, often miss out on the discussions about the revitalization of indigenous and African-derived traditions, crucial to understanding not only the region's religious past but also the present religious plurality and the various shapes and forms Christianity has taken in Latin America.[31]

Whereas the language barrier partially explains the limited interaction between scholars self-identified with the field of world Christianity and some of the recent developments in Latin American scholarship on religion, other factors also merit consideration. Judging by participation in world Christianity guilds and publication in world Christianity journals, monograph series, and edited volumes, the number of Latin American scholars of religion who identify world Christianity as their academic home is small indeed.[32] Thus, a large amount of the religious studies and theology literature that focuses on Latin America is produced by scholars who, for the most part, have not been involved in the theorizing of world Christianity. Consequently, fuller integration of Latin America into world Christianity scholarship demands more consistent engagement on the part of the world Christianity guilds and networks with the academic

---

30. See, for instance, Douglas Jacobsen, *The World's Christians: Who They Are, Where They Are, and How They Got There* (Oxford: Wiley-Blackwell, 2011), and Charles E. Farhadian, ed., *Introducing World Christianity* (West Sussex, UK: Wiley-Blackwell, 2012).

31. While my critique focuses mostly on the introductory textbooks to world Christianity, some books on these topics are available in English, such as Guillermo Cook, ed., *Crosscurrents in Indigenous Spiritualities: Interface of Maya, Catholic and Protestant Worldviews* (New York: Brill, 1997); Edward L. Cleary and Timothy J. Steigenga, eds., *Resurgent Voices in Latin America: Indigenous Peoples, Political Mobilization, and Religious Change* (New Brunswick, NJ: Rutgers University Press, 2004); Mark Z. Christensen, ed., *Translated Christianities: Nahuatl and Maya Religious Texts* (University Park, PA: Pennsylvania State University Press, 2014); Michel Androos, ed., *The Church and Indigenous Peoples in the Americas: In Between Reconciliation and Decolonization* (Eugene, OR: Wipf & Stock, 2019); and Raimundo C. Barreto and Roberto Sirvent, eds., *Decolonial Christianities: Latinx and Latin American Perspectives* (New Approaches to Religion and Power; New York: Palgrave MacMillan, 2019).

32. Some of the prominent Latin American or Latin Americanist scholars in world Christianity guilds include Ana María Bidegain, Daniel Ramirez, Carlos Cardoza-Orlandi, Luis Rivera-Pagán, Justo González, Paul Freston, Todd Hartch, Virginia Garrard-Burnett, Gastón Espinosa, Elaine Padilla, Philip Wingeier-Rayo, and Michel Androos.

study of religion in Latin America. Such a move would call for world Christianity scholars to bridge across different languages, academic disciplines, and other Latin American discourses. It is also important that scholars who identify world Christianity as their field of study engage more consistently with the area of Latin American studies to expand their theoretical and methodological tool kit in direct interaction with the scholarship produced in the region.

To exemplify how this kind of engagement can happen, I will turn to two important intellectual developments in Latin American academic circles that have impacted a variety of disciplines. These developments are the cultural and epistemological turns in Latin American studies, and their respective emphases on interculturality and decoloniality.

Engaging Latin American Intercultural and Decolonial Studies

The history of Christianity in Latin America cannot be disconnected from the violent European invasion of the world of Abya Yala, the Kuna name used by many Latin American indigenous peoples to refer to the region. Vitalino Similox Salazar, a K'aqchiquel Maya ecumenical leader, has referred to that encounter as "the invasion of Christianity into the world of the Mayas."[33] Others have described the first encounter of the indigenous peoples with Christianity as a "cultural genocide."[34]

The rise of indigenous voices on the eve of the commemorations of the five-hundredth anniversary of the "first evangelization" at a time when indigenous lives and lands continued to be systematically violated throughout Latin America led many to realize that the genocide against the indigenous peoples in the region was still an ongoing event. The resurgence of indigenous voices and faces in public discourse and the articulation of theological narratives in their own voices confronted many Latin American Christians with the need to reassess the meaning of Christian mission and evangelization. As part of this process, cultural differences and racial discrimination and injustice began to get more attention among scholars of Latin American Christianity. Concomitantly, indigenous movements in countries like Mexico, Guatemala, Ecuador, and Bolivia gained steam, advancing the call for these respective states' full acknowledgment of indigenous cultures and languages, and for the

---

33. Vitalino Similox Salazar, "The Invasion of Christianity into the World of the Mayas," in Guillermo Cook, ed., *Crosscurrents in Indigenous Spirituality: Interface of Maya, Catholic and Protestant Worldviews* (Leiden: Brill, 1997), 35.

34. See Guillermo Cook, "Introduction: Brief History of the Maya Peoples," in Cook, *Crosscurrents in Indigenous Spirituality*, 15.

protection of indigenous rights, through the articulation of multinational, multicultural, and multilingual national identities, in an effort to give full citizenship to people who, despite being the earliest settlers in those lands, have often been treated as second-class citizens. Such a political move was matched by the rise in academia of an intercultural discourse emphasizing respect, solidarity, conviviality, dialogue, and collaboration.[35]

To the struggle for the recognition of cultural rights and the right to self-determination on the part of indigenous nations that have survived five centuries of a genocidal devastation, we can add the struggle of other marginalized groups like women and black Latin Americans who also began to develop distinctive discourses as subjects (instead of only objects) in theological and religious studies in the region. The beginning of the 1990s, therefore, marked the moment when Latin American theological and religious studies, which in the previous three decades had focused mostly on socioeconomic and political liberation, began to pay greater attention to culture, adding critical cultural analysis to its theoretical and methodological tool kit. That is, for instance, the starting point of a Latin American intercultural theology that, on top of denouncing and resisting oppression, has also constructively advanced universally relevant values through dialogical initiatives centered on the engagement of formerly marginalized communities (in contrast to hegemonic top-down impositions of "the truth").[36] Beginning as an indigenous mobilization in response to the church's plans to commemorate five hundred years of evangelization, that anniversary became a turning point that placed the Latin American original peoples and other marginalized groups at center stage. Many learned at that time that Latin American indigenous peoples had long engaged Christianity on their own terms. Thereafter, important

---

35. Roberto E. Zwetsch, "Apresentação," in Roberto E. Zwetsch, ed., *Conviver: Ensaios Para uma Teologia Intercultural Latino-Americana* (S. Leopoldo, Brazil: Editora Sinodal/EST, 2015), 17–23, at18.

36. See Orlando Espín, "Intercultural Thought," in Orlando O. Espín and James B. Nickoloff, eds., *An Introductory Dictionary of Theology and Religious Studies* (Collegeville, MN: Liturgical Press, 2007), 639–45, at 643. Espín differentiates between universally valid and universally relevant truth claims. Behind his rationale is the assumption that truth seeking is a cultural and an intercultural process. In line with decolonial concerns with the colonial/modern universalization of local histories, he affirms that no single culture should be "considered as the definitive locus of truth." Instead, through intercultural dialogue contrasting truth claims can demonstrate universal relevance. By that Espín means that a "truth claim may be offered, from within a specific culture or group, to others who may find the claim to be useful, suggestive, or even true, thereby opening for and within the recipients perspectives (for example, questions and themes, answers and solutions, practices and approaches) that had hitherto remained closed, confused, or ignored."

conversations recentering indigenous peoples and cultures in Christian life and theology continued to take place.

One of the individuals who seems to have heard the indigenous concerns with the destruction of the environment—the great house—and the uprooting of their cultures is former Argentinian cardinal Jorge Mario Bergoglio, since 2013 Pope Francis, the first from the global South. In a visit to San Cristóbal de Las Casas, Mexico, in 2016, Pope Francis asked the indigenous people of Chiapas for forgiveness for the way they were treated and excluded by the church. Prior to that, in a visit to Bolivia, he likewise acknowledged the grave sins committed against the indigenous people in the name of God. In the past couple of years, Pope Francis's rhetoric has moved beyond the initial apologies to validating indigenous cultures as they are, calling for a truthful intercultural dialogue. As Michel Andraos notes:

> Francis advocates for a truly intercultural dialogue where Indigenous peoples, their traditions, wisdom, cultures, and spiritualities are the main partners. He concludes his address with a plea for Indigenous peoples to shape the culture of the church and contribute to building "a Church with an Amazonian face, a Church with a native face."[37]

Pope Francis's call for the indigenous peoples to help shape the church, and for the church to be a church with an Amazonian face, is a significant development in response to the call for a cultural conversion of Christianity to the indigenous other. The evolution of his intercultural turn can be seen more clearly in the Amazon Synod (2019). In his postsynodal exhortation, Francis makes clear that he has heard the cry of the Amazon peoples, expressing great concern not only with the environment but also with the preservation of the indigenous cultures, which he sees as being at serious risk. This Special Assembly of the Synod of Bishops for the Pan-Amazon Region (2019) interrogated the mission of the church vis-à-vis the peoples of the Amazon, calling for a new path of evangelization. Pope Francis responded to the synod's conclusions with the apostolic exhortation *Querida Amazonia* (2020), reinforcing the synod's radical call to "an integral conversion." Such conversion turns listening to the cry of the poor and the cry of earth into the starting point for a renewed pastoral journey.

---

37. Michel Andraos, "Introduction," in Michel Andraos, ed., *The Church and Indigenous Peoples in the Americas: In Between Reconciliation and Decolonization* (Studies in World Catholicism 7; Eugene, OR: Cascade Books, 2019). Kindle edition.

Pope Francis's response to the synod's findings openly acknowledges the colonial roots of the devastation of the Amazon environmental system and its diverse peoples and calls for a radical openness to interreligious and intercultural dialogue with the indigenous peoples, the river dwellers, and the *quilombola* communities. Whatever the limits of this exhortation, it offers a possible roadmap for a renewed relationship with the peoples and cultures of the Amazon.

Along with a section devoted to what he calls social and ecological dreams, Francis allocates an entire chapter of his exhortation to what he calls "cultural dreams." Advocating for the rights of the indigenous peoples, he stresses the need to care for their roots, calling for an intercultural dialogue that takes the indigenous roots seriously:

> Starting from our roots, let us sit around the common table, a place of conversation and of shared hopes. In this way our differences, which could seem like a barrier or a wall, can become a bridge. Identity and dialogue are not enemies. Our own cultural identity is strengthened and enriched as a result of dialogue with those unlike ourselves.[38]

Elsa Támez's critique only three decades ago that the church while managing to "be sensitive to the poor" had great difficulty being sensitive "to the other" highlights the significance of this shift.[39] It is worth noting that despite his position as the head of the Roman Catholic Church, Francis is a former Latin American pastor formed in the context of the theological debates taking place in the region since the early 1960s.[40] The value of these gestures and statements on the part of the first Latin American pope lies mainly in the fact that he has listened to the voices of the inhabitants of the Amazon and other indigenous peoples and engaged them as a primary source for theological reflection and pastoral praxis. He acknowledges their agency and sees no future for a church that does not listen to the voice of the poor—the true agents of salvation. Moved by the unending suffering of the indigenous peoples, and listening to what they

---

38. Pope Francis, "Post-Synodal Apostolic Exhortation 'Querida Amazonia,'" http://www.sinodoamazonico.va.

39. Elsa Támez, "The Bible and 500 Years of Conquest," in R. S. Sugirtharajah, ed., *Voices from the Margin: Interpreting the Bible in the Third World*, 25th Anniversary Edition (Maryknoll, NY: Orbis Books, 2016), 22–23.

40. Pope Francis's former professor, Argentinian theologian Juan Carlos Scannone, has written about the influence of the Argentine school known as "theology of the people" on Pope Francis, particularly evident in his apostolic exhortation *Evangelii gaudium*. See Juan Carlos Scannone, "Pope Francis and the Theology of the People," *Theological Studies* 77, no. 1 (2016): 118–35.

have been saying to the Christian churches, Francis seems to be willing to make a move until recently unthinkable: to propose an intercultural dialogue that takes indigenous cultures as a valid starting point. Such an intercultural engagement must occur on at least three levels—social, cultural, and ecological—and aims at a deep moral conversion. There is an ethical urgency in such a call for intercultural dialogue. From the perspective of the peoples of the Amazon, this call is a matter of life or death. Shouldn't these conversations also be placed at the center of world Christianity forums? This appeal to interculturality through Latin American lenses shows that conversations about indigeneity and Christianity have profound ethical implications. Such ethical emphasis is terribly needed in the field of world Christianity.[41]

The cultural turn in Latin American Christianity has been accompanied by an epistemological turn: the epistemic decolonial turn.[42] This was a theoretical move—a step further than the previous one—that shifted attention to the multiple loci of enunciation of those formerly neglected subjects, emphasizing not only their cultural and social location but also the validity and centrality of their knowledge and ways of knowing.[43] The decolonial turn has challenged homogenizing understandings of Latin America, elevating its *otros saberes*—that is, ways of knowing deeply connected to the experiences and histories of subaltern peoples—to the same level of knowledge normally deemed acceptable by academic and Chris-

---

41. For more on these ethical concerns, see Raimundo C. Barreto, "Human Rights Discourse and Interculturality: Insights from the Margins," *Reflexus: Revista de Teologia e Ciências da Religião* 12, no. 20 (2018): 543–65; and "Pistas Sobre o Pensamento Ético-Social Protestante Latino-Americano," *Reflexus: Revista de Teologia e Ciências da Religião* 12, no. 18 (2017): 307–36. A concern with the "ethical" has also been raised by other scholars in conversation with this field. Thomas Seat, an emerging world Christianity scholar, has discussed the centrality of translatability in the field on ethical grounds. Thomas Seat, "Why World Christianity's 'Translation Principle' Matters in Theory and in Practice, and Why We Should Rethink Translatability in Terms of Social Practice," a paper presented at the second World Christianity Conference at Princeton Theological Seminary, "Currents, Perspectives, and Methodologies in Ethnography for World Christianity," March 15–18, 2019, Princeton, NJ.

42. See Ramón Grosfoguel, "The Epistemic Decolonial Turn: Beyond Political-Economy Paradigms," *Cultural Studies* 21, no. 2–3 (2007): 211–23.

43. Ibid., 211. As Grosfoguel highlights, this move began to take place during a dialogue between the Latin American Subaltern Studies Group and the Asian Subaltern Studies Group in 1998. Some of the participants were concerned with the colonial epistemology of the U.S. Area Studies schema, which, while studying Latin American subjects, still privileged the Western theoretical apparatus. As such, it ended up producing knowledge about the subaltern, underestimating "ethnic/racial perspectives coming from the region." The decolonial turn that resulted from that split sought to transcend that Eurocentric epistemology, or decolonize it and its canon, by prioritizing the critique of Eurocentrism coming from "subalternized and silenced knowledges."

tian gatekeepers. As Nelson Maldonado-Torres rightly states, the decolonial turn "is about making visible the invisible and about analyzing the mechanisms that produce such invisibility or distorted visibility."[44] In other words, it examines and exposes the "mechanisms that not only determine *what* is theory but *who can and cannot* produce it," creating "spaces that serve as sites for producing theory, knowledge, and philosophy."[45]

In Latin America, scholars of religion not only interrogate the history of Christianity on the continent by means of advancing a new historiography, but they also problematize the meaning of "world" in world Christianity, suggesting the possibility of alternative worlds, which can help expand the horizons of world Christianity in fresh ways. The intellectual origins of the "decolonial turn" can be traced to the efforts of "Third World" networks such as CEHILA (Comisión para el Estudio de la Historia de las Iglesias en América Latina y el Caribe) and EATWOT (Ecumenical Association of Third World Theologians), which contributed to moving Christian narratives away from Eurocentric bias, reinventing Christianity on the basis of the diverse experiences and ways of knowing of "Third World" peoples. Enrique Dussel, whose contributions as a historian and a philosopher were important for the rise of decolonial theory, was one of the founders of CEHILA.[46] Founded in the early 1970s, CEHILA has unapologetically advanced Latin American historiographies, proposing a rereading of the history of the Latin American church that replaces a Eurocentric historiography with not only a situated history but one that privileges the Latin American impoverished peoples as interpreters of religious experience.

Dussel was also among the "Third World" Christian thinkers who contributed to the formation of EATWOT, a network of mostly global South theologians who embodied the idea of a "Christian Bandung" envisioned by people like Dom Hélder Câmara.[47] These regional and inter-

---

44. Nelson Maldonado-Torres, "On the Coloniality of Being," *Cultural Studies* 21, nos. 2–3 (2007): 262.
45. Ibid., 262, as cited in Raimundo Barreto and Roberto Sirvent, "Introduction," in Raimundo Barreto and Roberto Sirvent, eds., *Decolonial Christianities: Latinx and Latin American Perspectives* (Cham, Switzerland: Palgrave MacMillan, 2019), 1–21, at 6.
46. For more on these connections, see my essay "Decoloniality and Interculturality in World Christianity: A Latin American Perspective," in Dorottya Nagy and Martha Frederiks, eds., *The Study of World Christianity: Approaches, Methods and Cases* (Leiden: Brill, 2021).
47. This is a reference to the 1955 Afro-Asian conference in Bandung, Indonesia, which many credit as the birthplace of the Third World Movement. In the spirit of the League against Imperialism (Brussels, 1927), political leaders from Africa and Asia met to unite the hopes of the peoples of the "Third World" not only in their struggle against colonialism and imperialism but also in the formulation of an ideology that would help them to create an entirely new world. See Vijay Prashad, *The Darker Nations: A People's History of the Third World* (New Press People's History; New

regional articulations and their impact on Christian praxis and theology around the world need to be further explored as part of the intellectual genealogy of the field of world Christianity, to borrow a term recently used by Dale Irvin.[48]

While more consistent interaction with Latin American theoretical and methodological contributions to the study of religion, history, and theology is still needed in the field of world Christianity,[49] Latin American scholarship—directly and indirectly—has not been completely absent in the conceptualization of our field of study. In his important 2008 article "World Christianity: An Introduction,"[50] Dale Irvin engages with insights advanced by Latin American scholars such as Enrique Dussel, Anibal Quijano, Gloria Anzaldúa, and Walter Mignolo.[51] Irvin's argument that modernity has drawn "upon knowledge and power from peoples on all continents" resembles Dussel's understanding of transmodernity.[52] Turning to modernity's "cross-cultural and trans-regional practices," Irvin shows that "already at its inception" modernity contained "various forms of consciousness and perceptions that can be called global."[53] These insights are similarly present in some of the CEHILA's contributions to a Latin American historiography of Christianity.[54]

Likewise, in Irvin's important call for world Christianity to move beyond the old divide between "church history" and "mission history,"

York: New Press, 2007), Kindle edition. For more on Câmara and his idea of a Christian Bandung, see Raimundo C. Barreto, "Vatican II, Medellín, and Latin American Ecumenism: A Brazilian Protestant Perspective," *Journal of World Christianity* 9, no. 2 (2019): 187–202.

48. Irvin, "World Christianity: A Genealogy."

49. It is also my conviction that Latin American scholarship on Christianity can greatly benefit from more interaction with the burgeoning field of world Christianity. Because of that, as I have pointed out earlier, I have been involved in a series of initiatives to bridge the two, including through the organization of conferences on both ends, facilitating mutual translation and joint publications, and encouraging institutional partnerships and exchanges with scholars and institutions in Latin America, which, although not self-identifying with world Christianity, are doing things that can be considered equivalent and complementary to the most recent developments in the field of world Christianity.

50. Dale Irvin, "World Christianity: An Introduction," *Journal of World Christianity* 1, no. 1 (2008): 1–26.

51. He quotes several Latin American scholars in that essay, in particular Walter Mignolo and Enrique Dussel.

52. See, for instance, Enrique Dussel, "Transmodernity and Interculturality: An Interpretation from the Perspective of Philosophy of Liberation," *Transmodernity* 1, no. 3 (2012): 28–59.

53. Irvin, "World Christianity," 7.

54. See, for instance, Enrique Dussel, *The Invention of the Americas: Eclipse of "the Other" and the Myth of Modernity*, trans. Michael D. Barber (New York: Continuum, 1995).

he refers to Mignolo's analysis of the modern/colonial fissure, conceived as "border thinking."[55] Thus, one of the most influential essays in the field of world Christianity, although never noted for that reason, is enriched by a theoretical interaction with transmodern and decolonial theories originating among Latin American scholars. This is not the only case where that kind of interaction occurs. It suffices, though, to exemplify how the theorization of world Christianity can benefit from a more concerted interaction with the theoretical and methodological contributions coming from Latin America and its diaspora in terms of understanding both Christianity/religion and "the world."

Conclusion

While I have shown that world Christianity can benefit from adding Latin American scholarship to its theoretical and methodological tool kit, particularly the Latin American and Latinx contributions on interculturality and on decoloniality, some meaningful interaction has already taken place—even on the level of the theorization of the field. As a burgeoning field of study, world Christianity can greatly benefit from both the continuous inclusion of neglected histories and narratives (side by side with the transnational and transcontinental interactions that form them) and further engagement with theoretical and methodological insights and frameworks emerging among regional studies of religion/Christianity across the globe. While the histories of Latin American Christianity are increasingly finding their way into this rising field, there is a long path ahead as far as bringing more Latin American scholars, scholarship, and academic institutions into sustained conversation with the world Christianity guilds and networks.

---

55. Irvin, "World Christianity," 13ff. In footnote 28, Irvin says, "Historical analysis, cultural reflection, and social theory remain inadequate without attending to the presence of this border," using Mignolo's notion of the colonial difference to explain it, quoting directly from him as follows: "The colonial difference is the space where *local* histories inventing and implementing global designs meet *local* histories, the space in which global designs have to be adapted, adopted, rejected, integrated, or ignored." Here, Irvin is quoting from Walter Mignolo's *Local Histories/Global Designs: Coloniality, Subaltern Knowledges, and Border Thinking* (Princeton, NJ: Princeton University Press, 2000), ix. While he also engages W. E. B Dubois's notion of double consciousness and Gloria Anzaldúa's notion of *mestiza* consciousness, his argument that "distinctive natures of local histories give shape to a distinctive type of border thinking that follows along the modern/colonial divide" clearly draws on Mignolo's insights. While this is an important concept in Irvin's essay, it is not often picked up in the many references to his influential essay.

9

World Christianity in a Chinese Christian Perspective

PAN-CHIU LAI

In recent years, publications and academic programs under the name of "world Christianity" have mushroomed in the North Atlantic world. It is thus very natural to raise a question as to whether or not world Christianity should be seen as a discourse or field that derives its rationale and emphases in relation to North Atlantic academic structures or norms. Since I am not working in the North Atlantic, it is not appropriate for me to answer the question directly. Instead, I would like to explain why, as a Chinese Christian theologian working in Hong Kong, I adopted the discourse of world Christianity and to a certain extent participated in the promotion of this discourse or field. My explanation is based primarily on my observations and experiences of the Chinese explorations of the significance of world Christianity for the study of Christianity.

World Christianity and Chinese-Christian Identity

The relationship between Christianity and Chinese culture has troubled Christian missionaries and Chinese Christians since the introduction of Christianity into China. According to textual and archaeological evidence, some Syrian missionaries of the Church of the East reached China through the Silk Road in the seventh century, and the church they established was called *Jingjiao* (literally, "luminous religion"), which adopted certain Chinese expressions associated with Buddhism and Daoism in their theological discourses. It was not perceived to be a threat to the Chinese cultural tradition. In fact, some of its writings were even included in the Chinese Buddhist canon.[1] However, the contemporary popular

---

1. The texts can be found in Taishō Tripiṭaka (大正新脩大藏經) 54, no. 2143, available online: http://tripitaka.cbeta.org/T54n2143_001.

Chinese perception of Christianity was shaped mainly by Roman Catholicism and Protestantism, which arrived in China much later. Nowadays, Roman Catholicism and Protestantism are officially and conventionally recognized as two different religions—the former is called "Tiān zhǔ jiào" (天主教, literally "religion of the Lord of Heaven"), and the latter "Jī dū jiào" (基督教, literally "religion of Christ").

As both Roman Catholicism and Protestantism were perceived to be imported from overseas, they were often labeled pejoratively as "foreign religions" (yáng jiào 洋教), which literally means "religions from overseas." For the more educated Chinese, Christianity as a "Western" religion represented the spiritual core of Western culture, intertwined with Western imperialistic powers. In order to reduce the cultural resistance to Christianity, many missionaries, church leaders, and theologians endeavored to "indigenize" (běn sè huà 本色化) Christianity into China in various ways—liturgical, theological, organizational, artistic, architectural, musical, etc. These attempts at indigenization often assume that there is a "transcultural" gospel being wrapped in a Western jacket, which can and should be replaced by Chinese clothes in order to make the gospel acceptable to the Chinese. However, since the idea of indigenization tends to assume a stereotyped and stark contrast between Chinese culture and Western culture, efforts at indigenization may in turn reinforce the perception that Christianity as a religion is "Western" and thus needs to be indigenized. It is interesting to note that even though Christianity is recognized by some contemporary Confucian scholars as part of Chinese culture,[2] the Chinese government keeps on emphasizing that religions, including particularly the "foreign" religions such as Protestantism and Catholicism, should be "Sinicized" or "China-tized" (zhōng guó huà 中國化). These political slogans assume that Christianity remains a "foreign" or "Western" religion.

In 2001, I examined the issue concerning Christianity and Chinese culture with a largely historical and cultural perspective in an article published in *Studies in World Christianity*, one of the major journals promoting the study of Christianity in non-Western worlds.[3] After reviewing the development of Chinese Christian theology as well as the corresponding development of Chinese culture, I made references to works by Dale

---

2. For instance, Tu Wei-ming 杜維明, *Ti shi ruxue: rujia dang dai jia zhi de jiu ci dui hua* 體知儒學: 儒家當代價值的九次對話 [*Embodied Knowing: Conversations on the Modern Value of Confucianism*] (Hangzhou: Zhejiang University Press, 2012), 36.

3. See Pan-chiu Lai, "Development of Chinese Culture and Chinese Christian Theology," *Studies in World Christianity* 7, no. 2 (2001): 219–40; reprinted in Yang Huilin and Daniel H. N. Yeung, eds., *Sino-Christian Studies in China* (Newcastle: Cambridge Scholar Press, 2006), 280–303.

Irvin and Justo L. González to challenge the discourse of Christianity as a Western religion and the related program of indigenization. Their works highlight that, from a historical perspective, the Christian tradition has never been monolithic. In terms of numbers, European Christians in fact had never been the majority until the middle of the fourteenth century. Furthermore, since the 1970s, the number of Christians in Europe and America has decreased in relation to those outside these areas. Furthermore, today's Christianity is polycentric, with its centers of resources in North America and Western Europe and its centers of vitality, evangelistic zeal, and theological creativity in Asia, Africa, and Latin America.[4]

In the world Christianity approach, Christianity as a whole is considered a cross-cultural and multilingual movement, with significant diversity among the various forms of Christianity in different contexts. For this reason, it is possible to use the plural form ("world Christianities") in order to highlight the plurality or diversity among the various forms of Christianity. This pluralistic understanding of Christianity assumes that no particular form of Christianity should be considered as the ideal form of Christianity. Neither the "Western / Latin" form of Christianity, nor the "Eastern / Greek," nor the earliest Palestinian Christianity, nor the contemporary North Atlantic Christianity should be taken as the universal norm to be imposed on the other Christian churches. In other words, no particular representation of the Christian faith in a particular language, culture, or denominational tradition can be regarded necessarily superior to the other representations in other languages, cultures, or denominational traditions.

For me, this understanding of Christianity can clarify the issue of whether becoming a Christian means the adoption of Western culture or betrayal of Chinese culture and provides a theoretical basis for the integration of the Chinese cultural and Christian religious identities.[5] I further strengthen this understanding of Christianity with theoretical support from the Chinese cultural tradition, especially Confucianism. I argue that the transmission of the tradition concerns primarily the "heart-mind" (心 xin) instead of a particular text or doctrinal formula articulated in a particular language. This can offer a fruitful approach to understanding the continuity and ecumenicity of the Christian tradition.[6]

---

4. Ibid., 235; cf. Dale Irvin, *Christian Histories, Christian Traditioning* (Maryknoll, NY: Orbis Books, 1998), 86–99, 104, 106–22; Justo L. González, "The Changing Geography of Church History," in Gary Macy, ed., *Theology and the New Histories* (Maryknoll, NY: Orbis Books, 1998), 23–32, here 26–28.

5. Pan-chiu Lai, "Inheriting the Chinese and Christian Traditions in Global Context: A Confucian-Protestant Perspective," *Religion & Theology* 10, no. 1 (2003): 1–23.

6. Pan-chiu Lai, "Confucian Understanding of Humanity and Rationality in

Corresponding to this Chinese understanding of the transmission of "heart-mind" is the Christian affirmation of the Holy Spirit. The Holy Spirit is often associated with the preservation of Christian unity (Eph 4:1–6). Yet, according to the Book of Acts, at Pentecost, it is also the Holy Spirit who caused people to hear the disciples speaking to them in their own respective languages or dialects, rather than in just one particular language or dialect (Acts 2:1–11). Furthermore, the Holy Spirit dispersed the disciples to different places and thus pluralized the Christian churches in geographical, linguistic, racial, and cultural terms. The unity or ecumenicity of Christianity to be brought forth by the Holy Spirit should thus assume and preserve rather than negate the diversity among the Christian communities. The transmission of the Christian tradition should be primarily about the Spirit of the tradition rather than a particular text or historical form of Christianity. The Christian churches in various locations can thus articulate their theologies according to their own respective cultures, spiritual traditions, and socio-political contexts, and may share their theological and spiritual heritages with their fellow Christians from some other contexts through open and friendly theological dialogue, on equal footing.[7]

To summarize, the discourse concerning "world Christianity" highlights the conceptual difference between "world Christianity" and "Western Christianity," or that between "Christianity as a world religion" and "Christianity as a Western religion." On the one hand, this challenges the adequacy of the conventional assumption concerning Christianity as a Western religion. On the other, it provides a more adequate understanding of Christianity that can affirm the compatibility of the cultural identity and the religious identity of Chinese Christians.

World Christianity and Sino-Christian Theology

The question concerning Christianity and the relationship between Chinese and Western cultures appeared in an entirely different way after the implementation of the Chinese government policy of reform and opening-up. During the 1980s, there was a "culture fever" (文化熱 wén huà rè) in Mainland China. Many Chinese intellectuals endeavored

---

Conversation: A Chinese Christian Perspective," in Markus Mühling et al., eds., *Rationality in Conversation: Philosophical and Theological Perspectives* (Leipzig: Evangelische Verlagsanstalt, 2016), 321–35, here 346.

7. Pan-chiu Lai, "Sino-Theology, Bible and the Christian Tradition," *Studies in World Christianity* 12, no. 3 (2006): 266–81; reprinted in Pan-chiu Lai and Jason Lam, eds., *Sino-Christian Theology: A Theological Qua Cultural Movement in Contemporary China* (Frankfurt-am-Main: Peter Lang, 2010), 161–77.

to reflect critically on Chinese culture and became enthusiastic in introducing Western intellectual ideas into China. Some of these intellectuals became attracted to Christianity, especially the role of Christianity in Western culture, and even looked to it as a sort of salvation or cure to the illness of Chinese culture. A small number of them were called "cultural Christians" for they identified themselves as Christians without any church affiliation.[8] In addition to their efforts in translating many Western theological texts into Chinese, they also proposed a new theological agenda—called Sino-Christian theology or simply Sino-theology (漢語神學 hàn yǔ shén xué)—in order to differentiate it from the aforementioned indigenous theology promoted by the Chinese churches.[9]

The term "Sino-theology," which means literally "Han-language theology" or "Chinese language theology," highlights the role of language, as opposed to the notions of culture, ethnicity, or nationality associated with the term "Chinese" and implied by the concepts of indigenous theology (本色神學 běn sè shén xué), Chinese theology (華人神學 huá rén shén xué), or China theology (中國神學 zhōng guó shén xué), respectively. Whereas indigenous theology assumes a positive and yet instrumentalist view of Chinese culture, some advocates of Sino-theology take a rather critical stand on the Chinese cultural tradition.[10] Given its emphasis on the role of language in theology, Sino-theology pays particular attention to its relationship with the theologies of other languages, especially the Western languages. Since many of the advocates of Sino-theology are involved in the translation of Western theological texts into Chinese, a natural question arises: Is Sino-theology or theology in the Chinese language merely Chinese translation of Western theology?[11]

It is generally acknowledged that the development of Chinese theology has been influenced by various Western theologies rather than the other way round. However, a close scrutiny of the relevant theological lit-

---

8. Fredrik Fällman, *Salvation and Modernity: Intellectuals and Faith in Contemporary China*, rev. ed. (Lanham, MD: University Press of America, 2008).

9. See Lai and Lam, *Sino-Christian Theology*; Naomi Thurston, *Studying Christianity in China: Constructions of an Emerging Discourse* (Leiden: Brill, 2018).

10. See further Liu Xiaofeng, "Sino-Christian Theology in the Modern Context," in Huilin and Yeung, *Sino-Christian Studies in China*, 52–89.

11. This question was discussed at an international conference, "Translation and Reception: Encounter of Christianity and Chinese Culture," organized by China-Zentrum e. V. (Sankt Augustin, Germany) and the Institute of Sino-Christian Studies (Hong Kong), held at the European Academy in Berlin, December 6–9, 2001. The conference papers were published together as Daniel H. N. Yeung 楊熙楠 and Paul Rabbe 雷保德, eds., *Fān yì yǔ xī nà: dà gōng shén xué yǔ hàn yǔ shén xué* 翻譯與吸納: 大公神學與漢語神學 [*Translation and Adoption: Ecumenical Theology and Christian Theology in Chinese*] (Hong Kong: Institute of Sino-Christian Studies, 2004).

erature translated or written in Chinese during the twentieth century may show that it is not a zero-sum game between the translation of Western theological works into Chinese and the articulation of original Chinese theologies. In fact, instead of passively receiving what was exported from the West, the Chinese theologians translated the Western works selectively and creatively according to their understanding of the Chinese context, and the translated works in turn inspired some original Chinese theological works. In other words, Chinese theology has its own potential to make distinctive contributions to international theological discourse. One may expect that healthy interactive exchanges between Chinese and Western theologies can enrich the ecumenicity of the Christian tradition and reinforce the idea of world Christianity.[12]

With this vision, I have explored various ways to contribute to the global development of Christian theology. Just as I have shared my strategy of teaching global theology with my colleagues in the North Atlantic context,[13] I would now like to focus on my experience of theological research.

In my experience, some of the recent theological developments in the North Atlantic region are particularly receptive to theological contributions beyond the region, especially as this relates to issues of religious plurality and other global public issues. These are precisely the areas in which Chinese Christian theologians can make distinctive contributions, because they make use of the Chinese cultural, philosophical, and religious heritage in exploring theology of religions, interreligious dialogue, comparative theology, etc.[14] Due to their particular socio-political context, Chinese Christian theologians can also make distinctive contributions to

---

12. See Pan-chiu Lai, "Theological Translation and Transmission between China and the West," *Asia Journal of Theology* 20, no. 2 (October 2006): 285–304; for a revised and updated version, see Pan-chiu Lai, "Reconsidering Theological Exchange between China and the West," *International Journal for the Study of the Christian Church* 19, nos. 2–3 (2019): 103–9.

13. See Pan-chiu Lai, "Teaching Global Theology with Local Resources: A Chinese Theologian's Strategies," in Kwok Pui-lan, Cecilia Ganzaléz-Andrieu, and Dwight N. Hopkins, eds., *Teaching Global Theologies: Power and Praxis* (Waco, TX: Baylor University Press, 2015), 91–104, with notes on 190–94.

14. My recent contributions include Pan-chiu Lai, "Religious Diversity and Public Space in China: A Reconsideration of the Christian Doctrine of Salvation," in Simone Sinn and Tong Wing Sze, eds., *Interactive Pluralism in Asia: Religious Life and Public Space* (Leipzig: Evangelische Verlagsanstalt, 2016), 43–58; "Tillich's Concept of Ultimate Concern and Buddhist-Christian Dialogue," in Ka-fu Keith Chan and Yau-nang William Ng, eds., *Paul Tillich and Asian Religions* (Berlin: de Gruyter, 2017), 47–67; and "Karl Barth and Universal Salvation: A Mahayana Buddhist Perspective," in Christian T. Collins Winn and Martha Moore-Keish, eds., *Karl Barth and Comparative Theology* (New York: Fordham University Press, 2019), 85–104.

the discussions in such areas as political theology, church and state relationship, ecological theology and public theology.[15]

In short, rather than contributing to the prevailing understanding of Christianity as a Western religion, the discourse of world Christianity can better support theological exchanges on equal footing among theologians from different parts of the world. This may eventually benefit theological responses from the Christian churches in China as well as in the North Atlantic to pressing global issues of public concern.

World Christianity and Christian Studies in China

The world Christianity discourse is already receiving attention in the Chinese-speaking world. The Chinese translation of Philip Jenkins's *The Next Christendom* was published in 2003—only one year after its original English version in 2002.[16] Based on a few studies of world Christianity, Zhao Lin 趙林, a philosophy professor of Wuhan University, has analyzed the demographic distribution of the global Christian population, especially the rapid growth of the Christian population in the non-Western world. For Zhao, given the cultural, political, religious, and social contexts of China, especially the Confucian (cultural) soft-resistance and the Communist (political) hard-resistance to Christianity, it is unlikely that Christianity in China will experience an explosive growth comparable to that seen in some other countries or regions. In view of both the global resurgence of Christianity and the particular situation of contemporary China, Zhao suggests that Chinese Christianity has to creatively transform itself and then the Chinese culture.[17] Since Zhao's interest is on the growth of

---

15. My recent contributions in this area include Pan-chiu Lai, "Forgiveness, Reconciliation and Peace-Building: A Sino-Christian Perspective," in Pauline Kollontai, Sue Yore, and Sebastian Kim, eds., *The Role of Religion in Peacebuilding: Crossing the Boundaries of Prejudice and Distrust* (London: Jessica Kingsley Publishing, 2018), 35–51; "Ecological Theology as Public Theology: A Chinese Perspective," *International Journal of Public Theology* 11, no 4 (2017): 477–500; "The Christian Story of God's Work—A Chinese Christian Response," in Ernst Conradie and Hilda Koster, eds., *T & T Clark Handbook of Christian Theology and Climate Change* (London: Bloomsbury, 2020), 480–89; and "Subordination, Separation, and Autonomy: Chinese Protestant Approaches to Religion-State Relation," *Journal of Law and Religion* 35, no. 1 (June 2020): 1–16.

16. Philip Jenkins, *The Next Christendom: The Coming of Global Christianity* (Oxford: Oxford University Press, 2002). Chinese translation: Fēi lì pǔ. Zhān jīn sī 菲立浦. 詹金斯, *Xià yī gè jī dū wáng guó: Jī dū zōng jiào quán qiú huà dí lái lín* 下一個基督王國: 基督宗教全球化的來臨, trans. Liáng yǒng ān 梁永安 (Taibei: lì xù wén huà 立緒文化, 2003).

17. Zhao Lin, "Glocalization of Christianity and the Responding Strategy of Sino-Christian Theology," *Logos & Pneuma* 41 (Autumn 2014): 163–84 (in Chinese with abstract in English). In addition to the book by Jenkins mentioned earlier, Zhao makes

the Christian population in the non-Western world, however, the implications of other aspects of world Christianity might have been overlooked.

It seems to me that the significance of the study of world Christianity for Christianity in China is far more multifaceted. As opposed to Zhao, my interest in world Christianity is primarily related to the understanding of Christianity as a cross-cultural and multilingual movement, rather than its global phenomenal growth. This prompts me to make two suggestions. First, in the development of Sino-Christian theology, one should pay more attention to the spiritual and theological traditions of marginal groups that are within Western Christianity but ignored by the stereotype of Western Christianity. For example, Celtic Christianity has its own spiritual tradition that differs from other parts of Western Christianity, but is very relevant to Sino-Christian theology. Second, scholars advocating Sino-Christian theology should also explore the significance of Sino-Christian theology for the non-Chinese world, instead of focusing exclusively on the development and theological indigenization of Christianity in China.[18]

It is quite understandable that Chinese scholars of Christianity tend to focus their studies on Christianity in China or issues directly related to China, but there is a very serious drawback or limitation to this approach. Christianity in China consists of mainly Catholicism and Protestantism, while the Orthodox churches are very tiny and marginalized in the Chinese-speaking world. It is thus quite easy for Chinese scholars to overlook the Eastern Orthodox churches, which are also ignored sometimes in the stereotyped discourses on Western Christianity. There are some Chinese studies of Orthodox Christianity, with a few interesting Chinese explorations of Orthodox theology, but the limitations of the existing Chinese studies of Orthodox churches are also quite glaring. For example, such studies exhibit certain limitations, such as a poor understanding of the Orthodox churches' "mystical" doctrines, including the doctrine of deification, as well as neglect of the Orthodox churches' extensive experience of living under totalitarian regimes.[19] The value of the latter for Christianity in Communist China is rather obvious, and the

---

extensive references to Todd M. Johnson and Kenneth R. Ross, eds., *Atlas of Global Christianity, 1910–2010* (Edinburgh: Edinburgh University Press, 2009).

18. Lai Pinchao 賴品超 (= Pan-chiu Lai), "Glocalization Strategies of Sino-Christian Theology: A Response to Prof. Zhao Lin," *Logos & Pneuma* 41 (Autumn 2014): 185–98 (in Chinese with abstract in English).

19. Pan-chiu Lai, "Chinese Explorations of Orthodox Theology: A Critical Review," *International Journal of Sino-Western Studies* 14 (June 2018): 27–41; an expanded version was published with permission in *International Journal for the Study of the Christian Church* 18, no. 4 (December 2018): 315–31.

former's relevance to Chinese Christianity cannot be ignored. It is interesting to note that some of the studies exploring the significance of the doctrine of deification for Chinese Christian theology are done by scholars associated with the field of world Christianity. For example, Alexander Chow's exploration of the doctrine of deification for Sino-Chinese Christian theology, especially its dialogue with the Confucian understanding of the unity between humanity and Heaven, has been published as part of a book series titled *Christianities of the World*.[20] My explorations of the significance of the doctrine of deification for the dialogue with Confucianism are done with the understanding that the doctrine of deification is more "ecumenical" than exclusively "Greek-Eastern"; this challenges the stereotype of "Latin-Western" Christianity and the presumed opposition between "Western" and "Eastern/Asian/Oriental" religious traditions represented by Christianity and Confucianism, respectively.[21]

In short, the discourse of world Christianity, with its emphasis on the global or *glocal* perspective, may serve as an important reminder that the academic study of Christianity should not be restricted to the churches typically associated with China. For the Chinese studies of Christianity, the discourse of world Christianity is more beneficial because it covers Christianity as a whole and overcomes the tendency to study Christianity in China in isolation from the global church. Chinese scholars seem to be quite open to this kind of research. For example, Wang Zhixi 王志希, a young scholar now teaching at Shantou University, China, seeks to integrate the perspectives of "global Christianity" and "reception history" in the study of the reception history of the Bible.[22] This is significant because how the Bible was interpreted and received in China has become a focus of interest in international academia.[23] In addition to how Chinese interpretations of the Bible were shaped by Chinese contexts, an

---

20. Alexander Chow, *Theosis, Sino-Christian Theology, and the Second Chinese Enlightenment: Heaven and Humanity in Unity* (New York: Palgrave Macmillan, 2013).

21. Pan-chiu Lai, "Christian Transformation of Greek Humanism and Its Implications for Christian-Confucian Dialogue," *Korea Journal of Systematic Theology* 22 (2008): 245–69; "Shaping Humanity with Word and Spirit: Perspectives East, West and Neither-East-Nor-West," in Anselm K. Min and Christoph Schwöbel, eds., *Word and Spirit: Renewing Christology and Pneumatology in a Globalizing World* (Berlin: de Gruyter, 2014), 131–49.

22. See Wang Zhixi, "'Reception History of the Bible' from the Perspective of Global History: Toward the Integration of 'Global History of Christianity' and 'Reception History,'" *Fujen Religious Studies* 31 (Autumn 2015): 143–70 (in Chinese with English abstract).

23. See Chloë Starr, ed., *Reading Christian Scriptures in China* (London: T & T Clark, 2008); K. K. Yeo, ed., *Oxford Handbook of Bible in China* (Oxford: Oxford University Press, 2021).

even more interesting exploration concerns how to engage the biblical texts and the Chinese religious texts in mutually critical comparison or dialogue. A bilingual journal titled *Journal of Comparative Scripture* 比較經學 has been launched specifically for this kind of research.²⁴

The global reception of the Reformation is another interesting topic, especially in light of the many publications and academic conferences commemorating its five-hundredth anniversary. I presented three papers about the Reformation at three different conferences from 2017 to 2018. At a conference held in Beijing in September 2017, I presented a paper in Chinese criticizing the misunderstandings of the doctrine of justification by faith assumed by some Chinese Protestant church leaders, who advocate "diluting" the doctrine in order to "Sinicize" Christianity. In addition to clarifying their misinterpretations of the doctrine and arguing that it is neither necessary nor desirable to dilute or neglect the doctrine, the paper introduces the Finnish interpretation of Martin Luther and explains how it may offer an interpretation of the doctrine and how it can address some related concerns of Chinese Christians in a positive and better way.²⁵ At a conference held in Hong Kong in September 2017, I presented a paper in English offering a critique of the ecological heritage of the Reformation from a Chinese Christian perspective. Through analyzing the prevalent evaluations of the ecological heritage of Protestantism in Western context, the Chinese perception of the Christian ecological heritage, and the Chinese Protestant ecological discourses, the paper argues that in terms of its "letter" or doctrinal formula, including particularly its anthropocentric soteriology, the theological heritage of Protestantism as a whole is ambivalent regarding its potentialities for ecological theology. However, in terms of its "spirit," the Protestant notion of continuing reform can be valuable for the development of Christian ecological ethics in the contemporary world, including the contemporary Chinese context.²⁶ In a more positive manner, I presented a paper titled "Divine Love and Human Love: An Asian Ecumenical Revisit of Martin

---

24. See You Bin 游斌, ed., *Journal of Comparative Scripture* 1, no. 1 (2013), jointly published by Institute of Comparative Scripture and Interreligious Dialogue, Minzu University of China (Beijing), and Institute of Sino-Christian Studies (Hong Kong).

25. An English version of the conference paper was published as Pan-chiu Lai, "Justification by Faith and Protestant Christianity in China: With Special Reference to the Finnish Interpretation of Luther," *International Journal of Sino-Western Studies* 16 (June 2019): 21–33.

26. The paper was presented at the International Conference on the Reformation's Culturally Transformative Influences and Impacts: European and Asian Cultural Perspectives, held at Hong Kong Baptist University, September 22–23, 2017. The paper will be published as Pan-chiu Lai, "Ecological Heritage of Protestantism in Chinese Christian Perspective," *Ching Feng* N.S. 19 (2020): 21–47.

Luther's Heidelberg Disputation 1518" in Hong Kong in 2018. The paper revisits Luther's criticism of St. Thomas Aquinas on the issue concerning the relationship between divine love and human love, and proposes how the nondualistic Chinese way of thinking can resolve to a certain extent the dispute that sparked the theological divergence between Protestantism and Roman Catholicism.[27]

All three papers concern the Chinese reception of the Reformation: the first one attempts to rectify some of the Chinese misinterpretations by clarifying the positions of the Reformers; the second offers a critical evaluation of the ecological heritage of the Reformation from a Chinese Christian perspective; and the third aims to provide a Chinese solution to a problem developed during the Reformation. In different ways or directions, these three papers exhibit how the theological exchange between China and the West can be reciprocally beneficial to both parties. They also indicate how the Chinese responses to the Reformation(s) can enrich studies of the global receptions of the Reformation(s).

World Christianity, Religious Studies, and Cultural Studies

In Mainland China, theology as an academic discipline and theology departments are excluded from the university system. The academic study of Christianity is usually conducted under the umbrella of religious studies, which is recognized as a branch of philosophy. The study of Christianity is thus expected to be more or less in line with the norm(s) adopted by the academic studies of other religions, especially Chinese religions, and is significantly different from the approach or method of theological studies practiced in the independent seminary. Compared with the denominational approach adopted by Catholic or Protestant theological seminaries, world Christianity, due to its emphasis on the global perspective, should be more compatible with the university setting. This is a rather obvious advantage for the adoption of the world Christianity approach in Chinese academia. A question to be explored is whether and how the discourse of world Christianity can contribute to religious studies.

I teach in the Department of Cultural and Religious Studies at the Chinese University of Hong Kong. For certain historical reasons, the department comprises three divisions: cultural studies, religious stud-

---

27. The paper was presented at International Conference on the Asian Ecumenical Movement, co-organized by the Centre for Catholic Studies (CUHK) and Tao Fong Shan Christian Centre, held at the Chinese University of Hong Kong, April 12–13, 2018. It was published as Pan-chiu Lai, "Divine Love and Human Love: An Asian Ecumenical Revisit of Luther's *Heidelberg Disputation* (1518)," *Hong Kong Journal of Catholic Studies* 9 (December 2018): 30–59.

ies, and theology.²⁸ The unique composition of the department provides a rather special environment for the study of Christianity. As a scholar doing research in the field of interreligious encounter and dialogue, I find that the discourse of world Christianity can enrich religious studies, especially the study of non-Christian religions.

The discourse of world Christianity places Christianity in a global context and invites the study of Christianity from the perspective of globalization. This approach is quite different from the prevalent China-centered approach to the study of Chinese religions that is adopted, even in some existing Chinese publications, with regard to the encounter between Chinese and "foreign" religions in China. A volume I edited that reviews the encounter between Chinese and non-Chinese religions in China from the perspective of the globalization of culture counters this approach. The book argues that among the three models of globalization of culture—Westernization, clash of civilization, and hybridization—the last model can best explain the data of the historical encounters among the religions involved.²⁹ This hybridization proposes that the encounter between different religions and cultures produces change within each religion and, thus, preserves the link between pluralization and globalization. This understanding of religion as a cross-cultural process matches very well the understanding of religious movements assumed by the discourse of world Christianity.

The discourse of world Christianity, with its emphasis on Christianity as a multilingual and cross-cultural movement, also counters the "Orientalist" approach to the study of religions. The debate sparked by Edward Said's (1935–2003) critique of Orientalism³⁰ prompts Richard King to reexamine the studies of "Eastern" religions. He raises questions

---

28. The story behind this rather unique case is that the university was formed in 1963 by combining three existing higher education colleges, including Chung Chi College, which was founded as a Christian college with theological training included. It was decided that theology can be taught at the university on a self-financing basis, without any subsidy from the government. Since then, theology was taught together with religious studies. In 2004, the department of religion was merged with the cultural studies programs from another department to form a new department of cultural and religious studies.

29. Lai Pinchao 賴品超, ed., *Cóng wén huà quán qiú huà kàn zhōng wài zōng jiào jiāo liú shǐ* 從文化全球化看中外宗教交流史 [*History of the Exchange between Chinese and Foreign Religions in the Perspective of Globalization of Culture*] (Hong Kong: Centre for the Study of Religion and Chinese Society, Chung Chi College, the Chinese University of Hong Kong, 2018).

30. See Edward W. Said, *Orientalism: Western Conceptions of the Orient* (Harmondsworth: Penguin, 1995), 1–28. For a brief survey of the debate, see Harry Oldmeadow, *Journey East: 20th Century Western Encounters with Eastern Religious Traditions* (Bloomington, IN: World Wisdom, 2004), 3–19.

about whether the studies of Eastern religions betrayed the characteristics of the Orientalist approach criticized by Said, including: "textualism" (which identifies a religion with a set of "sacred" texts); "essentialism" (which tends to assume a dualistic demarcation between the "East" and the "West"); and the colonial ideology (which legitimates Western pride of cultural superiority and even colonial power).[31] It is interesting to note that some scholars of Eastern religions might do it the other way around—adopting the strategies of textualism, essentialism, dualistic demarcation between the East and the West, etc., with the aim of strengthening their nationalistic ideology and cultural pride vis-à-vis Western culture.[32] Considering the emphasis on the multilingual and cross-cultural character of world Christianity, it is quite obvious that world Christianity is in a better position to resist the above-mentioned characteristics of the Orientalist approach to religions, plus the justification of cultural pride of either Eastern or Western culture. In short, the discourse of world Christianity counters the Orientalism or "reverse Orientalism" involved in the comparison or dialogue of religions or cultures[33] and can enrich the research of religious studies and cultural studies.

Concluding Remark

It is my hope that the personal witness outlined above illustrates that whether or not the discourse or field of world Christianity derives its rationale and emphases in relation to North Atlantic academic structures or norms, it can and should be adopted in the Chinese context because the discourse of world Christianity will benefit the future development of Christian studies as an academic discipline in the Chinese-speaking world.

---

31. See Richard King, *Orientalism and Religion: Postcolonial Theory, India, and "the Mystical East"* (London: Routledge, 1999).

32. See Bernard Faure, *Chan Insights and Oversights: An Epistemological Critique of the Chan Tradition* (Princeton, NJ: Princeton University Press, 1993), 52–88.

33. For my critique of Orientalism and reverse Orientalism in Buddhist-Christian studies, see Pan-chiu Lai, "Timothy Richard's Buddhist-Christian Studies," *Buddhist-Christian Studies* 29 (2009): 23–38; Lai Pinchao, "Being and Non-being: Paul Tillich, Buddhist-Christian Dialogue, and Sino-Christian Theology," *Logos & Pneuma* 43 (2015): 29–50 (in Chinese with English abstract).

10

Incorporating Middle Eastern Christianity into World Christianity

DEANNA FERREE WOMACK

The Middle East was already home to a multiplicity of Christian traditions by the time it became a prime target for Western missions, starting with the arrival of European Catholic orders in the sixteenth century. As a result of Catholic missionary activity, the region's Christian landscape had become even more diverse by the time Protestant evangelists settled there in the 1820s and thereafter established new churches of the Reformed tradition. These Western missionaries encountered denominationally, liturgically, culturally, and ethnically distinct Christian communities that hailed from North Africa to West Asia and spoke or worshiped in Arabic, Coptic, Armenian, Persian, Greek, and Syriac, among other languages. Middle Eastern Christians contributed to the early globalization of Christianity, initiating the Syrian-heritage churches of India by the second century and sending missionaries to China in the seventh century.[1] By the early twentieth century, Middle Eastern Christian populations had begun migrating to Europe and to North, Central, and South America, expanding this global reach even further. Middle Eastern Christianity has thus taken on a plurality of expressions across time and space, within the region and in other parts of the globe. For far

---

* This chapter is an adapted and expanded version of an earlier publication: Deanna Ferree Womack, "Middle Eastern Christianity in the Context of World Christianity," in Mitri Raheb and Mark A. Lamport, eds., *The Rowman & Littlefield Handbook of Christianity in the Middle East* (Lanham, MD: Rowman & Littlefield, 2020), 548–58. Reprinted with permission.

1. Philip Jenkins, *The Lost History of Christianity: The Thousand-Year Golden Age of the Church in the Middle East, Africa, and Asia—and How It Died* (New York: HarperCollins, 2008), 64–68.

too long, however, English language scholarship has given Middle Eastern Christians fleeting attention.

Even with the growing interest in Middle Eastern Christian studies over the past two decades,[2] broader scholarship on Christianity rarely engages with the complexities of Middle Eastern church traditions or considers why such traditions matter for Christianity as a whole, past and present. Historical surveys of Christianity typically recognize the place and importance of Middle Eastern churches in the early Christian movement, but the focus turns quickly to Christianity in Europe—a paucity of treatment seemingly justified by the view that the Middle Eastern Christian population is a dwindling remnant. Such neglect of Middle Eastern Christianity across the centuries, and particularly in recent historical and contemporary studies, is evident even in the field of world Christianity. This chapter therefore examines why the Middle East remains so marginal to the field and considers what scholars of world Christianity and scholars of Middle Eastern Christianity might gain by coming into closer conversation with each other. The first section considers why such collaborations are so rare; the remaining three sections each offer a reason why it makes good sense to think about Middle Eastern Christians in the global context of Christianity and within the study of world Christianity itself.

Scholarly Neglect of Middle Eastern Christianity

In studies on the Middle East, according to Akram Khater, "religious minorities have been relegated to the farthest margins of the scholarly field, inadvertently reinforcing neo-Orientalist imaginings of the Middle East as a monolithic historical and contemporary space."[3] In other words, conceptions of the Middle East as "the Islamic world" have often prevented scholars from giving Middle Eastern Christianity the attention it deserves throughout all time periods, and not just up until the Islamic conquests of the seventh century. Khater is among the small, yet growing number of scholars who have made Middle Eastern Christian studies an area of research within Middle East studies in the past decade or so.[4] Another

---

2. Deanna Ferree Womack, "Christian Communities in the Contemporary Middle East: An Introduction," *Exchange* 49, nos. 3–4 (2020): 189–213.

3. Akram Fouad Khater, *Embracing the Divine: Passion and Politics in the Christian Middle East* (Syracuse, NY: Syracuse University Press, 2011), 4. Khater spoke specifically about the dearth of English-language scholarship on Middle Eastern Christianity.

4. Movement in this direction in the early 2000s was reflected in a roundtable published in the *International Journal of Middle East Studies* in 2010 under the title "How Does New Scholarship on Christians and Christianity in the Middle East Shape How We View the History of the Region and Its Current Issues?" See Akram Fouad Khater,

way to challenge such simplistic imaginings about the region would be to study Middle Eastern Christianity in conversation with current work in world Christianity, something that few books on Middle Eastern Christianity have endeavored to do, with the exception of some texts like Philip Jenkins's *The Lost History of Christianity*.[5] Most general introductions to the field of world Christianity do give attention to the Middle East. But, while some include nuanced histories of Christianity in the region, others have, perhaps inadvertently, reinforced the notion that Middle Eastern Christianity has essentially disappeared.

Textbooks commonly used to teach about world Christianity convey varying images about the Middle East. Some, like Dale Irvin and Scott Sunquist's two-volume *History of the World Christian Movement*, give consistent treatment of Middle Eastern Christians and their diversity throughout church history.[6] Because of their wide scope, the two volumes focus mainly on the realities of Muslim political rule over Christians in the region rather than on particularities of church practice or local traditions. Yet readers understand Middle Eastern Christianity as an enduring part of global Christian history. This approach encourages further study of Middle Eastern traditions, whereas books that emphasize Christianity's eclipse in the Middle East or its disappearance from the region signal that further study may be unnecessary—at least when it comes to contemporary Christianity.

In making the important points that religions such as Christianity die in some locales and are reborn in others and that Christian history outside of the West should not be overlooked, Philip Jenkins suggested that Christianity in the Middle East has been lost. His book's full title conveys this message clearly: *The Lost History of Christianity: The Thousand-Year Golden Age of the Church in the Middle East, Africa, and Asia—and How It Died*. The

---

"Introduction," *International Journal of Middle East Studies* 42, no. 3 (2010): 471; Fiona McCallum, "Christians in the Middle East: A New Subfield?," *International Journal of Middle East Studies* 42, no. 3 (2010): 486–88; Womack, "Christian Communities," 198–208.

5. Another important exception, a study of contemporary Middle Eastern Christianity published within a world Christianity book series, is Kenneth R. Ross, Mariz Tadros, and Todd M. Johnson, eds., *Christianity in North Africa and West Asia* (Edinburgh: Edinburgh University Press, 2018). And although the following volume focuses mainly on Christian-Muslim contexts outside of the Middle East, it recognizes the important contributions David Kerr made to the study of world Christianity as a scholar of Middle Eastern Christianity: Stephen R. Goodwin, ed., *World Christianity in Muslim Encounter: Essays in Memory of David A. Kerr*, vol. 2 (London: Continuum, 2009).

6. Dale T. Irvin and Scott W. Sunquist, *History of the World Christian Movement*, vol. 1. *Earliest Christianity to 1453* (Maryknoll, NY: Orbis Books, 2001); Irvin and Sunquist, *History of the World Christian Movement*, vol. 2. *Modern Christianity from 1454–1800* (Maryknoll, NY: Orbis Books, 2012).

text itself consistently emphasizes that Middle Eastern Christianity has, to repeat one recurrent theme, fallen into total and utter "oblivion."[7] The book does recognize a Middle Eastern Christian diaspora and notes that "at least some [Christian] groups still survive as sturdy minorities" in the region. But Middle Eastern Christians today might contest the view that "Middle Eastern Christianity has, within living memory, all but disappeared as a living force."[8] In reality, the Christian population in the region numbers nearly 19 million and has continued to experience slow numerical growth since the early twentieth century, despite severe hardships, persecution, and high emigration rates.[9] Jenkins's work is invaluable for linking Middle Eastern Christianity and world Christianity because it highlights a history that has been largely lost to Western Christian memory and motivates readers to study Middle Eastern Christian communities after the rise of Islam. At the same time, drawing attention mainly to the loss of Christian sociopolitical power and declining numbers can render actual living communities of the Christian Middle East nonexistent and thus discourage studies on recent history and contemporary Christian practice in the region.[10]

I have dwelt at some length on *The Lost History of Christianity* because of the strong influence the book has had on world Christianity circles and because so many other texts in this field convey similar notions. Some predict a bleak future for the Christians of the Middle East by describing them as "surviving, but just barely,"[11] or as reaching "near

---

7. Jenkins, *Lost History of Christianity*, 4, 32, 34, 75, 222.

8. Ibid., 174, 229. The book also explains, "Middle Eastern Christians, in short, tried every possible tactic to survive and flourish, and their efforts have largely failed" (168).

9. Todd M. Johnson and Gina A. Zurlo, *World Christian Encyclopedia*, 3rd ed. (Edinburgh: Edinburgh University Press, 2020), 933; Todd M. Johnson and Gina A. Zurlo, eds., *World Christian Database* (Leiden: Brill), https://www.worldchristiandatabase.org/. Whereas Christianity had 5.8 million adherents in the Middle East in 1900 and 8.4 million in 1970, there were 18.8 million Christians in the region in 2020. Even excluding the 4.39 million Christians in the Gulf states, a predominantly migrant population from outside the region, the number of indigenous Middle Eastern Christians continues to grow. Lower birth rates and high emigration rates have slowed this growth, and certain communities and regions (like the Assyrian Christian homelands in Iraq) have experienced negative growth. Yet the data overall do not substantiate claims that Christianity is near extinction in the Middle East.

10. Jenkins's fascinating chapter on the "ghosts" of Christianity that linger in Islamic architecture and Muslim ritual practices similarly suggests that it is difficult to find a living trace of Christianity in the Middle East. Jenkins, *Lost History of Christianity*, 173–206.

11. Douglas Jacobsen, *The World's Christians* (Malden, MA: Wiley-Blackwell, 2011), 69. The chapter is titled "The Middle East and North Africa: Barely Surviving." See pp. 67–87.

extinction."[12] Others emphasize what has been lost by noting the "inevitable decline"[13] of Christianity in the region since the seventh century or by describing the Middle Eastern church as "vanished almost entirely"[14] and "utterly crushed."[15] Still other world Christianity texts helpfully note cycles of "growth and persecution"[16] and of "promise and failure."[17] The most comprehensive and nuanced treatments of Middle Eastern Christianity, however, come from edited volumes on world Christianity that incorporate work by scholars of the Middle East. These works recognize Middle Eastern Christians' contemporary struggles, but they also show definitively that Christianity in the Middle East is not dead today and that these ancient traditions are also carried on by immigrant communities outside the region. In Charles Farhadian's *Introducing World Christianity*, for example, Heather Sharkey describes Middle Eastern Christianity as "persisting" in the region, explaining that "vibrant Christian communities remain and take pride in rich histories on which they build."[18] In another volume, *Relocating World Christianity*, Naures Atto demonstrates that for Assyrian Christians from Iraq, deep-rooted memories of genocide and recent traumas of dispossession and migration provide a "powerful counterweight to the more frequently told triumphalist story of the explosive worldwide growth of Christianity in recent decades."[19] Atto also sheds light on the realities of Middle Eastern Christians living in North America and Europe—where most Assyrians today have settled—and

---

12. Frederick W. Norris, *Christianity: A Short Global History* (Oxford: Oneworld Publications, 2002), 5. Norris recognizes that Asian Christianity "is recovering from near extinction at the end of the thirteenth-century Mongolian peace." His chapter covering the history of Christianity in North Africa and West Asia also uses the same expression: "Crusades to the Near Extinction of Asian Christians, 1100–1500" (108–36).

13. Dana L. Robert, *Christian Mission: How Christianity Became a World Religion* (Malden, MA: Wiley-Blackwell, 2009), 24.

14. Dyron B. Daughrity, *Rising: The Amazing Story of Christianity's Resurrection in the Global South* (Minneapolis: Fortress Press, 2018), xiv.

15. Dyron B. Daughrity, *To Whom Does Christianity Belong? Critical Issues in World Christianity* (Minneapolis: Fortress Press, 2015), 36.

16. Sebastian Kim and Kirsteen Kim, *Christianity as a World Religion: An Introduction* (London: Bloomsbury Academic, 2008/2016), 28.

17. Lamin Sanneh, *Disciples of all Nations: Pillars of World Christianity* (Oxford: Oxford University Press, 2008), 58.

18. Heather J. Sharkey, "Middle Eastern and North African Christianity: Persisting in the Lands of Islam," in Charles E. Farhadian, ed., *Introducing World Christianity* (Malden, MA: Wiley-Blackwell, 2012), 7.

19. Naures Atto, "The Death Throes of Indigenous Christians in the Middle East: Assyrians Living under the Islamic State," in Joel Cabrita, David Maxwell, and Emma Wild-Wood, eds., *Relocating World Christianity: Interdisciplinary Studies and Local Expressions of the Christian Faith* (Leiden: Brill, 2017), 281.

the importance of understanding their lives outside the Middle Eastern context.

Such studies of particular Middle Eastern Christian communities are part of the wider story of world Christianity, past and present. As evidenced in several book series, journal issues, and new monographs and dissertations that span from the ancient Near East to the contemporary Arab world, the area of Middle Eastern Christian studies has experienced tremendous growth in English-language publishing since the late 1990s, with Coptic studies often leading the way.[20] Yet despite this reality, few scholars of Middle Eastern Christianity identify world Christianity as an academic home. Monographs on Middle Eastern Christianity rarely engage the subject of global Christianity, and prominent world Christianity conferences feature sessions on the Middle East sporadically. For example, my survey of the Yale-Edinburgh Group on World Christianity and the History of Mission conference programs for a five-year span, between 2015 and 2019, showed only four full panels and six additional presentations on Christianity in the Middle East or on missionaries to the region.[21]

Why is this the case, especially since broad studies of world Christianity usually endeavor to address the Middle East? Among other reasons, one could name:

- enduring presumptions about the Middle East as the Islamic world
- discussions in the field of world Christianity that tend to gravitate toward population growth
- the overwhelmingly Protestant character of world Christianity studies, when very few Middle Eastern Christians are Protestants[22]

---

20. Womack, "Christian Communities," 198–209. On Coptic studies, see Nelly van Doorn-Harder, "Finding a Platform: Studying the Copts in the 19th and 20th Centuries," *International Journal of Middle East Studies* 42, no. 3 (2010): 479–82; Febe Armanios, "Approaches to Coptic History after 641," *International Journal of Middle East Studies* 42, no. 3 (2010): 483–85.

21. The newer Princeton Theological Seminary conferences on world Christianity included three presentations on the Middle East in 2019 and one presentation in 2018. Deanna Ferree Womack's *Protestants, Gender and the Arab Renaissance in Late Ottoman Syria* (Edinburgh: Edinburgh University Press, 2019), places Middle Eastern Christianity in the context of world Christianity and missions. A number of other historical studies have addressed Western missions across the region, including Melanie E. Trexler, *Evangelizing Lebanon: Baptists, Missions, and the Question of Cultures* (Waco, TX: Baylor University Press, 2016); Emrah Şahin, *Faithful Encounters: Authorities and American Missionaries in the Ottoman Empire* (Montreal and Kingston: McGill-Queen's University Press, 2018).

22. On world Christianity as "a largely Protestant preoccupation," see Joel Cabrita and David Maxwell, "Relocating World Christianity," in Cabrita et al., *Relocating World Christianity*, 14.

- the reality that most Middle Eastern Catholics are not Roman Catholic, making them less familiar within Western academia

In addition, although scholars of world Christianity challenge Eurocentric notions about church history, some still tend to think of world Christianity as connected with modern Western missions. This excludes many Christian traditions in the Middle East that existed before the rise of Islam and long before European and American Christians embarked on missionary work to the region. Despite these various reasons for neglect, I will now discuss three reasons why it *does* make sense to study Middle Eastern Christianity within the context of world Christianity.

Reason 1: World Christianity Attends to Marginalized Christian Populations

Scholars of world Christianity speak often about the "shift in the center of gravity" of the Christian population from the "global North" to Africa, Asia, and Latin America since the early twentieth century.[23] This notable growth is one reason for the turn from studying Christianity as a European tradition to studying Christianity as a worldwide movement. Yet the field of world Christianity developed for another, more fundamental purpose as well: to challenge Eurocentric notions that had so long defined the way Christians in the West and many other parts of the globe understood Christianity. Eurocentric thought patterns had obscured the reality of Christianity as a diverse, worldwide movement. So scholars like Andrew Walls and Lamin Sanneh called attention to "global South," Christians whose stories had been overlooked. The astounding growth of Christianity in places like sub-Saharan Africa in the twentieth century reinforced the need for new research, but this research was also critical because for so long scholars had treated Christians outside of Europe and North America as marginal to the faith.

The field of world Christianity brings new attention to these long-neglected Christian communities. Dale Irvin explained that the field "is particularly concerned with underrepresented and marginalized communities of faith, resulting in a greater degree of attention being paid to Asian, African and Latin American experiences; the experiences of mar-

---

23. For examples of this repeated catchphrase, see Andrew Walls, *The Cross-Cultural Process in Christian History* (Maryknoll, NY: Orbis Books, 2002), 30–33, 64, 85, 118; Sanneh, *Disciples of All Nations*, xxiii; Ogbu U. Kalu, "Changing Tides: Some Currents in World Christianity at the Opening of the Twenty-First Century," in Ogbu U. Kalu and Alaine Low, eds., *Interpreting Contemporary Christianity: Global Processes and Local Identities* (Grand Rapids, MI: Eerdmans, 2008), 4.

ginalized communities within the North Atlantic world; and the experiences of women throughout the world."[24] So numbers alone do not—or at least should not—drive research on world Christianity. Otherwise, numerical dominance would become the criterion for determining what forms of Christianity are worth studying. Then some Christian communities—such as those in or from the Middle East—would be entirely written out of the global Christian story.

As I argued in my book on Syrian Protestants, "If the recent shift from studying Western missionary activity to studying global Christianity means attending to marginalized communities, then regions like the Middle East should not be overlooked because of their smaller Christian populations or because existing Christian communities predate the modern missionary movement."[25] Although it is understandable that most scholars follow the numbers, Devaka Premawardhana recently called for a different research agenda, one that is not fixated on church growth (in his case on pentecostal growth in Africa). In his words, in order to uncover the story that statistics alone cannot convey, we need to shift "from the centers of global Christianity to the fringes."[26]

We fail to do justice to the global scope of Christianity or to local Christian particularities if we neglect such peripheries, like communities that are declining or that otherwise do not fit the mold of world Christianity as the field is often conceived. That includes communities in the Middle East like Arabic or Armenian-speaking Protestants, who have never been in the majority; it includes Maronites, whose history and liturgy distinguishes them from most other Catholics; and it includes Copts, who are minoritized in Egypt yet outnumber all other Arab Christians combined.[27] Studying such traditions would help expand the boundaries of world Christianity and keep the field rightly focused on the whole of Christian faith, practices, and traditions in all of their diversity.

Reason 2: World Christianity Explores Global Christian Diversity

The Protestant tone of most studies in world Christianity is one reason why some scholars of Middle Eastern Christianity have not engaged with the field. A minority of Middle Eastern Christians are Protestant, overall

---

24. Dale T. Irvin, "World Christianity: An Introduction," *Journal of World Christianity* 1, no. 1 (2008): 1–2.
25. Womack, *Protestants, Gender and the Arab Renaissance*, 336.
26. Devaka Premawardhana, *Faith in Flux: Pentecostalism and Mobility in Rural Mozambique* (Philadelphia: University of Pennsylvania Press, 2018), 8, 10–11.
27. Womack, "Christian Communities," 197.

and country by country; and Catholics are not the majority of Middle Eastern Christians either. As previously noted, the largest community by far is Coptic Orthodox, numbering 8.4 million in Egypt alone.[28] In Lebanon and Iraq, Catholics make up the greatest segment of the Christian population, but most are not Roman Catholic. The largest Lebanese Catholic group is Maronite, and most Catholics in Iraq are Chaldean (of Assyrian heritage). Across the Levant, one finds a significant number of Greek Orthodox Christians too.[29] Yet apart from Greek Orthodoxy—which is rarely represented in studies of world Christianity—most Middle Eastern Christians come from traditions that are unique to the Middle East. Others, like the Armenian Catholic and Armenian Evangelical churches, originated in the region before spreading to Armenia and elsewhere.[30] Therefore, the study of Christianity in the Middle East and of Middle Eastern Christian migrants around the globe can help convey the full diversity of world Christianity that would otherwise be missed.

The ecclesial and liturgical diversity within Middle Eastern Christianity challenges Eurocentric imaginings of Christianity and upsets assumptions about the faith being divided into Roman Catholic, Greek Orthodox, and Protestant segments. The Coptic Orthodox Church, Armenian Apostolic Church, Syriac Orthodox Church, and the Assyrian Church of the East all serve as reminders (along with the Syrian Orthodox churches of India and the Ethiopian Orthodox) that Christianity was richly varied long before the faith spread throughout Europe. Middle Eastern Christian diversity is also cultural, ethnic, national, and even transregional. Not all Middle Eastern Christians are Arab, for instance, and not all Christians who call the Middle East home are originally Middle Eastern. A major example are the Armenians, whose families have resided in the Middle East for generations or even centuries but who still trace their heritage to Armenia.

Stretching across parts of North Africa, West Asia, and southeastern Europe, the Middle East itself defies the continental divisions typically used to categorize world Christianity.[31] Handbooks on Christianity in Asia, for example, may include West Asia but have difficulty describ-

---

28. Johnson and Zurlo, *World Christian Encyclopedia*, 267.

29. Out of 2,005,629 Christians in Lebanon in 2015, 1,613,061 were Catholic (mainly Maronite and Melkite). Of 332,757 Christians in Iraq that same year, 185,972 were Catholic. Johnson and Zurlo, *World Christian Database*.

30. For example, Syriac Christianity spread to India, and, much later, Armenian Protestant churches emerged first in the Middle East (and not in Armenia itself) before spreading to Armenian communities elsewhere.

31. I refer to western Turkey as a continentally European region included in the Middle East.

ing Arab Christianity without referencing Egypt, which is home to so many Arab Christians, including migrants from other parts of the Middle East.[32] Volumes on Christianity in Africa have the opposite challenge of addressing North African Christianity in relation to sub-Saharan African Christianity. This often means setting aside North African–West Asian ties and contemporary Christianity in places like Egypt, and focusing on early church history in North Africa.[33] Likewise, when it comes to studies on Christianity in Europe, the small community of contemporary Armenian, Catholic, and Greek Orthodox Christians in European Turkey are unlikely to receive much attention.

Often overlooked because of their small numbers, Middle Eastern Christians complicate neat regional divisions of the world and of global Christianity. The very location of the Middle East at the intersection of three continents is a reminder that civilizations overlap with one another, especially along the peripheries. Linking east with west and north with south, Middle Eastern Christianity disrupts normative assumptions and signals that movements, networks, and interrelations ought to receive more attention within the study of world Christianity.

Reason #3: World Christianity Examines Global Christian Interconnections

Some scholars speak about world Christianities in the plural, emphasizing that expressions of Christianity vary between distinct local contexts.[34] To prevent dominant groups from imposing their normative understandings of Christianity on everyone else, we must attend to such particularities—ecclesial, liturgical, cultural, historical, etc. Otherwise minority groups like Middle Eastern Christians would remain largely overlooked. Yet we should not—and in many cases simply cannot—study diverse forms of Christianity in complete isolation from each other.[35] Beyond theological arguments about world Christian unity, local expressions of Christianity

---

32. Herman Teule noted this difficulty and included Egyptian Christianity in Herman G. B. Teule, "Christianity in Western Asia," in Felix Wilfred, ed., *The Oxford Handbook of Christianity in Asia* (Oxford: Oxford University Press, 2014), 27.

33. For example, three of the thirty-three chapters in *The Routledge Companion to Christianity in Africa* focus on North Africa, but only in the section on historical perspectives. See Elias Kifon Bongmba, ed., *The Routledge Companion to Christianity in Africa* (New York: Routledge, 2016). These chapters center on early church history and end before the modern period. In contrast, most chapters on sub-Saharan Africa center on modern or contemporary Christianity.

34. See Peter C. Phan, "Doing Theology in World Christianities: Old Tasks, New Ways," in Cabrita et al., *Relocating World Christianity*, 115–42.

35. Cabrita and Maxwell, "Relocating World Christianity," 21–25.

around the globe are practically linked and even entangled. In this age of migration, churches in the global South send pastors to serve congregations abroad—just as churches in Europe and the United States once supplied African and Asian congregations with missionary pastors (and still sometimes do).[36] As Dale Irvin observed, "world Christianity as a field of study is at its best when studying things that are crossing (transcultural, transconfessional, transreligious) or things that take place in the interstices (intercultural, interconfessional, interreligious)."[37] Klaus Koschorke similarly spoke of global Christian history as a story of "multidirectional transcontinental interactions."[38] Attending to the history and contemporary experiences of Middle Eastern Christians makes such global Christian interconnections apparent in a number of ways.

First, Christianity was a boundary-crossing, global movement from the beginning. Noting the diversity of the crowd gathered at Pentecost in Acts 2, Arab church leaders often emphasize that Arabic was one of the languages spoken in Jerusalem on that day.[39] Early Christians also engaged in transregional travel. The apostle Paul journeyed to Greece and Italy from Palestine and planned a trip to Spain; and the missionary travels of Mark the evangelist and the apostle Thomas are central to Coptic Christianity in Egypt and to Syrian Christianity in India, respectively. Later, the (Assyrian) Church of the East sent missionaries to India and China, demonstrating the global reach and polycentric nature of Christianity by the medieval era. In that period Syriac Christianity was a third center of world Christianity along with Latin and Byzantine Christianity.[40] Vibrant Syrian Christian traditions in India today, especially in the state of Kerala, demonstrate the uninterrupted nature of these transregional linkages.[41] Thus, Middle Easterners made Christianity global long before the advent of modern missions.

---

36. For an example of Middle Eastern churches sending clergy to serve American congregations, see Yvonne Haddad and Joshua Donovan, "Good Copt, Bad Copt: Competing Narratives on Coptic Identity in Egypt and the United States," *Journal of World Christianity* 19, no. 3 (2013): 212–13.

37. Irvin, "World Christianity: A Genealogy," 18.

38. Klaus Koschorke, "Transcontinental Links, Enlarged Maps, and Polycentric Structures in the History of World Christianity," *Journal of World Christianity* 6, no. 1 (2016): 29.

39. Colin Chapman, "Christians in the Middle East—Past, Present and Future," *Transformation: An International Journal of Holistic Mission Studies* 29, no. 2 (2012): 91.

40. Koschorke, "Transcontinental Links," 35.

41. Arun Jones, "Christianity in South Asia," in Farhadian, *Introducing World Christianity*, 93, 97–98; Sonja Thomas, *Privileged Minorities: Syrian Christianity, Gender, and Minority Rights in Postcolonial India* (Seattle, WA: University of Washington Press, 2018), 24–28.

Second, the modern movement of Christians to and from the Middle East links this early globality to the transnational networks within world Christianity today. In addition to centuries-old ties between the Maronites of Lebanon and Rome, a plurality of Middle Eastern Catholic traditions emerged between the sixteenth and nineteenth centuries through contact with Italian, French, and other Roman Catholic missionaries.[42] A Protestant presence in the Middle East arose in the nineteenth century (with the work of British, American, and German missionaries, among others), and Russian Orthodox missionaries cultivated new connections with Arab Orthodox communities then as well.[43] By the early twentieth century, advances in world travel enabled significant numbers of Middle Eastern Christians to migrate to Europe and North America. Some relocated for economic reasons. Many Lebanese peasants, for example, labored for years as peddlers in the Midwestern United States and then returned home with their earnings.[44] Others traveled for education—missionaries recruited some of these scholars, like the Jesuit Louis Cheikho (1857–1927), who trained as a priest in France before returning to Ottoman Syria. Another Syrian, the Greek Orthodox poet Mikhail Naimy (1889–1988), studied at Russian Orthodox schools in Syria and then attended a theological seminary in the Ukraine. Naimy later migrated to New York, the site of a large Syrian colony and a popular destination for Syrian intellectuals, like the Maronite authors Khalil Gibran and Amin al-Rihani.[45] Still other Arab migrants found new homes in Latin America, where for some of them, a common Catholic affiliation may have helped ease the transition.[46]

---

42. Lucette Valensi, "Inter-Communal Relations and Changes in Religious Affiliation in the Middle East (Seventeenth to Nineteenth Centuries)," *Comparative Studies in Society and History* 39, no. 2 (April 1997): 251–69; Bernard Heyberger, "The Development of Catholicism in the Middle East (16th-19th Century)," in Habib Badr, Suad Abou el Rouss Slim, and Joseph Abou Nohra, eds., *Christianity: A History in the Middle East* (Beirut: Middle East Council of Churches, 2005), 631–51; Khater, *Embracing the Divine*.

43. On American, British, and Russian missions in the region, see Deanna Ferree Womack, "Imperial Politics and Missionary Practices: Comparative Transformations in Anglo-American and Russian Orthodox Missions in Syria-Palestine," *ARAM* 25, nos. 1–2 (2013): 1–12.

44. Akram Fouad Khater, *Inventing Home: Emigration, Gender, and the Middle Class in Lebanon, 1870–1920* (Berkeley: University of California Press, 2001), 48–145.

45. Deanna Ferree Womack, "Syrian Christians and Arab-Islamic Identity: Expressions of Belonging in the Ottoman Empire and America," *Studies in World Christianity* 25, no. 1 (2019): 33, 41–43. On the Syrian colony in New York, see Linda K. Jacobs, *Strangers in the West: The Syrian Colony of New York City, 1880–1900* (New York: Kalimah, 2015).

46. Theresa Alfaro-Velcamp, *So Far from Allah, So Close to Mexico: Middle Eastern Immigrants in Modern Mexico* (Austin: University of Texas Press, 2007), esp. 64, 93–94.

Third, many Middle Eastern Christians take pride in or even depend on such ongoing global connections.⁴⁷ Some have understood themselves as fully part of Islamic society and maintained distance from Western Christianity. Yet in the words of Colin Chapman, others have felt that "the only way to maintain their identity as Middle Eastern Christians has been to be connected to a larger form of Christianity—as represented, for example, by Byzantium, the Crusaders, Roman Catholicism and the Protestant Churches."⁴⁸ This is increasingly true today, as warfare and genocide have led Arabs and other Middle Eastern Christians—like Armenians and Assyrians—to seek refuge among Christians elsewhere. Atto described the Assyrians of the twentieth century choosing to settle Europe or in North and South America, "where they expected to be welcomed with open arms as co-religionists."⁴⁹ Today, only a minority of Assyrians still live in their historic homeland. They are among the significant population of Christians of Middle Eastern heritage who now live outside the Middle East due to high emigration levels since the mid-twentieth century.

Fourth, and finally, while many Christians of Middle Eastern heritage have left their homelands, Christian populations have grown in some parts of the region. Increasing numbers of Christian refugees from sub-Saharan Africa have fled to the Middle East, for instance,⁵⁰ and economic opportunities have drawn higher numbers of Christians than ever before to the Persian Gulf states. There, Catholic, Protestant, and Orthodox migrant workers from South and Southeast Asia number in the millions.⁵¹

---

47. Cabrita and Maxwell, "Relocating World Christianity," 21. Other Christians around the globe also take pride in such transnational connections.

48. Chapman, "Christians in the Middle East," 101. Chapman draws on the work of George Sabra, who identifies two historical Arab Christian orientations: those who emphasize their Arab-Islamic identity and those who identify as Eastern Christians preserved through links with the West.

49. Atto, "The Death Throes of Indigenous Christians in the Middle East," 283.

50. United Nations High Commissioner for Refugees, "Fact Sheet: Egypt" (April 2019), https://www.unhcr.org/. As of April 2019, Egypt, a major destination country for asylum seekers and refugees, was host to nearly 59,000 documented refugees from Sudan and South Sudan as well as another 39,298 from other parts of Africa.

51. The Catholic expatriate community is particularly high, with 1,746,000 Catholics in Saudi Arabia (including Filipinos, Koreans, Indians, Europeans, and Arabs), 901,000 in the United Arab Emirates (mainly Filipinos and Arabs), 308,000 in Qatar (Filipinos and Arabs), and 372,000 in Kuwait (mainly Filipinos). The United Arab Emirates also has two large Indian denominations, the India Pentecostal Church of God (10,000 members) and the Mar Thoma Syrian Church (5,000) members. There are 8,000 members of the Mar Thoma Syrian Church in Kuwait. In Bahrain, the expatriate Catholic community of Filipinos, Indians, British, and Americans number 150,000. Indian Christians make up the majority of other congregations in the country—including the Malayalee Christian Congregation (9,500), the Church of South India (4,200), Mar Thoma Syrian Church (1,800), Orthodox Syrian Church of India (1,300), and the

Notably, Christians from India—where Syriac Christianity migrated centuries ago from Persia—have brought a diversity of Syrian and other Indian Christian traditions to the Gulf today.[52] Thus in the Middle East and among Christians of Middle Eastern heritage around the globe, we see transnational Christian networks that have persisted for centuries.

Conclusion

These transnational interconnections, rich diversity, and marginalization of Christians in and from the Middle East ought to make the region a focal point for scholars of world Christianity. Because the Middle East itself defies typical divisions of the world into continental regions, it can helpfully unsettle the ways we tend to conceive of and classify global Christian traditions. With openness to such reconceptualization and serious attention to the polycentric nature of Christian faith, the field of world Christianity could become a welcoming academic home for seasoned scholars and future students of Middle Eastern Christianity. This possibility, however, will depend in large part on scholars of world Christianity who are committed to making this field more inclusive. Leaders in the field will need to consider what forms of Christianity have been left out of previous studies and why. We will need to carefully address issues such as the Protestant focus of most world Christianity discussions and the bias toward new Christian communities that emerged during and after the modern missionary movement. The fixation of many world Christianity publications on rapid numerical growth is also an issue of concern, especially when coupled with the unfortunate assumption that Middle Eastern Christianity is dead, dying, or dwindling out of existence. Significant work is needed to shift perceptions about what counts in world Christianity and to reorient scholars' understandings of contemporary Christianity in the Middle East. In short, world Christianity will need to live up to its name by advancing the study of all forms of Christianity in all regions of the world.

St. Thomas Evangelical Church (400). Yemen's Christian population numbers 22,782. Oman's is 152,318, with 96,000 of these being Catholics (mainly Filipino migrant laborers). Johnson and Zurlo, *World Christian Database*.

52. Stanley J. Valayil C. John, *Transnational Religious Organization and Practice: A Contextual Analysis of Kerala Pentecostal Churches in Kuwait* (Leiden: Brill, 2018).

11

Generational Transitions and New Conceptions

HELEN JIN KIM

World Christianity has expanded as a field since the late-twentieth century, furnishing scholarly tools especially for the study of non-Western Christians, a previously neglected group, sometimes simplistically rendered as pawns of empire. The Africanist pioneers of the field, however, have argued for the agency of non-Western Christians, a lens that has served scholars studying regions beyond Africa as well as the disciplines beyond the immediate intellectual centers in which the field was created. This chapter reviews the evolution of world Christianity as a field and argues that its emphasis on the twin elements of local agency and transnationalism continue to provide a critical lens for a new generation of scholars studying Christianity in the non-Western world. Using the case study of transpacific Korean Christianity, this chapter shows how Africanists in the field of world Christianity advanced two insights that can propel this relatively underexplored area of study forward: (1) world Christianity does not see nonliberal movements in transpacific Korean Christianity solely through a reductionist lens;[1] and (2) world Christianity does not see transpacific Korean Christianity solely as the hand-

---

1. The term "nonliberal" is in reference to works such as anthropologist Saba Mahmood's *Politics of Piety*, in which she studies the piety movement in the Islamic revival in Cairo, Egypt. She shows how Muslim women crafted their sense of agency and selfhood beyond the boundaries of Western feminism and outside the gaze of the Western academy's secular liberalism. Similarly, as I show in the last section of this essay, the subjects of world Christianity—specifically within transpacific Korean Christianity—are often understudied because they fall outside the purview of Western assumptions of the secular liberal subject. Saba Mahmood, *Politics of Piety: The Islamic Revival and the Feminist Subject* (Princeton, NJ: Princeton University Press, 2011).

maiden of Western empire. As this chapter suggests, these insights are especially helpful for transpacific Korean Christianity as it lives in the tension betwixt and between the fields of world Christianity and ethnic studies—two fields largely divergent in their assessment of Christianity in general and Christian missions in particular.

Empire, Christian Missions, and the Pioneering Role of Africanists

Africanists from a variety of fields have critiqued the entrenched view of Western Christian missions as the handmaiden of Western empire. Political scientist David Abernethy, a specialist in sub-Saharan Africa, employs the "triple assault" metaphor to illustrate the collusion between missionaries, colonialism, and capitalism. This tripartite force of "coercive rule, commerce, and conversion," he claims, had a "triply threatening impact" that advanced the European colonization of non-European societies.[2] "The key to dominance was the spatial stretch of all three . . . ," including the work of missionaries, nonstate actors who were "instrumental in preparing many non-European societies for eventual subordination."[3] By any reckoning, the unholy trinitarian marriage of church, state, and private sector is deeply troubling. Moreover, Dianne Stewart—scholar of religion and specialist in African heritage traditions—argues, not only the institutional power of the church but also the missionary thinking embedded in Christianity itself was problematic: "There is an imperialistic trait in Christian theology, which is most audaciously portrayed in its missionary approach to Christian faith confession."[4] As anthropologists Jean and John Comaroff have also noted, the danger of cultural imperialism in the Western missionary encounter with South Africans was that it not only penetrated their thought but also consciousness itself, producing the "colonization of consciousness."[5]

The critique of cultural imperialism had a ripple effect in the academy and spurred the previously colonized to express their discontent through intellectual and political activism. In part, that led to the flourishing of new academic disciplines, including postcolonial studies, and the founding of

---

2. David Abernethy, *The Dynamics of Global Dominance: European Overseas Empire, 1415–1980* (New Haven, CT: Yale University Press, 2000), 231, 242.

3. Ibid., 236.

4. Dianne Stewart, *Three Eyes for the Journey: African Dimensions of the Jamaican Religious Experience* (New York: Oxford University Press, 2005), xxxiii.

5. Jean Comaroff and John Comaroff, *Of Revelation and Revolution*, vol. 1. *Christianity, Colonialism and Consciousness in South Africa* (Chicago: University of Chicago Press, 2008).

the first School of Ethnic Studies in 1968 at San Francisco State University. A growing generation of college students of color—African American, Asian American, Latino American, and Native American—mobilized politically by identifying with Third World struggles for decolonization and resistance to the Vietnam War. They allied with Marxist and Maoist struggles for justice and liberation and with the Third World Liberation Front to create a curriculum devoted to the histories and lives of communities of color in the United States and globally.[6] In their liberatory activism and intellectual projects, Christianity was largely seen as an imperial force that needed to be excised, along with a Eurocentric curriculum. In particular, with the characterization, and sometimes caricaturization, of Christian missionaries as the right arm of colonialism, missions became somewhat of an "embarrassing remnant of colonial history."[7] On an ecclesial level, some Christians would have even preferred to mute "the Great Commission," the Christian call to spread the good news to the world.[8]

At the same time, however, the critique of missionary imperialism also motivated a new generation of scholars, especially Africanists, to pioneer alternative ways of narrating this missionary past, ultimately creating world Christianity as a new field of study. As Joel Cabrita and David Maxwell write, "[M]any of the first-generation scholars of world Christianity—Andrew Walls, Lamin Sanneh, Kwame Bediako—have all been Africanists," who were primed by a "rich tradition of twentieth-century scholarship to emphasize indigenous agency and local cultural appropriations of Christianity."[9] Within the larger late-twentieth century context of Third World liberation, and the revolutionary critiques of the Eurocentric academy, not only ethnic studies but also world Christianity emerged. While ethnic studies broadly adopted the cultural imperialist argument that Christian mission was the handmaiden of empire, world Christianity reexamined this long-held assumption. Proponents argued that Christian mission was not irrevocably tainted by the stain of colo-

---

6. For an overview of the larger Asian American Movement of which the rise of ethnic studies was a part, see Michael Liu and Kim Geron, *The Snake Dance of Asian American Activism: Community, Vision and Power* (Lanham, MD: Lexington Books, 2008).

7. Dana Robert, "The Great Commission in an Age of Globalization," in Daniel Jeyaraj, Robert W. Pazmiño, and Rodney Lawrence Petersen, eds., *Antioch Agenda: Essays on the Restorative Church in Honor of Orlando E. Costas* (New Delhi: Indian Society for the Promotion of Christian Knowledge for Andover Newton Theological School, and the Boston Theological Institute, 2007), 8.

8. Ibid.

9. Joel Cabrita and David Maxwell, "Introduction: Relocating World Christianity," in Joel Cabrita, David Maxwell, and Emma Wild-Wood, eds., *Relocating World Christianity: Interdisciplinary Studies in Universal and Local Expressions of the Christian Faith* (Leiden: Brill, 2017), 19.

nialism. This means that while both fields value uncovering new non-Western and nonwhite narratives, they have largely advanced divergent approaches in their interpretation of the history of Christianity in general and Christian missions in particular.

To that end, field pioneering Africanists, such as Andrew Walls and Lamin Sanneh, mined a key question at the heart of world Christianity: Why was there a shift in the center of Christianity from the "global North" to the "global South" throughout the twentieth century, even amid the rise of British and American empires? Walls and Sanneh argued that, while the effects of Western Christian empire were, indeed, devastating and enduring, non-Western Christians also chose Christianity at record rates because they exercised a measure of indigenous agency.[10] Sanneh highlighted the vernacularization of Christianity, emphasizing the agency of indigenous people, even amid, and sometimes in spite of, the dangers of Western Christian empire. Indigenous believers, he argued, translated the Bible into their local tongue, adapting the Christian message to their own context and for their own needs.[11] African Christianity spread rapidly because Africans converted Africans, not primarily because white Westerners coerced them to do so. Meanwhile, historian Dana Robert advocated a granular case study model, as opposed to a generalized theoretical model, showing that not all missionaries colluded with colonial power. In some regions, Robert shows, missionaries advocated for indigenous liberation, and missionaries from some U.S. churches abdicated power, transferring authority to indigenous leaders.[12]

The interdisciplinary and Africanist-centered field of world Christianity provided a watershed intervention in the scholarly discourse. It produced new insights into the emergence of Christianity in the non-Western world in general and the agency of non-Western Christians in particular. To be sure, critiques of the collusion of Western Christian missions and empire remain as a general principle of knowledge in some fields of study. But, by emphasizing indigenous agency and leadership, world Christianity pioneers advanced an interpretation of the missionary encounter that moved scholarship beyond the sole focus on the trappings of Western Christendom. They did so not as an apologia for empire but as an intellectual endeavor seeking clarity and meaning about one of the

---

10. See, for example, Andrew Walls, *The Cross-Cultural Process in Christian History: Studies in the Transmission and Appropriation of Faith* (Maryknoll, NY: Orbis Books, 2002); Lamin Sanneh, *Translating the Message: Missionary Impact on Culture* (Maryknoll, NY: Orbis Books, 1989).

11. Sanneh, *Translating the Message*.

12. Dana Robert, *Christian Mission: How Christianity Became a World Religion* (Chichester, UK; Wiley-Blackwell, 2009), 84–95.

most powerful religious transformations of the twentieth century—the rise of Christianity in the "global South." In doing so, world Christianity scholars forged a path to reverse the academic temptation to reduce non-Western Christians into mere, or "duped," victims of empire.

Multiple Entry Points into World Christianity: Disciplinary Training

Since the origins of the field, new research centers for the study of world Christianity emerged, primarily in the West.[13] A critical cohort of scholars trained at these centers, primarily located at research universities connected to theological institutions. Sanneh, Robert, and Walls, for instance, have respectively spearheaded prominent world Christianity research centers, housed at Yale University's Divinity School, Boston University's School of Theology, and the University of Edinburgh's School of Divinity. Scholars continue to train at these hubs at the same time that a new generation, or cohort, of scholars enters the field through multiple entry points, whether it be in terms of their disciplinary training or regional focus.

In terms of disciplinary training, world Christianity emerged, in part, out of theologically aligned fields such as mission studies and ecumenical studies. Yet, today, explicitly nontheologically aligned fields, including anthropology, area studies, and a range of historical subfields, draw upon and expand the interdisciplinary study of world Christianity. Within the historical subfields alone, global history, diplomatic history, and U.S. history—just to name a few—are key entry points for the study of world Christianity, with a growing number of such scholars advancing the study of nonstate connections between the United States and non-Western and nonwhite Christians abroad. Thus, the Africanist-centered origins of world Christianity have laid an important foundation for scholars engaging the transnational historical study of American religions as well as regions of the world including and beyond the African continent.

With the broader "religious turn" in diplomatic history, world Christianity has become an invaluable resource to this subfield. As diplomatic historian Andrew Preston notes, religion had been neglected in the field for about the last decade. However, religion has had a burgeoning presence, especially with new interpretations about the relationship between missions, empire, and war; in particular, he cites the contributions of world Christianity scholars who have argued for the "agency and autonomy" of non-Western Christians.[14] His own work, *Sword of the Spirit, Shield of Faith,*

---

13. Cabrita and Maxwell, "Introduction: Relocating World Christianity," 1–2.
14. Andrew Preston, "The Religious Turn in Diplomatic History," in Frank

has paved the way for this "religious turn," and more recent works such as historian Lauren Frances Turek's *To Bring the Good News to All Nations: Evangelical Influence on Human Rights and U.S. Foreign Relations* (2020) continue to highlight not only this shift in diplomatic history but also the role of world Christianity in shaping these new narratives. Turek pinpoints the crucial role that faith-based, nonstate organizations and actors had in shaping U.S. foreign policy in the decades following the Cold War. She uses the contributions of world Christianity in order to draw connections between U.S. evangelical groups and the transnational relationships they forged with "their coreligionists abroad" to create "a diffuse yet energetic global network" that influenced diplomatic affairs.[15]

For Americanists, the broader "transnational turn" in the last twenty years has moved them to study linkages beyond the U.S. nation-state.[16] Thus, U.S. historians of religion have increasingly ventured into world Christianity, tracing transnational connections across the globe between U.S. Christians and nonwhite and non-Western Christians abroad. A few texts recently published by historians who study the transnational connection between American religions and world Christianity include Heather Curtis's *Holy Humanitarians: American Evangelicals and Global Aid* (2018); David Kirkpatrick's *A Gospel for the Poor: Global Social Christianity and the Latin American Evangelical Left* (2019); and David Swartz's *Facing West: American Evangelicals in an Age of World Christianity* (2020).[17] These

---

Costigliola, ed., *Explaining the History of American Foreign Relations* (New York: Cambridge University Press, 2016), 287, 288.

15. Lauren Frances Turek, *To Bring the Good News to All Nations: Evangelical Influence on Human Rights and U.S. Foreign Relations* (Ithaca, NY: Cornell University Press, 2020), 7.

16. Several fields and subfields, especially among Americanists, have taken heed of the transnational and global turn. See Eric Foner, "American Freedom in a Global Age," *American Historical Review* 106, no. 1 (February 2001): 1–16; Matthew Frye Jacobson, "More 'Trans-,' Less 'National,'" *Journal of American Ethnic History* 25 (Summer 2006): 74–84; Shelley Fisher Fishkin, "Crossroads of Culture: The Transnational Turn in American Studies," *American Quarterly* 57, no. 1 (March 2005): 17–57. Fishkin also contributed her thoughts on transnationalism in "Redefinitions of Citizenship and Revisions of Cosmopolitanism—Transnational Perspectives: A Response and a Proposal," *Journal of Transnational American Studies* 3, no. 1 (2011): 47–52.

17. Heather Curtis, *Holy Humanitarians: American Evangelicals and Global Aid* (Cambridge, MA: Harvard University Press, 2018); David Kirkpatrick, *A Gospel for the Poor: Global Social Christianity and the Latin American Evangelical Left* (Philadelphia: University of Pennsylvania Press, 2019); David Swartz's *Facing West: American Evangelicals in an Age of World Christianity* (New York: Oxford University Press, 2020). See also David Hollinger, *Protestants Abroad: How Missionaries Tried to Change the World but Changed America* (Princeton, NJ: Princeton University Press, 2017); David King, *God's Internationalists: World Vision and the Age of Evangelical Humanitarianism* (Philadelphia: University of Pennsylvania Press, 2019). Note, though, that while Hollinger and King

publications represent a growing area of study in which U.S. religions are analyzed in terms of global processes. They show that modern U.S. humanitarianism, social Christianity, and evangelicalism were shaped by networks forged with non-Western people and contexts. Influences moved in both directions, however unevenly.

As such, these texts highlight not only the dominance of U.S. empire in the non-Western world but also the power of nonwhite and non-Western actors and their organizations in shaping religion, politics, and culture in the United States and abroad. In particular, Melani McAlister's *The Kingdom of God Has No Borders: A Global History of American Evangelicals* (2018) works at these multiple intersections of diplomatic history, global history, American religious history, and world Christianity. She emphasizes the agency of non-Western Christians in the twentieth century—foundational intellectual assumptions within the world Christianity field—to show how they helped to shape U.S. Christianity, culture, and politics. McAlister writes, "African Christians have been a primary force in pivoting Christianity toward the global South, and their political concerns—from global poverty to gender politics—are now on the agenda of international evangelicalism." As such, she shows how the interaction between global evangelicals led "some conservative Protestants in the United States to understand themselves differently, as part of a truly global community. Globalizing views were not always liberal, certainly, but they were influential, reshaping the moral map for many believers."[18] The growing literature in diplomatic history, global history, and American history reveal the expansion of world Christianity into subfields not deeply connected with its historical or theological origins.

The transnational focus is a direction much-welcomed by scholars of world Christianity. Historian Jehu Hanciles argues for studying the transnational linkages forged especially by post-1965 African Christian transmigrants in the United States, who carry out their role as missionaries through ongoing connections between two nation-states. He writes, "Africa epitomizes the inextricable link between mission and migration: not only is it a major heartland of Christianity, but it is also a theater and source of international migrations."[19] To use a nation-state paradigm would be to miss a key component in understanding contemporary world Christianity: the transnational interdependence of missions and migra-

---

do provide a global context for the study of American Christianity, their primary aim is not necessarily to foreground the stories of non-Western Christians.

18. Melani McAlister. *The Kingdom of God Has No Borders: A Global History of American Evangelicals* (Oxford: Oxford University Press, 2018), 4.

19. Jehu Hanciles, *Beyond Christendom: Globalization, African Migration, and the Transformation of the West* (Maryknoll, NY: Orbis Books, 2008), 179.

tion. Cabrita and Maxwell also argue in their review of world Christianity that it is "precisely this attention to transnational networks and cross-cultural linkages that has been lost in recent scholarship's focus on cultural particularity."[20] They suggest that what is required is "a robust sense of global connections and networks more broadly, both imperial as well as entirely outside the remit of empire."[21] Cabrita's own work illustrates the power of these transnational connections between the United States and South Africa.[22] Indeed, these investigations into the transnational role of nonstate networks forged between U.S. Christians and Christians abroad indicate the growth and the multiple entry points into an expanding world Christianity field.

Yet, curiously, as noted, with the exception of a few chapters on India, Korea, and China in the aforementioned texts, few U.S. historians have fully immersed their studies in the region of Asia or prioritized Asian historical actors in their narratives.[23] Indeed, a robust transpacific approach to the study of Christianity in Asia and its linkages to the Americas is still relatively nascent. Using *transpacific Korean Christianity* as a case study, the next section examines how the insights of Africanist pioneers in the subfield of world Christianity, and the transnational turn among Americanists, can foster new avenues of intellectual exploration, especially when world Christianity intersects with ethnic studies.

New Regional Interests: A Transpacific Approach

Transpacific Korean Christianity is a helpful regional case study for examining modern transnational networks forged between Asia-Pacific and the Americas, due to the high concentration of Protestants in South Korea and the diaspora in the United States. For background, between 1950 and 1980, South Korea's Christian population grew from less than 5 percent to 20 percent of the population.[24] South Korean evangelical

---

20. Cabrita and Maxwell, "Introduction: Relocating World Christianity," 24.

21. Ibid., 24.

22. Joel Cabrita, *The People's Zion: Southern Africa, the United States, and a Transatlantic Faith-Healing Movement* (Cambridge, MA: Harvard University Press, 2018).

23. William Yoo, *American Missionaries, Korean Protestants and the Changing Shape of World Christianity, 1884–1965* (New York: Routledge, Taylor and Francis Group, 2017). Note that while Yoo does look at the transnational interactions between American missionaries and Korean Protestants, he does not necessarily foreground a "transpacific" lens for his study.

24. As Chung-Shin Park notes, by contrast, North Korea (the original hub of Christianity in Korea) had approximately 10,000 Protestants and 4,000 Catholics by the mid-1980s. Chung-Shin Park, *Korean Protestantism and Politics* (Seattle: University of Washington Press, 2003). Moreover, prior to the growth of Christianity in Korea

Protestantism "exploded," especially through global missionary activity and megachurches, with the nation earning the title of a "regional Protestant superpower."[25] Now, in the twenty-first century, South Korea sends out more missionaries per capita than any other country in the world.[26] Korean Americans, especially those who immigrated to the United States with the passage of the 1965 Hart-Cellar Act, also became majority Christian—about 70 to 80 percent—and fervent practitioners of evangelical Protestantism. Sociologist Rebecca Kim called collegiate Korean American evangelicals "God's whiz kids."[27] Today, men of Korean descent lead flagship American evangelical institutions, from the National Association of Evangelicals (NAE) to the Presbyterian Church of America (PCA). But with the exception of a few studies and scholars, world Christianity and ethnic studies have not been sufficiently braided together in a transpacific frame, especially historically.

There are several reasons that a transnational frame is still underutilized for the study of South Korean Protestant and Korean American Protestant communities. First, for the study of South Korean Protestants, a nation-based analysis has tended to dominate Korean studies in general and Korean religions in particular.[28] Second, for the study of Korean American Protestants, Korean American studies and Asian American

---

between 1907 and 1988, Confucianism, Buddhism, and Shamanism dominated the religious landscape of Korea. Timothy Lee notes that approximately 483,366 South Koreans, or about 1 percent of the population, claimed Confucianism as their religion in 1985. This figure contrasted with 8,059,624 (20 percent) for Buddhism and 8,354,679 (21 percent) for Christianity (combining Catholics and Protestants). Minister of Economic Planning Board, 13th Population and Housing Census of the Republic of Korea 153 (Seoul: Ministry of Economic Planning Board, 1985), 288, table 6. Timothy Lee, *Born Again: Evangelicalism in Korea* (Honolulu: University of Hawai'i Press, 2010), 155.

25. See Paul Freston's use of the term "regional Protestant superpower" in reference to South Korea, considering most Asian nations do not have sizable Christian populations, with the exception of the Philippines, which is mostly Catholic. Paul Freston, *Evangelicals and Politics in Asia, Africa and Latin America* (Cambridge, UK: Cambridge University Press, 2001), 61.

26. Rebecca Kim, *The Spirit Moves West: Korean Missionaries in America* (Oxford: Oxford University Press, 2015).

27. Rudy Busto, "The Gospel according to the Model Minority? Hazarding an Interpretation of Asian American Evangelical College Students," in David Yoo, ed., *New Spiritual Homes: Religion and Asian Americans* (Honolulu: University of Hawai'i Press, 1999), 178–79; Rebecca Kim, *God's New Whiz Kids? Korean American Evangelicals on Campus* (New York: New York University Press, 2006).

28. See the following key texts in the history of Korean Christianity; they primarily use the Korean nation-state frame in their works: Timothy Lee, *Born Again: Evangelicalism in Korea* (Honolulu: University of Hawai'i Press, 2010); Sung Deuk Oak, *The Making of Korean Christianity: Protestant Encounters with Korean Religions* (Waco, TX: Baylor University Press, 2013); Sebastian C. H. Kim and Kirsteen Kim, *A History of Korean Christianity* (Cambridge: Cambridge University Press, 2014).

studies more generally have tended to lack a robust analysis of the category of religion; and, when this is attempted, a nation-based framework is often evident.[29] Third, Asian studies and Asian American studies emerged through nonconverging intellectual genealogies, such that studies that bridge this divide still remain the exception, including in the historical field. In their edited volume *Encountering Modernity: Christianity in East Asia and Asian America,* historians Albert L. Park and David K. Yoo challenge the distinction between Asian and Asian American studies, especially as it pertains to the study of Christianity. They write, "Increasingly, the line between Asian and Asian American Studies has been blurred, reflecting the movements of people, goods, and ideas that have been taking place for some time between East Asia and the United States. The fields have distinctive legacies, but there is a convergence taking place that is opening up greater opportunities for conversation and dialogue."[30] They point to new possibilities for transpacific history, which largely emerged out of Asian American studies.

Lon Kurashige, Madeline Y. Hsu, and Yujin Yaguchi define transpacific history, in particular, as "transnational processes, persons, and events within and across the Pacific Ocean" and note that it tends to bridge "two or more conventional fields, including histories of the American West, U.S. immigration and ethnicity, U.S. diplomatic and international relations, Asian American Studies, East Asian Studies, and Pacific Islander studies."[31] Indeed, Park and Yoo's call for tracing Christian linkages between East Asia and Asian America is grounded in a larger transpacific turn in Asian American studies. Park and Yoo's intervention is not yet fully reflected in the scholarly literature, especially when it concerns religion in general and Christianity in particular. Indeed, the above definition of "transpacific history" could include the category of religion, including the role of religious actors and processes of migration, but it is not yet listed as a major category of analysis. Why? And, how can this be addressed?

---

29. I have especially expounded this point in Helen Jin Kim, "Reconstructing Asian America's Religious Past: A Historiography," in Khyati Joshi and David Yoo, eds., *Envisioning Religion, Race and Asian Americans* (Honolulu: University of Hawai'i Press, 2020), 13–41.

30. Albert L. Park and David K. Yoo, eds., *Encountering Modernity: Christianity in East Asia and Asian America* (Honolulu: University of Hawai'i Press, 2014), 7.

31. Lon Kurashige, Madeline Y. Hsu, and Yujin Yaguchi, "Introduction: Conversations on Transpacific History," *Pacific Historical Review* 83, no. 2 (May 2014): 183–88. The purpose of this special issue, according to the guest editors, was to bring greater coherence to the "emerging research area of 'transpacific history.'"

As briefly discussed, Asian American studies in particular, and ethnic studies in general, emerged out of the late-twentieth-century movements for social change, invested in a critique of American empire and its collusion with Christianity. Thus, the field has shied away from a robust treatment of the category of religion in general and has not made the full turn toward world Christianity. As noted above, world Christianity and ethnic studies both matured in the late-twentieth century, with a focus on people of color and/or non-Western societies. While it seems they would be in close conversation, these two fields are especially in tension when considering the entangled history of Christian missions. Asian American studies largely understands the history of Christian missions to be a history of missionary imperialism, so it tends not to portray Christian missions, Western or non-Western, in robust terms. However, how do scholars of Asian American studies and/or transpacific history, then, consider new and unexpected phenomenon, including that the next wave of Christian missionaries, in the aftermath of Western Christendom, are largely nonwhite and non-Western Christians? Chief among them are South Koreans, who, in the twenty-first century, send out the most missionaries per capita.[32] Yet the scholarly apparatus to study these missionary-focused communities, especially in transpacific historical or diasporic frame, is still an emerging area of study for a new generation and cohort of scholars. I submit that the Africanist foundations within the field of world Christianity, especially the role of indigenous agency and transnationalism, can provide a helpful critique of the transpacific historical lens that is prone to seeing these nonliberal communities through a reductive lens or omits their narratives completely, rendering a significant part of the past invisible.

Empire, Missions, Agency

Christian missions often serve as the pinnacle of piety for Christians with roots in the global South, including among Korean and Korean Americans. Social scientists such as Rebecca Kim and Judy Ju Hui Han, who have spearheaded transnational studies of South Korean and Korean American Protestant communities, have asked, To what extent did zealous Korean and Korean American Christian missionaries and their projects also fall prey to empire? Was it the work of Western missionaries—especially the theological impulse to make converts or spread the gospel—or was it Western empire's cultural trappings, and its intransigent belief in racial superiority, that made missions a colonizing force? Are contemporary

---

32. Kim, *The Spirit Moves West*.

Korean and Korean Americans pursuing a noncolonial form of Christian missions, given its stained heritage?

Kim and Han have laid the groundwork to address these questions in their critique of race and empire as it is infused in the missionary work of those of Korean descent. Though, as noted above, contemporary South Koreans send out the most missionaries per capita in the world, rendering them a powerhouse in the Christian missionary world, in the United States they have had to contend with deeply rooted racism and a church that views mission as a Western prerogative. In the study of "reverse missions"—the non-Western effort to evangelize the West—although there has been considerable promise for Korean missionaries' influence in America, it has been highly circumscribed. As Rebecca Kim shows, Korean missionaries in the United States wield a distinctly Korean faith, but their intention to convert white Americans, seen as the most prized of converts, is largely fruitless, because as immigrants they cannot overcome U.S. racial hierarchy.[33] Her findings provide an empirical basis for what historian Hanciles has concluded: "[W]hile non-Western Christians now represent the face and future of global Christianity," due to prevailing attitudes of Western superiority, "the church in the non-Western world does not yet constitute its main driving force."[34] Moreover, as Ju Hui Judy Han has shown, contemporary Korean/American missionaries ride the coattails of U.S. empire, replicating developmentalist racist arguments about Africans and others in Third-World nations.[35] Korean Christian missionaries have possibly adopted a Eurocentric theology of missions, inherited from U.S. missionary and cultural dominance. Some have carried with them the white supremacist logics learned from the legacies of the white-over-black racial hierarchy embedded within the U.S. military and culture in Korea, including within Korean Christianity.[36]

Kim and Han have effectively charted a path for scholars of transpacific Korean Christianity to investigate the status of their missionary

---

33. Kim, *The Spirit Moves West*. Through her close study of University Bible Fellowship (UBF), Kim discovered the enduring influence of "American global Christianity" and found that though UBF prizes evangelizing white college students, their work ultimately "clashes with the dominant white American culture and racial hierarchy" (169).

34. Hanciles, *Beyond Christendom*, 385.

35. Ju Hui Judy Han, "Shifting Geographies of Proximity: Korean-led Evangelical Christian Missions and the U.S. Empire," in Carole McGranahan and John F. Collins, eds., *Ethnographies of U.S. Empire* (Durham, NC: Duke University Press), 205–7.

36. For a discussion of the American white-over-black racial hierarchy in Korea, see Nadia Kim, *Imperial Citizens: Koreans and Race from Seoul to LA* (Stanford, CA: Stanford University Press, 2008).

work, but these studies can be expanded to address questions such as the following: To what extent are ideas of American racial hierarchy infused into transpacific Korean Christian missionary work? How do belief, practice, gender, and region modify the extent to which modern Korean missionaries are subject to adopting ideas of American racial ideology and to what extent do they object to them? Further data can be uncovered, especially expanding into global South to global South connections that those missionaries of Korean descent forge in Latin America, Africa, and throughout Asia, especially using a historical frame.

To expand these studies, further engagement with world Christianity is also necessary. The foundational tools forged through an Africanist-centered world Christianity are helpful for other regions of study, especially the insight that transpacific Korean Christianity is more than the handmaiden of empire. While the critique of ethnic studies tends to emphasize the power of structure, especially the structures of race and empire, the world Christianity model tends to emphasize the power of agency. To simply lump the subjects of transpacific Korean Christianity into either category is to construct a binary that does not always fully reflect the everyday lives of these subjects on the ground. Moreover, the balance between agency and structure can change over time depending on context. As Nami Kim argues, missionary forms of Korean Christianity cannot be understood merely as "Western export" or "indigenous response free from global power structures."[37] To overlay a specific theory onto the granular data, including archival data, about how research subjects forge their lives and worlds would be to silence some of the surprising voices discovered in ethnographic or archival studies. The data often call for negotiation with the tensions between agency and structure to provide a clear-eyed analysis. Thus, the critique of race and empire in ethnic studies can be brought into productive conversation with the emphasis of local agency in world Christianity.

In the study of Christianity in Korea, for instance, scholars have long debated the role of U.S. missionaries in the birth, growth, and success of the tradition. Yet, through the lens of world Christianity, arguing against the "colonization of consciousness," scholars have emphasized the concept of hybridity and a "third way" to argue for an indigenous form of Korean Christianity. Sung-Deuk Oak argues that Korean Christians in the late-nineteenth and early-twentieth centuries hybridized Korean religious cultures, Chinese Protestantism, and Anglo-American Protestant-

---

37. Nami Kim, "A Mission to the 'Graveyard of Empires'? Neocolonialism and the Contemporary Evangelical Missions of the Global South," *Mission Studies: Journal of the International Association for Mission Studies* 27 (2010): 20.

ism to create a uniquely Korean form of Christianity.[38] Similarly, Deok Joo Rhie has long emphasized that early Korean Christianity represented a "third way" that hybridized indigenous Korean traditions with Western Christianity to create Korean Christianity.[39] As such, Korean Christians cannot be reduced to Western puppets and automatons. Therefore, to see Christianity only as the handmaiden of Western empire or Korean Christians as the unwitting instruments of empire involves an incomplete reading of historical data and narratives. It may fall prey to treating the cross-cultural expansion of Christianity as a unidirectional dynamic, ignoring the profound impact of indigenous agency, appropriation, and aspirations on the outcomes.

Ultimately, studies that emphasize local nonwhite and non-Western agency prevent the historian's tendency to focus on a global American Christianity that omits the role of nonwhite and/or non-Western figures. Preston, for instance, has emphasized the dominant and global role that American Protestantism continues to have within and without the nation.[40] Mark Noll has also emphasized that global faith reflects American Christianity.[41] While these studies are right to emphasize the expansive historic and contemporary force of American Christianity with the rise of American empire, they do not effectively decenter this force in their studies. They unwittingly reinforce white-led global American Christianity by leaving the hegemonic voices as the central subjects of study and critique. Therefore, an emphasis on the nonwhite and non-Western Christian voices that have emerged from the rise of world Christianity are a necessary countervailing force to decentering these voices, and emphasizing agency is key. And while world Christianity emphasizes the role of local agency, the critique of Asian American studies also provides that local agents cannot be viewed simply as free-floating global agents, unencumbered by empire, thus providing a productive tension.

---

38. Oak, *The Making of Korean Christianity*.

39. Deok-Joo Rhie, *A Study on the Formation of the Indigenous Church in Korea, 1903–1907* (History of Christianity in Korea Research Institute, 2000). (Korean original; my English translation of title).

40. Andrew Preston, "Defender of the Faith: The United States and World Christianity," in Joel Cabrita, David Maxwell, and Emma Wild-Wood, eds., *Relocating World Christianity: Interdisciplinary Studies in Universal and Local Expressions of the Christian Faith* (Leiden: Brill, 2017).

41. Mark Noll, *The New Shape of World Christianity: How American Experience Reflects Global Faith* (Downers Grove: IVP Academic, 2009).

"Nonliberal" Subjects

Another significant challenge to studying transpacific Korean Christianity, in particular, may be that these Korean "nonliberal" subjects are an unwelcome category for those whose primary scholarly gaze is shaped through a secular liberal or progressive lens. Their stories may be overlooked because they are not seen as morally and politically redemptive stories, from a secular or liberal-to-progressive Western gaze. However, if scholars paint those who do not fit their political, social, or theological visions as one-dimensional or reductive characters, then the full landscape of the past will remain unknown. This leads to the second contribution of world Christianity to transpacific Korean Christianity: world Christianity does not see nonliberal Christian movements in transpacific Korean Christianity solely through a reductionist lens.

To be sure, while there are indeed minority threads of "progressive" or "liberal" forms of transpacific Korean Christianity, the dominant mode is an evangelical, charismatic and/or fundamentalist style of Christianity. To use a phrase from anthropologist Susan Harding, an expert on American fundamentalism, these subjects may be deemed the "repugnant cultural other." As Harding notes, her study of white American fundamentalists often elicited looks of disdain from her colleagues, raising questions about her own theological and/or political commitments. Her subjects are not palatable for Western secular academic scholars, for they do not champion progressive or liberal causes.[42] In fact, they are largely nonliberal subjects who do not fit neatly into the categories of Western secular liberalism.[43] In much the same way, the nonliberal subjects of transpacific Korean Christianity who espouse evangelical, fundamentalist, and/or charismatic forms of Christianity may have been, thus far, sidelined from transpacific history because they are deemed culturally, politically, or theologically "repugnant." Indeed, anthropologist Devaka Premawardhana argues that, from a world religions perspective, the subjects of world Christianity may be deemed as such because they practice "alien" forms of Christianity that may unsettle the West. Yet he suggests that the subjects of world Christianity require careful study, nonetheless, for they defamiliarize knowledge:

> Christianity is assumed to be in all cases familiar. Its internal multiplicities, its own strangenesses, get swept away. The result-

---

42. Susan Harding, "Representing Fundamentalism: The Problem of the Repugnant Cultural Other," *Social Research* 58, no. 2 (Summer 1991): 373–93.
43. See note 1.

ing flattened, monolithic Christianity is confined to its modern Western expressions, an unwarranted reduction in any time period, but most certainly today. Given not only its presence but its preponderance in the global South, Christianity can no longer be taken for granted as familiar.[44]

In relegating these nonliberal subjects of transpacific Korean Christianity to the shadows of history, knowledge about how they have shaped, and continue to shape, the modern world is rendered inaccessible—but their ghosts nevertheless haunt us. Better to know that they are there, and to investigate who they are in the full historical drama.

The reality is that, as it pertains to the extant literature on transpacific Korean Christianity, the stories have not been fully documented and the data itself have not been fully uncovered in the Western academy. Simply put, the full gamut of stories have not even been told. Scholars of transpacific Korean Christianity, as well as those practitioners within the community—and, to be sure, those outside of the community—do not yet know all of the stories that exist or how to analyze them. Scholars and practitioners do not fully know yet which archives to access and do not yet have an archive of those stories in secondary sources. If one only sees the religious past through one-dimensional historical characters, their full stories—and adequate critique of them—will remain lost. So as to build a full historical landscape, all characters from the past need to come alive.

Conclusion

This chapter has reviewed the formation of world Christianity and argued that the Africanist pioneers of the field have laid a foundation that can help to advance new and emerging areas of research, including the case study of transpacific Korean Christianity. Transpacific Korean Christianity sits at the intersection of multiple fields. Given that world Christianity and ethnic studies have emerged through nonintersecting intellectual genealogies, this chapter has offered methodological avenues through which these two fields can be put into productive conversation, especially as the former emphasizes agency and the latter structure. World Christianity's focus on agency offers nonreductive ways—including but also going beyond the category of empire—to approach the study of transpa-

---

44. Devaka Premawardhana, "Christianity Becomes Unfamiliar," *Harvard Divinity Bulletin* (Winter/Spring 2011): 31.

cific Korean Christianity, which is primarily composed of missionary-focused Christian movements, including evangelical, charismatic, and/or fundamentalist styles of Christianity. The pioneers of world Christianity have set a path that should be tested and critiqued among a new generation of scholars, including in relatively nascent areas of research such as transpacific Korean Christianity.

Contributors

Raimundo César Barreto Jr. is a Brazilian-born scholar of world Christianity who teaches in the history department at Princeton Theological Seminary. He is one of the conveners of the Princeton World Christianity Conference and the general editor of the Fortress Press series World Christianity and Public Religion.

Carlos F. Cardoza-Orlandi is Frederick E. Roach Professor of World Christianity at the Department of Religion, Baylor University. His teaching and research interests focus on the interpretations of the movement of the Christian religion in Latin America and the Caribbean, particularly Christianity's interplay with Amerindian religions, Creole Caribbean religions, and *Espiritismo*. Among his publications is the award-winning book *To All Nations from All Nations: A History of the Christian Missionary Movement* (with Justo L. González) (Nashville, TN: Abingdon, 2013).

Gemma Tulud Cruz is senior lecturer in theology at the Australian Catholic University. She is author of the forthcoming book *Christianity across Borders: Theology and Contemporary Issues in Global Migration*.

Dyron Daughrity has authored ten books and numerous articles on the study of religion. He is an academic editor for three international presses and is a professor of religious studies at Pepperdine University in Malibu, California.

Jehu J. Hanciles is D. W. and Ruth Brooks Professor of World Christianity and director of the World Christianity Program at Candler School of Theology, Emory University. He has written and published on issues related to the history and globalization of Christianity with a focus on migration. His most recent book is *Migration and the Making of Global Christianity* (Grand Rapids, MI: Eerdmans, 2021).

Contributors

Helen Jin Kim is assistant professor of American religious history at Emory University's Candler School of Theology. She completed her MDiv and PhD at Harvard University and her BA at Stanford University. Helen Jin Kim studies U.S. history and religion, with a focus on the Pacific and Asian America. She is author of a forthcoming book on U.S. evangelicals and South Korean Protestants in the Cold War era (Oxford University Press).

Kirsteen Kim (PhD, Birmingham, UK) holds the Paul E. Pierson Chair in World Christianity and serves as associate dean for the Center for Missiological Research at Fuller Theological Seminary, USA. She is co-author, with Sebastian C. H. Kim, of *Christianity as a World Religion* (2nd ed., 2016) and *A History of Korean Christianity* (2015). Her research contributions also include monographs and articles on Indian and Korean theologies, intercultural pneumatology, and mission, evangelism, development, and religious studies.

Paul Kollman, CSC, is a priest of the Congregation of Holy Cross and associate professor of theology at the University of Notre Dame. His academic interests include world Christianity, African Christianity, and mission studies. He is past president of the American Society of Missiology, and from 2016 to 2022 serves as president of the International Association for Mission Studies.

Kwok Pui-lan is Dean's Professor of Systematic Theology at Candler School of Theology at Emory University. Her publications include *Postcolonial Imagination and Feminist Theology*; *Introducing Asian Feminist Theology*; and *Discovering the Bible in the Non-Biblical World*.

Pan-chiu Lai is professor of religious studies and director of the Centre for the Study of Religious Ethics and Chinese Culture, The Chinese University of Hong Kong. He has published extensively in the research areas of interreligious dialogue, modern Christian thought, and Chinese Christian theology. His representative publications include *Towards a Trinitarian Theology of Religions: A Study of Paul Tillich's Thought* (1994); *Mahayana Christian Theology* (in Chinese, 2011); and *Sino-Christian Theology in the Public Square* (in Chinese, 2014).

Dana L. Robert is the Truman Collins Professor of World Christianity and History of Mission, and director of the Center for Global Christianity and Mission at the Boston University School of Theology. Her books include *Christian Mission: How Christianity Became a World Religion*.

Contributors

Shobana Shankar is associate professor of history at Stony Brook University. She is author of *An Uneasy Embrace: Africa, India and the Spectre of Race* (2021), and *Who Shall Enter Paradise: Christian Origins in Muslim Northern Nigeria, c. 1890–1975* (2014). She co-edited *Religions on the Move* (2013) and *Transforming Religious Landscapes in Africa: The Sudan Interior Mission, Past and Present* (2018).

Emma Wild-Wood is senior lecturer in African Christianity and African indigenous religions and codirector (with Alex Chow) of the Centre for the Study of World Christianity at the University of Edinburgh. Previously she has worked in Congo, Uganda, and Cambridge. Her recent publications include *The Mission of Apolo Kivebulaya: Religious Encounter and Social Change in the Great Lakes c. 1865–1935* (2020) and (coedited with Alex Chow) *Ecumenism and Independency in World Christianity: Historical Studies in Honour of Brian Stanley* (2020).

Deanna Ferree Womack is assistant professor of history of religions and multifaith relations at Emory University's Candler School of Theology. Her research combines the study of Middle Eastern Christianity with commitments to Christian–Muslim dialogue. She is author of *Protestants, Gender and the Arab Renaissance in Late Ottoman Syria* (Edinburgh: Edinburgh University Press, 2019), and *Neighbors: Christians and Muslims Building Community* (Louisville, KY: Westminster John Knox Press, 2020).

Gina Zurlo (PhD, Boston University) is codirector of the Center for the Study of Global Christianity at Gordon-Conwell Theological Seminary (South Hamilton, MA). She is co-editor of the *World Christian Database* (Brill) and co-author of the *World Christian Encyclopedia*, 3rd ed. (Edinburgh: Edinburgh University Press).

Index

Academic Association for Theology, 50
academic freedom, 124
Adogame, Afe, on reverse mission, 94
Africa
  discourse on transformative/redemptive masculinity in, 88
  significance in shaping the field of world Christianity, 29
African Council of Churches, 31
African Initiated Churches, 87
Africanist agenda, in field of world Christianity, 29, 30
Africanists
  pioneering role in field of world Christianity, 186–89
  and reverse mission model, 100
Ahlstrom, Sydney, 6
Ahmadiyya (Islamic) sect, 111, 112
Akrofi-Christaller Institute of Theology, Mission, and Culture, 25
Althaus-Reid, Marcella, 25
Amazon Synod (Special Assembly of the Synod of Bishops for the Pan-Amazon Region, 2019), 152
American Christianity, historic force of, 198
American history, contribution of world Christianity to, 191
American Society of Church History, and world Christianity, 15
Anderson, Gerald, and origin of world Christianity field, 12, 13
Andover-Newton Seminary, 8
anthropology of religion, and education in world Christianity, 70
Armenian Apostolic Church, 179
Armenian Evangelical churches, 179
Armenians, in the Middle East, 179
Asia
  ethnolinguistic diversity in, 132
  geographic, cultural, and demographic statistics, 119, 120
  as global economic force, 119, 120
  religions of, 120
Asian Christianity, methodology in study of, 123–32
Asian Women's Resource Centre for Culture and Theology (Protestant), 89
Assyrian Church of the East, 179, 181
Atto, Naures, 35, 175
  on Middle Eastern diaspora Christianity, 175, 176, 183
Auerbach, Erich, on Goethe and world literature, 99

Balasundaram, Franklyn, and contextual Asian theology, 123, 124
bandits, and Christian mission in Northern Nigeria, 110, 111
Barringer, Terry, 30
Bediako, Kwame
  and Africanist scholarly agenda, 29
  and emergence of field of world Christianity, 29, 36, 146, 187
  as founder of the Akrofi-Christaller Institute of Theology, Mission, and Culture, Ghana, 25
  and growth of Christianity in Africa, 36
  on translatability of Christian faith, 143, 144
beliefs, Muslim and Christian, gray areas, 103, 104
believers/nonbelievers, and teaching world Christianity, 19
Berger, Peter, 8, 9, 10, 18
Bergoglio, Jorge Mario. *See* Francis, Pope
"Bible women," 86
Bliss, Catherine, 30
bodily comportment, and differences between religions, 106–10
Boko Haram, 105
  violence against women and girls, 106
border thinking, 157, 157n55
borderlands, 101, 101, 105
Boston College, 8
Boston University, Center for Global Christianity and Mission, 96
Boston University School of Theology, 7, 8, 16, 18, 20, 22, 189
  preparation for world Christianity students, 81, 82

bullock-cart Christology, 121

Cabrita, Joel
  on Africanists and world Christianity, 187
  on cultural particularity and world Christianity, 192
  on "world Christianity," 75, 97, 114, 187
Cambridge Centre for Christianity Worldwide, 49–50n25
Cardoza-Orlandi, Carlos F., 27, 38, 41
  and world Christianity curriculum, 39
Carey, William, and collection of social-scientific data, 79
Caribbean Council of Churches (CCC), 31
Carpenter, Joel, and history of world Christianity, 12, 13, 26
Center for Global Christianity and Mission, xix, 16, 18, 20
Center for Missiological Research (CMR), xiv, xv, xvi, xvii
Center for the Study of Global Christianity, 16, 18, 20
Center for the Study of World Christianity (CSWC), xiv
Centre for the Study of Christianity in Asia (Singapore), 16, 30
Centre for the Study of Christianity in the Non-Western World (CSCNWW), xiv, 4, 14, 24, 47
Chaldean Christians, in the Middle East (Iraq), 179
Cheah, Pheng, and world literature, 99
Cheetham, David, 50, 51
Chia, Edmund, on birth of Christianity in Asia, 120
Chinese Christian Posters Project (Boston University), 96

Chinese culture, relationship with Christianity, 158–61
Christian Bandung, 155, 155n47, 156
Christian movements, worldwide, range and variety, 28
Christianity
  areas of interest to scholars of globalization and development, 51, 52
  as an Asian religion, 120
  center of, shift from global North to global South, 20, 27, 83, 89, 93, 141, 177, 188, 191
  comparative, 5, 6, 21
  as institutional migrant, 91
  interconnectivity among local expressions, 180–84
  interdisciplinary focus on Asia, Africa, and Latin America, 16
  local expressions of, 29
  loss of, in Middle East, 173–75
  persistence and growth in Middle East, 174, 174n9, 175, 176, 183
  as world-building system, 10
Christians
  demographics, 83
  in Northern and Southern Nigeria, 102
Church of England Zenana Missionary Society, 84, 85
Circle of Concerned African Women Theologians, 31, 89, 127, 128
Coe, Shoki, and contextuality, 77
collaboration, among world Christianity scholars, 40, 41
colonial ideology, and Orientalist approach, 170
colonialism, 7, 29, 46, 75, 93, 131, 139n3, 186, 187

Columbia University, and American sociology, 80
Comisión para el Estudio de la Historia de las Iglesias en América Latina y el Caribe (CEHILA), 155, 156
confessional diversity, in world Christianity faculty, 59
Congregation for the Doctrine of the Faith, investigation of theologians, 124, 124n19
conquest, and the Christianization of Latin America, 147
Conrad, Sebastian, on global history, 100, 101
contextual theology, 31
  Asian, 123
contextuality, 77
conversion to Islam, forced, and marriage, 106
Coptic Orthodox, in the Middle East, 179
Costas, Orlando, and missiology, 8, 8n13
Cruz, Gemma Tulud, on gender and religion in global migration, 95
Cruz, Tito, on Asian self-identification, 132
cultural analysis, in Latin American theological and religious studies, 151, 152
cultural anthropology/area studies, and field of world Christianity, 47, 48
cultural Christians (in China), 162
Currents in World Christianity Project (CWC), 15, 26, 46

Daly, Mary, and Christian feminism, 87
Daughrity, Dyron, 35

Day Missions Library, 12, 14, 25, 30
decentering European theology, and world Christianity, 54, 55, 56, 57, 177
decolonialism, and Latin American Christianity, 154–57, 154n43
decolonizing the curriculum, 39
deification, in Chinese Christian theology, 165, 166
development, and world Christianity, 51, 52, 53
dialogue, and Asian Christianity, 126, 127
digital humanities, 96
diplomatic history, contribution of world Christianity to, 189, 190
doctrine, perspective of world Christianity on, 55, 56
Dussel, Enrique, on decolonialism in Latin American religious experience, 155

Ecclesia in Asia (apostolic exhortation of John Paul II), 125
Ecclesia of Women in Asia (Catholic), 89
Ecumenical Association of Third World Theologians (EATWOT), 31, 155
ecumenism, and field of world Christianity, 49, 75
ecumenists, prominence in field of world Christianity, 30
Emory University, Global Christianity program, xvii, xviii
employment, for students of world Christianity, 44, 45
environmentalism, and Latin American indigenous concerns, 152, 153, 154
Episcopal Divinity School, 8
epistemologies, Asian, 124, 125

essentialism
  cultural, 135, 136
  and Orientalist approach, 170
Ethiopian Orthodox Church, 179
ethnography, 36
Europe, decentering of, and Middle Eastern Christianity, 177
European Society for Intercultural Theology and Interreligious Studies (ESITIS), 50, 51
evangélicos, theologies and practices of, 38

faculty, for courses in world Christianity, 59
Federation of Asian Bishops' Conferences (FABC), on Asian Christianity, 122
feminism, Christian, 87, 88
feminist theology, world Christianity perspective on, 87, 88
Forman, Charles, 5, 6
Francis, Pope, and Latin American indigenous concerns, 152–54
Friedli, Richard, 49
"From Christendom to World Christianity" (1992 conference), 14, 25
Fuller Theological Seminary School of Intercultural Studies/School of World Mission, xiv, xv, xvi, 15, 44, 44n1, 47, 48

gender studies, interdisciplinary character of, 86, 87
genocide, cultural, and Latin American Christian origins, 150
geographical diversity, in world Christianity faculty, 59
German Association for Mission Studies (DGMW), 50
Ghar Wapsi (Home Coming) reconversion movements, 33

Index 209

global history, contribution of world Christianity to, 189–91
Global Research Institute, xiv
global South, as epicenter of world Christianity, 20, 27, 83, 89, 93, 141, 177, 188, 191
global/globalization studies, 99, 100, 101
globalism
 and world Christianity, 51, 52, 53; resistance to, 16, 17
Goethe, Johann Wolfgang von, 99
Gordon-Conwell Theological Seminary, 8, 16, 18, 20
 preparation for world Christianity students, 81, 81
Greek Orthodox, in the Middle East, 179

Hanciles, Jehu
 on African migrant-missionary movement, 93, 94
 on de-Europeanization of American churches, 92
 on transnational focus in world Christianity, 191
Handsome Lake, 3
Harvard Divinity School, 8
Harvard University, Digital Collections, 96
Hastings, Adrian, and Africanist scholarly agenda, 29
heart-mind, 160, 161
 and Holy Spirit, 161
Hefner, Robert, and comparative studies of conversion, 9
helicopter Christology, 121
Henry Martyn Centre in the Cambridge Theological Foundation, 49–50n25

hermeneutics
 Gadamerian, 56, 57
 non-Western intercultural, 125, 126
Hick, John, and theologies of religious pluralism, 53
historians, prominence in field of world Christianity, 30
Hollenweger, Walter, 49
Holy Spirit, and unity, 161
Hutchinson, Mark, 15
hybridity, in study of Christianity, 33, 34, 42, 48, 169, 197, 198
hybridization
 and encounter between Chinese and non-Chinese religions in China, 169
 and Korean Christianity, 197–98
hymns, Christian, and political protest, 63, 64, 69, 71, 72, 73

imagination, comparative, and preparation of scholars of world Christianity, 68–71
immigrant churches, vitality, 92, 93
imperialism
 in Christian missions, 186–88
 and South Korean Christian missionaries, 195–97
Indians, and Christian conversion, 33
indigeneity
 as approach to world Christianity, 29
 and Latin American Christianity, 150, 151
indigenous believers, and shift of Christianity to global South, 188
indigenous peoples, Latin American, and Pope Francis, 152, 153, 154

indigenous principle, 143
Institute for the Study of American Evangelicals, 12
Institute for the Study of Economic Culture, 8
Institute on Culture, Religion, and World Affairs (CURA), 8n14, 10, 12n23, 18, 18n42
institutions of world Christianity, 37, 38. *See also under individual college and university listings*
interconnectedness, in study of Christianity, 32–35
intercultural theology, 31
  and ecumenism, 50
  and world Christianity, 49, 50
interculturality, in Latin American studies, 150–54
interdisciplinarity
  and Asian perspective on Christianity, 131, 132
  in field of world Christianity, 30, 77, 78, 189
International Missionary Council, 49
  merger with World Council of Churches, 30
interreligious theology, 31
intersectionality, and Asian perspective on Christianity, 131
Irvin, Dale
  definition of world Christianity, ix
  on the field of world Christianity, 142, 156
  on the origins of world Christianity, 16, 30, 45
  on world Christianity and marginalized Christian communities, 177, 178
  on "world" in world Christianity, 142, 143

Jenkins, Philip, on the loss of Christianity in the Middle East, 173, 174
Jesus, divinity of, 105
Jingjiao ("luminous religion"), 158
journals, with African perspective on world Christianity, 29

Kärkkäinen, Veli-Matti, 56
Khater, Akram, on Middle Eastern Christianity, 172
Khrist Bhakla Movement, 34
Kim, Ai Ra, on Korean Christianity in the United States, 94, 95
Kings, Graham, on the world Christianity field, 49–50n25
Korea, role of U.S. Christian missionaries, 197, 198
Korean Christianity
  evangelical, charismatic, and fundamentalistic as dominant mode, 199
  and the power of agency, 197
  transpacific, 192–200
Koschorke, Klaus
  comparative approach to world Christianity, 34
  on global Christian history, 181
  and non-Western Christianity, 15, 26
  on polycentric nature of world Christianity, 15, 26, 141
Koyama, Kosuke, on raw materials for Christian theologizing in Asia, 123

Lai, Pan-chiu, on Christianity in East Asia, 38
Lam, Carrie, 64
language
  barriers to Latin American scholars, 146, 147, 149
  role in Sino-theology, 162

Latin American Council of
    Churches, 31
Latourette, Kenneth Scott, 5, 12, 14,
    25
Lee, Moon-jang, on Western influence in non-Western Christianity, 121
LGBTQ issues, 89
liberation theology
    and contextualized Christian
        experience, 31
    and Latin American scholarship,
        147, 148
Lindbeck, George, 5, 6
local agency, in field of world
    Christianity, 29
local/global, 5, 9, 13, 14, 16, 17, 18,
    20, 22, 29, 43, 77, 78, 82, 83, 93,
    101, 166

Mackie, James, 31, 32
Mahdism, 104, 105
Mallampalli, Chandra, on translatability in an Indian milieu, 33
marginalized peoples, and Middle
    Eastern Christianity, 177, 178
Margull, Hans, 49
Maronites, in the Middle East
    (Lebanon), 179, 182
marriage, politics of, in Northern
    Nigeria, 109, 110
    of Christians and Muslims in
        Northern Nigeria, 107–9
Martin, David and Bernice, 9
masculinity studies, 88
Maxwell, David
    on Africanists and world Christianity, 187
    on the term "world Christianity," 75, 97, 114
    on world Christianity's focus on
        cultural particularity, 192

Mbiti, John, 30
Middle Belt, Nigerian, and Christianity, 102, 103
Middle East
    diversity of Christianity in, 171,
        178–80
    as Islamic world, 172
Middle Eastern Christianity
    demographics, 178, 179
    global interconnectivity of, 181,
        182
    scholarly neglect of, 172–77
Middle Eastern Christians, as part
    of Islamic society, 183
migrants
    female, experience of, 94, 95
    statistics, 90, 91
migration
    and American Catholic Church,
        92
    and evangelical churches, 92
    of Middle Eastern Christians,
        182–84
    and world Christianity, 35
migration studies, and world
    Christianity, 90–95
minority voices, neglect of, in
    cultural approach to world
    Christianity, 48
missiology
    employment prospects for students of, 45
    Protestant, project of world
        evangelization, 52
"mission," problems with use of
    term, 44
mission history, and origins of field
    of world Christianity, 14, 17,
    46, 47
mission studies, 11, 12, 26, 50, 52
    title change to world Christianity, 27, 76

212 Index

missionaries
   collection of social scientific data, 78, 79
   female, 84, 85, 86
   South Korean, 193, 195, 196, 197
missionary enterprise, Protestant and Catholic, 78, 79
Mohanty, Chandra Talpade, on discursive nature of Asian scholarship, 125
Mothers' Union, 85, 86
Muhammad Yusuf, 105
multiple belonging, 34

Nagy, Dorottya, on world-mindedness, 98
Neill, Stephen, 30
Nestorian Christianity, 120
Newbigin, Lesslie, 30
The Next Christendom (Philip Jenkins), 16, 26
Nobili, Roberto de, 127
nonliberal subjects/movements, 185n1, 199, 200
   and study of transpacific Korean Christianity, 199, 200
"non-Western," and normativity of Eurocentrism, 24, 25
North Atlantic Missiology/Missionary Project, 15, 26, 46
North Korea, Christian population, 192n24
Northern and Southern Nigeria, Christians in, 102

Orientalism, in study of religions, 169, 170
Orthodox theology, Chinese studies on, 165, 166
Orthodoxy, Eastern, 35, 36
orthoproxy, and Asian approach to world Christianity, 132–37

Overseas Ministries Study Center (OMSC), 4, 12–15

Padilla, Elaine, 56
patriarchy, Asian, 135
pentecostales, theologies and practices of, 38
Pew Charitable Trusts, role in developing the field of world Christianity, 11–15, 26, 46,
Phan, Peter, 56
   and field of world Christianity, 16, 16n38
   on history of mission, 130
   investigation by Congregation for the Doctrine of the Faith, 124, 124n19
   on migration and world Christianity, 91, 92
   participatory method of, 41
   on sources for theologizing, 122
   on the teaching of world Christianity, 129, 130
   on world Christianities, xi n9, 18, 19
plurality, religious, in Latin America, 148, 149
Pobee, John, 30
polygamy and monogamy, in Northern Nigeria, 109
Poon, Michael, 30
poor, in Latin American theologizing, 141
postcolonialism, and world Christianity, 141–45
praxis
   in African women's theologies, 128
   in Latin American intellectual traditions, 140, 141
Princeton Theological Seminary, 15, 36

Protestantism, as "foreign religion" in China, 159
Puritan tradition, end of, in American religion, 6

Querida Amazonia (apostolic exhortation of Pope Francis, 2020), 152–54

Rah, Soong-Chan, on immigrant churches, 92
Redemptoris missio (papal encyclical), 11
Reformation, Chinese reception of, 167, 168
relational reflexivity, 42
religious interlopers, in Northern Nigeria, 112, 113
religious media, uncontrollability, in Northern Nigeria, 112
religious studies
  as academic discipline in Mainland China, 168, 169
  origins, 53
  and world Christianity, 53, 54
research agendas, of world Christianity, 28–32
Research Enablement Program (REP), 13, 14, 26
ressourcement theology, historical approach of, 56
reverse mission, 93, 94, 100
  Korean, 196
revitalization movement, 3, 4
Rhodes, Alexander de, 127
Ricci, Matteo, 127
Ro, Bong Rin, on contextualization of Asian theology, 123
Robert, Dana
  on links of mission history to world Christianity, 46
  on missionaries advocating for indigenous liberation, 188

Roman Catholicism, as "foreign religion" in China, 159
Rouse, Ruth, 30

Samartha, Stanley, 31
  on helicopter and bullock-cart Christology, 121
Sanneh, Lamin, 46
  and Africanist scholarly agenda, 29, 187
  on Christianity's encounter with Islam and African traditions, 76, 77
  and emergence of field of world Christianity, 8, 12, 15, 25, 26, 146, 187, 188
  focus on global South, 177, 188
  focus on local institutions and local agents, 76, 188
  and translatability theory, 11, 29, 33
  on "world" and "global," 97, 98
  on world Christianity as a historical discipline, 46
  on world Christianity or Christianities, 19
  on "world" in world Christianity, 17
Scholars Initiative for Studies in Mission and International Christianity, 12
scholars of world Christianity, preparation for, 64, 65
scholarship, Asian, 125, 126
  publication of, 129
scholarship, Latin American, centered in North Atlantic, 145, 146
scholarship, on world Christianity, in China, 165, 166
scholarship, religious, Latin American, 146–48, 156, 156n49

scholarship, translations into Spanish and Portuguese, 147, 148
School of Ethnic Studies, San Francisco State University, 187
Schreiter, Robert J., and Catholic contextual theology, 77
secret believers, in Northern Nigeria, 111, 112
secular academy, and world Christianity theological studies, 40
self-identification, Asian, 132
Selley Oak colleges, 25, 26
seminaries, African, 37
Seton, Rosemary, 30
sexuality, and world Christianity studies, 89
Sharkey, Heather, growth of Christianity in Middle East, 175
Sino-theology, 162
slaves, freed female, in Northern Nigeria, 106, 107
"small traditions," Asian, 125
Smalley, Martha, 30
Smith, Jonathan, on comparison and classification in religion, 69, 70
Smith, Wilfred Cantwell, and comparative history of religion, 53
social ethics, Christian, 80
social studies, of religious communities, 54
social-scientific data, collection by missionaries, 78, 79
sociology
  academic and applied, 79
  Christian, 80
  and mission studies, 81
  religious roots, 80, 81
sociology of religion
  and education in world Christianity, 70
  and world Christianity, 78–83

sociology of religion students, comparison with world Christianity students, 81
South Korea
  growth of Christian population, 192
  as Protestant superpower, 193
specialization, and preparation for scholars of world Christianity, 66, 67, 68
Stanley, Brian, 15, 25, 32, 46
Strasburg, James, on indigenous contexts in world Christianity, 121
Sugirtharajah, R. S., 26
Syrian Orthodox churches, of India, 179, 181
systematic theology, perspective of world Christianity on, 55, 56

testimonio/testimony, and world Christianity, 41, 42
textualism, and Orientalist approach, 170
theologians, African, and indigeneity of African Christianity, 144
theological awareness, and preparation for scholars of world Christianity, 71, 72
theology
  as academic discipline in Mainland China, 168
  contribution of Chinese Christian theologians, 163, 164
  implicit/explicit, 71
Theology and Mission in World Christianity (book series), 56
Thomas (apostle), mission to India, 130
Thomas, M. M., 31
transcultural concerns, in study of Christianity, 32, 33

Index 215

"translatability" theory, 11, 29, 33, 143
translation, of Western theological works: into Chinese, 162, 163; into Spanish and Portuguese, 147, 148
transnational approach, to world Christianity, 34–36
transnational turn, in U.S. religious history, 190, 191
transnationalism
   in South Korean and Korean American studies, 193–95
   in world Christianity studies, 190–92
transpacific history, 194
Trinity Theological College (Singapore), 16
triple dialogue, and Asian Christianity, 126, 127

University of Aberdeen, 4, 16, 24
University of Chicago, and American sociology, 80
University of Edinburgh, 4, 13, 14, 15, 24, 189
University of Notre Dame, World Religions/World Church (WRWC) program, 65, 66

Wallace, Anthony F. C., on revitalization movements, 3, 4
Walls, Andrew, 105
   and Africanist scholarly agenda, 29, 187, 188
   and cultural anthropology/area studies, 47
   and emergence and history of field of world Christianity, 4, 12, 13, 16, 24, 25, 36, 40, 97, 146, 187, 188, 189
   focus on global South, 177
   on growth of Christianity in Africa, 36
   on interaction of Christianity with local cultures, 76
   and translatability theory, 11, 33
   on the universal and the local in Christianity, 97
   on world Christianity or Christianities, 19
   on "world" in world Christianity, 17
Wang Zhixi, and Chinese biblical interpretation, 166
Weston Jesuit School of Theology, 8
Wheaton College, 12
women
   Christian, respectability in Northern Nigeria, 106
   Christian, role in developing American sociology, 80
   as guardians of culture, 94, 95
   local, role in Christian missions, 85, 86
   multireligious history in Northern Nigeria, 106–10
   participation in Christian missions, 84, 85, 86
   role in immigrant churches, 94, 95
   slaves, conversion to Christianity in Northern Nigeria, 106, 107
   visibility/invisibility, in Northern Nigeria, 106
women/girls, Christian, loss of social value in Northern Nigeria, 108, 109
Women's Christian Temperance Union, 85
women's studies/gender studies, and world Christianity, 83–90

Index

"world"
  as coded term for non-Western, 76
  meaning, 99, 100
  in the term "world Christianity," 142, 143, 155

world Christianities, xi, xii, 18, 19, 160, 180

world Christianity
  in academia, xi, xiii, 4
  Asian perspective, 119–37
  Chinese perspective, 158–70
  definition, ix
  as a field of study, 20
  focus on marginalized Christians, 177, 178
  historic and geographic scope, 35, 36
  as historical discipline, 46, 47
  history of discipline, 4–10, 24–28
  Latin American perspective, 138–57
  and local/global dynamic, 82, 83
  methods of study, 82
  Middle Eastern perspective, 171–84
  new directions in the field, 32–36
  origins and use of the term, 14, 76
  as revitalization movement, 4
  polycentric nature, 15, 26, 38, 39, 46, 47, 49, 92, 96, 141, 142, 160, 181, 184
  reasons for appearance and development of the field, 73, 74
  research centers, 189
  study of, in China, 169
  teaching of, Asian perspective, 129–31

world Christianity program
  curriculum considerations, 58, 59
  learning outcomes, 57, 58

World Council of Churches, support for world Christianity institutions, 31

world literature, 99

World Missionary Conference (Edinburgh, 1910), 52

world religions paradigm, 53, 54

"world" vs. "global," xviii, xviii n18, xix n19, xix n20, 98

"worlding" of Christianity, 98, 100–103, 110–15

Yale-Edinburgh conferences, 14, 24, 25, 46

Yale University
  Divinity School, 12, 14, 15, 25, 189
  Religious Studies Department, 5

Yung, Hwa, on theologizing in the Asian church, 122

YWCA, 85

Zhao Lin, on Christianity in China, 164

Zhou Yun, on "Bible women," 86

www.ingramcontent.com/pod-product-compliance
Lightning Source LLC
Chambersburg PA
CBHW071408300426
44114CB00016B/2224